IMAGES
of America

ESOPUS

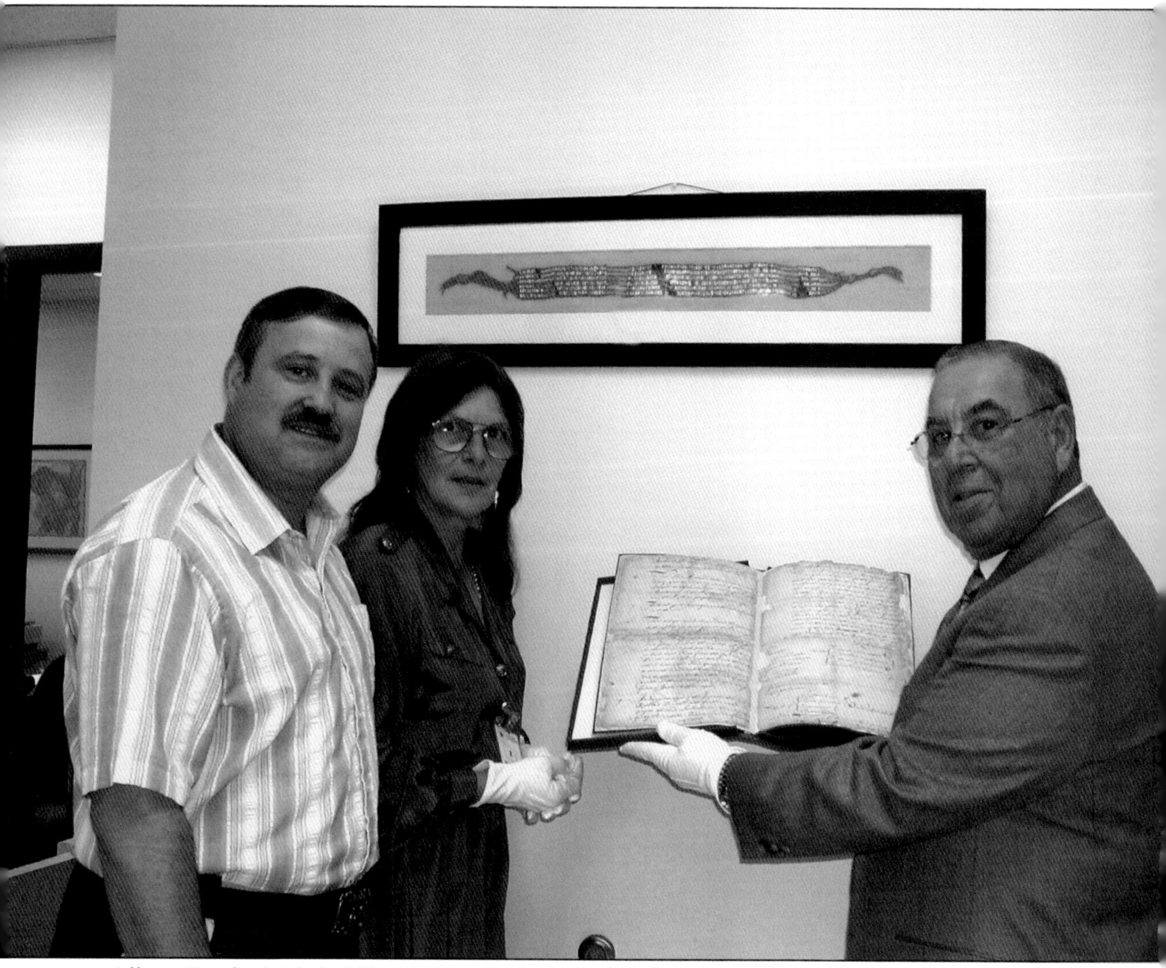

Albert Spada (right), Ulster County clerk, holds the original 1665 Richard Nicolls–Esopus Indian Treaty. The sewan wampum belt that accompanied the treaty hangs in a frame on the wall above. For 36 years, Spada has set the tone with high standards of preservation and maximum accessibility to county records. Working with the accommodating staff at the clerk's office, authors Karl R. and Susan B. Wick (left) spent many hours immersed in researching primary documents. It was here that they discovered a treasure trove of new information about the earliest inhabitants of Esopus. (Photograph by Phyllis McCabe.)

IMAGES
of America

ESOPUS

Karl R. and Susan B. Wick

ARCADIA
PUBLISHING

ISBN 978-0-7385-1188

Published by Arcadia Publishing
Charleston, South Carolina

Printed in the United States of America

Library of Congress Catalog Card Number: 2003101274

For all general information, contact Arcadia Publishing:
Telephone 843-853-2070
Fax 843-853-0044
E-mail sales@arcadiapublishing.com
For customer service and orders:
Toll-Free 1-888-313-2665

Visit us on the Internet at www.arcadiapublishing.com.

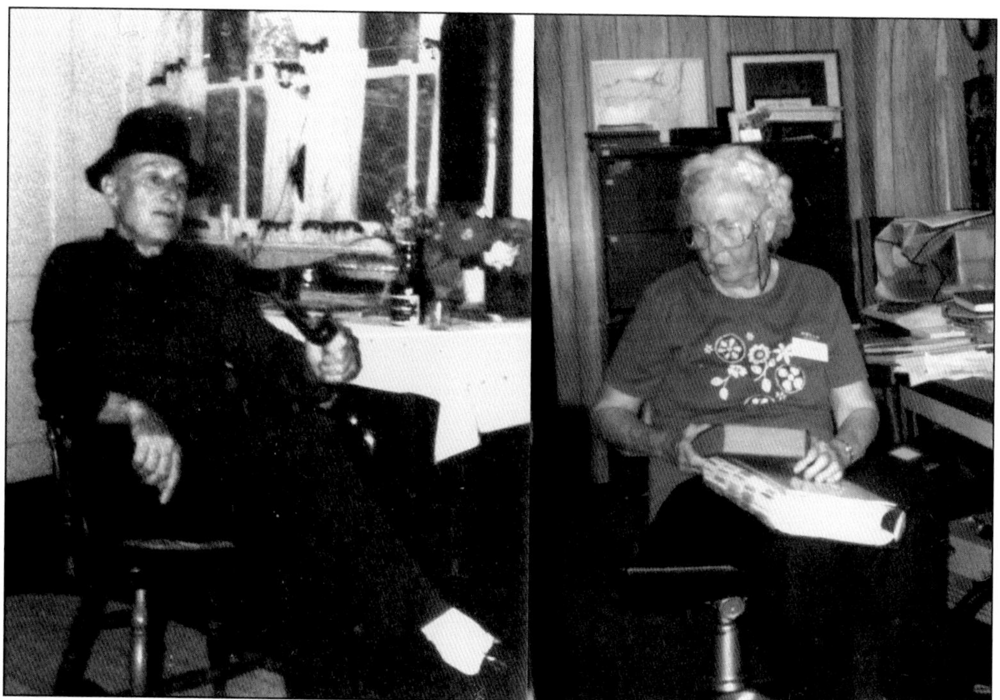

We dedicate this book to Samuel Haines Carman (1901–1990) and to Dorothy Dumond. "Uncle Sam" was the St. Remy historian and Karl's mentor for 30 years. Dot is a former historian for the town of Esopus. She is selfless in her dedication to history and is an inspiration to both of us. Without the knowledge, enthusiasm, and attitude of these two fine individuals, this volume would never have been conceived.

CONTENTS

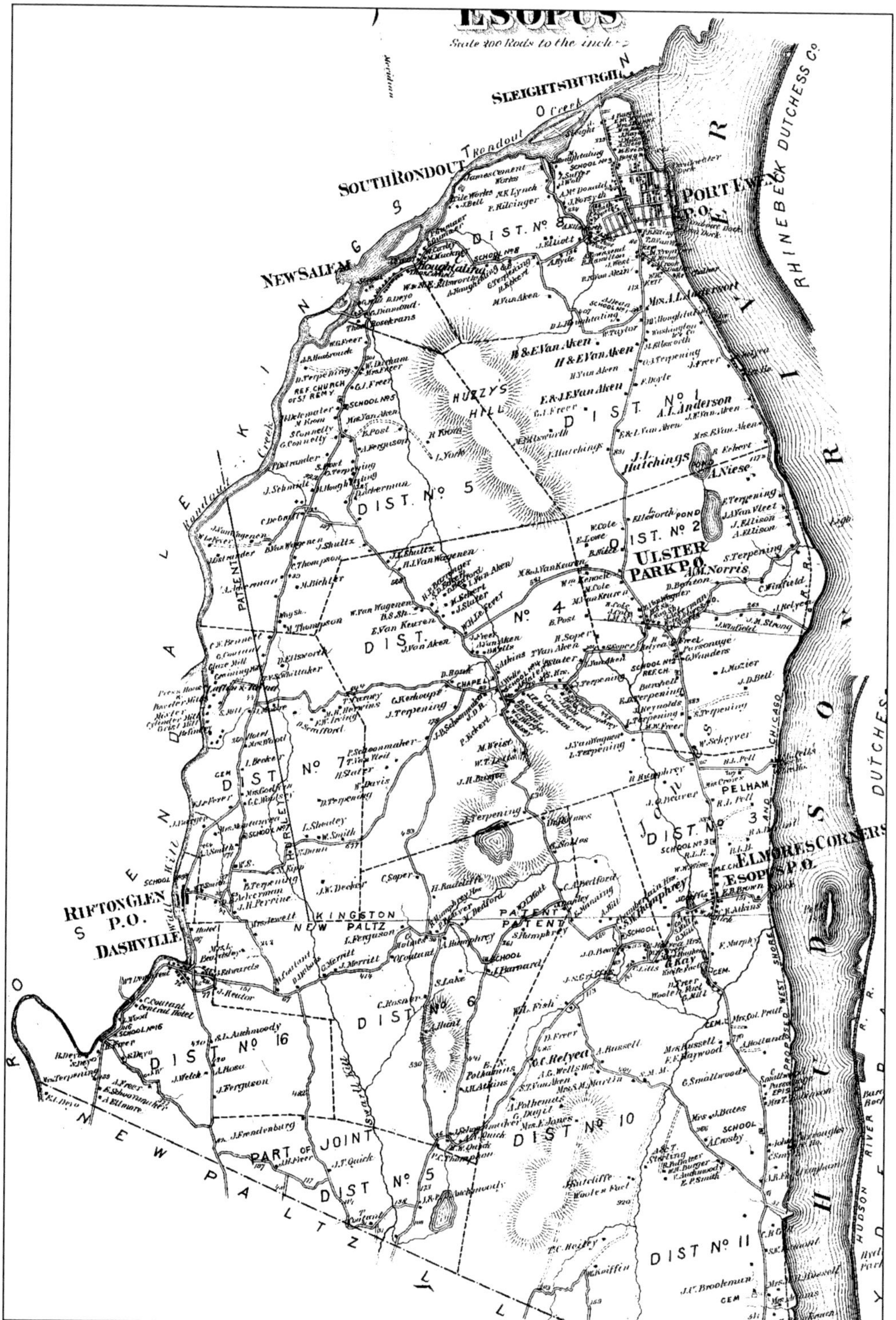

Shown is a map of Esopus. (William LeFever Krom collection; courtesy of Don and Shirley Ayers Briggs.)

INTRODUCTION

Esopus: "place of the small river or wellspring of creation" where Amerindians made wampum belts and treaties. Esopus: safe harbor and fertile valley to shelter generations of immigrants and "native Americans." A place where Indian traders had been running bartering posts for two years by the time the New Netherland Company officially received its charter in 1615.

In the mid-1600s, New Netherlands law called for "all persons to keep good fences and gates" and for "everyone to inclose [*sic*] his lot within four months and build a house on the same in one year, or forfeit it." And so Dutch colonists Jan VanVliet, Peter Vanauken, the Freer clan, and others set about establishing freeholds. They cleared the fields and used the stone to satisfy the law. The permanence of stonework appealed to their thrifty, practical natures. Maintained with care, these structures would last through many generations. Walls of stone made safe havens and reflected the Dutch determination to build communities capable of withstanding the storms of time. The sturdy Dutch worked hard, men and women side by side. When their work was done, they shared good fellowship, a generous meal, and liberal libation. Their thrift and prudent stewardship quickly led to a prosperous and thriving community.

Augustus Van Buren makes the following observations:

> It may be safely asserted that the first settlement in Ulster County was made at Esopus in 1652 or 1653. Many of these pioneers came from the Manor of Rensselaerswyck. That princely domain, embracing most of the present counties of Rensselaer, Columbia and Albany except Fort Orange and the land lying immediately about it; over which the patroon, Kilian van Rensselaer, ruled a feudal lord. Why did they come? Mayhap it was the wanderlust that lay in the blood. Perhaps the fertile valley of the Esopus Creek, ready for the plow, attracted them. Perchance there was a broader, a deeper reason. The patroon was the chief magistrate of his estate. From the decrees of his courts there was practically no appeal. He had the first right to purchase the products raised by his tenants who must grind their grist at his mill and could not hunt or fish without his license. The tenants of the manor farms were, in large measure, but the vassals of the patroon. Perhaps it was to escape all this, to own themselves, that they left Rensselaerswyck. Perhaps it was their desire to be able to put their foot down upon a spot of ground and say to all the world, "this is mine," that induced them to come to the land of the Esopus.

When the New Netherlands colonies were asked to kowtow to a system of patroonships, the inhabitants of Esopus said, "No thank you. We will not bow to overlords, not even if they be our countrymen." Compatriots of independence, entrenched behind a bulwark of stubborn Dutch determination, they dug in their heels and demanded there be freeholds and home rule. These settlers held the keys to the kingdom of Esopus—the major food producer for the whole colony and the seat of very lucrative fur trading. These sons and daughters of Holland merchants had not come to New Netherlands out of desperation, but to found a new world based on free enterprise.

When the British came in 1652, there was no visible resistance to their conquest. While local Dutch officials remained in office, British soldiers replaced the Dutch at the fort. This was a good plan because while the Dutch were worthy merchant traders and farm folk, their temperament did not lend itself to a soldier's way of life. If by chance those British soldiers should step out of line, freehold governance did provide for redress. The power of the Dutchmen's established trade with the local Indians, who were no friends to the British, was surely a deciding factor in this retention of self governance. The Dutch had found kindred spirits in the Lenape.

Van Buren goes on to say, "Women's rights and the rights of women [*sic*] were well recognized. It was not necessary for the squaws to organize a suffragette party. They usually got what they wanted. The secret of their great influence probably lay in the fact that each of them was an excellent cook, and each wife became the mother of a lusty brood of papooses."

From the matriarchal leadership of Lenape women to suffragette Sojourner Truth to St. Cabrini and many, many others, equality for women marches through the Valley of Esopus and its generations.

That women were afforded the opportunity to be equal partners, there is no doubt. The Dutch rewarded diligent effort regardless of sex or birth order. All had the right to avail themselves of the courts, exercise religious freedom, own real property, and obtain a public education. The right to choose would be an inherent right, maintained by all, for themselves, and for the generations to come.

From *Southeastern New York*, we learn the following:

> Various as the strains of immigrants were during the seventeenth and eighteenth centuries, all succumbed more or less to the ever pervasive and persuasive Dutch influence. Even the New Paltz French, who struggled to keep their language and French Church, gave up after fifty years, allowed their children to speak Dutch and engaged Dutch pastors. Dutch was a familiar language in Ulster County homes almost up to the present time. The strong organization of the Dutch Reformed Church in the country from 1659 had something to do with this, but equally influential, no doubt, was the evident merit of the Dutch scheme of life; the abundance, thrift and neatness of their households, their tolerance, easy going attitude toward disputable points of belief and morals; their practical good sense.

In later generations, German, Irish, and other Europeans came with families to ply their crafts among the boatyards, icehouses, brickyards, breweries, and farms of Esopus. What magnet drew these immigrants of so many generations? They saw a land made rich with fertile Dutch stewardship. They saw safe harbor in a Dutch sea of tolerance where dissimilar convictions were allowed to flourish, as long as values of thrift, good sense, and stewardship were fervently embraced and a sturdy work ethic was maintained.

From its inception as a trading post, Esopus was regulated, licensed, and taxed concerning intoxicating beverages. With religious and home consumption exempt from taxation, the Esopus freeholders quickly traded tea for home-pressed cider. The "gold of them thar Hussey Hills" would often be a treasure trove of stills. Smugglers, scalawags, and rumrunners have long plied their trade by lantern light among the coves of Kit Davit's River. A kaleidoscope of cultures joined ranks in bootlegging the contraband. The Ark of J.I.B. is a case in point. This Prohibition-era social hall was built on the deck of a barge (called a "boating bar"). It would be towed out into the Hudson for a boisterous good time of gambling, dancing, and drinking bootleg hooch. "Far away from the long tentacles of the law. And what did the initials J.I.B. stand for? Why Jews, Irish, and Binnewaters of course! A Binnewater was the local designation for a Protestant. And as the name implies, all were welcome on the Ark of J.I.B.," said Wilson Tinney in an April 2003 interview.

And so it goes in Esopus, from the banks of the Wallkill, Rondout, and Black Creek to the shores of the mighty Hudson, the river that runs both ways. With melding visions of diversity, the sons and daughters of immigrants shape our destiny.

One

THE EARLY DAYS

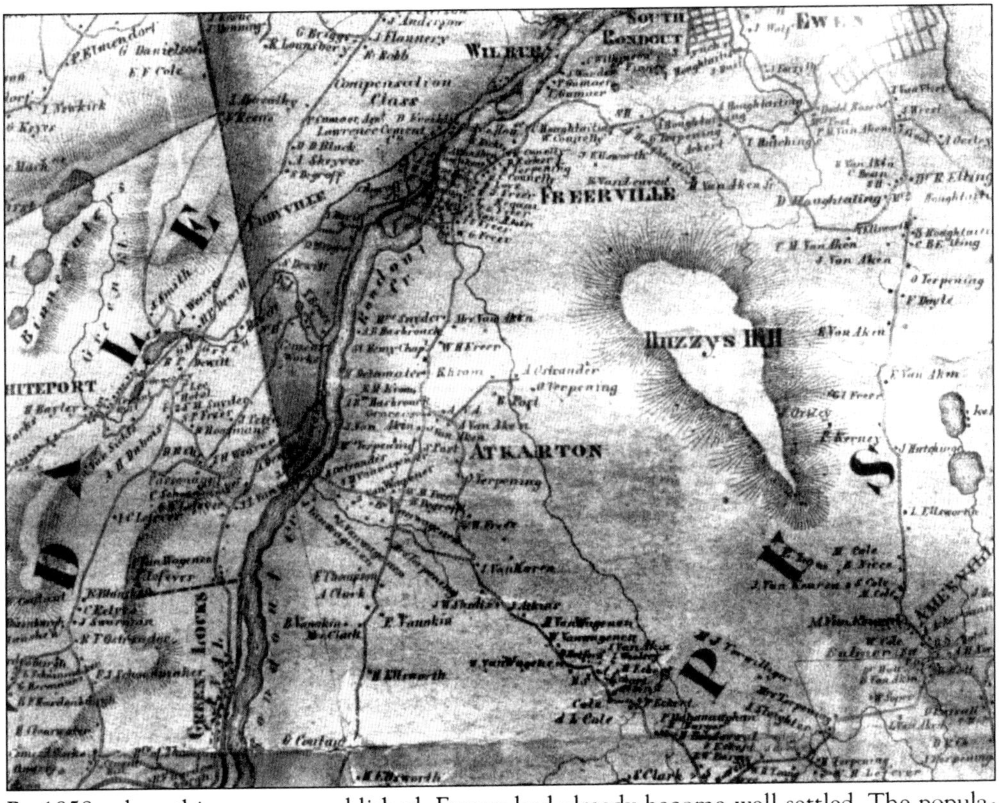

By 1858, when this map was published, Esopus had already become well settled. The population was 4,700, up from about 740[1] in Revolutionary times, and would stay near that number for the next 90 years.[2] Not until the latter half of the 20th century did population eventually double. This chapter will explore town history in the 16th and 17th centuries, when European settlement was still in its infancy. The first well-documented explorer to visit Esopus was, of course, Henry Hudson, who explored the great North River in 1608. He was probably not the first European visitor, however. A French trading post was established south of Albany in 1540. Jean Allefonsce (a ship's pilot) made reference to this outpost in his journal of 1542.[3] The first known European settler of Klyne (Little) Esopus was Christoffel "Kit" Davits. Kit Davits was a true pioneer. He carved a home or two out of the wilderness, trapped, explored, and traded with and translated for the natives. He got into a bit of mischief as well.

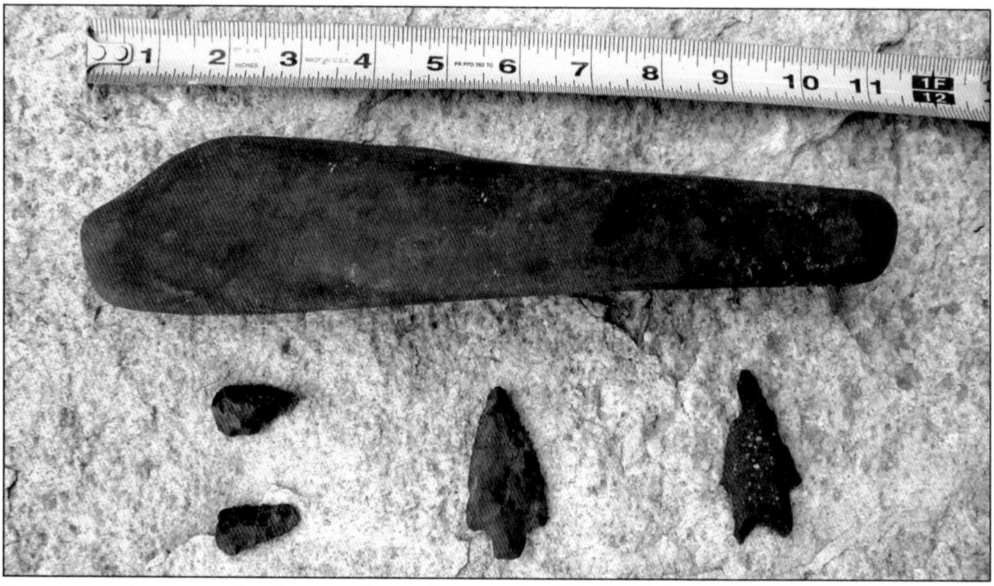

Esopus was home to the Lenape for millennia prior to Hudson's famous voyage. Sadly, the Lenape did not leave us any written records. They did, however, leave oral and archaeological histories for us to study: locally found Amerindian artifacts. The large pestle and grinder, made for someone who is left-handed, is still used by the author to grind corn for ceremonial purposes. The two larger points (bottom right) are from the Hudson River area and are courtesy of David Cummins of Esopus Landing.

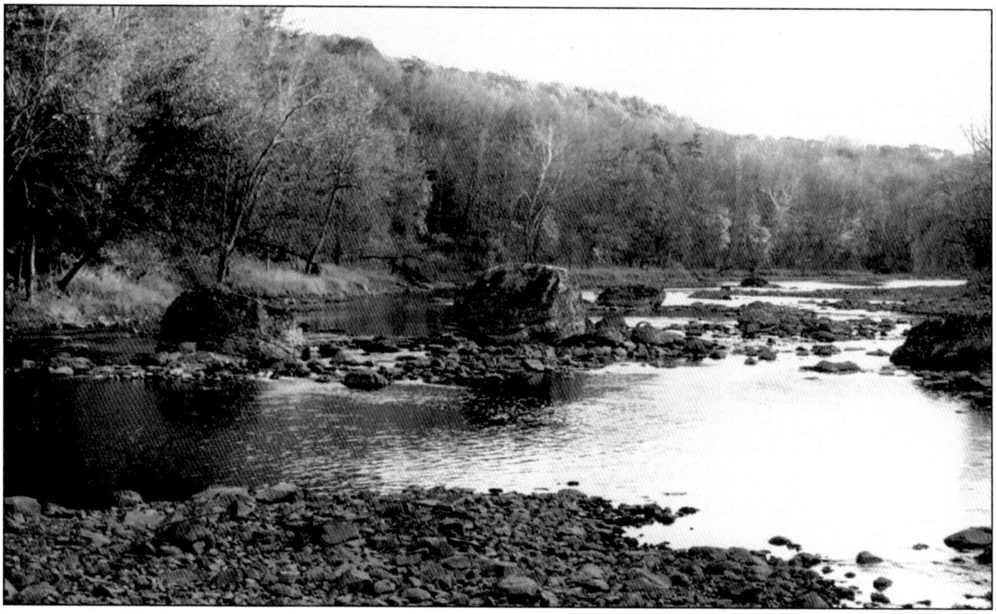

Mogowasinck, a great glacial boulder, sits in the Rondout Creek among the remains of Amerindian fishing weirs and overlooking locks No. 2 and No. 3 of the abandoned Delaware and Hudson Canal. Mogowasinck is an ancient monument marking the boundaries of clan fishing grounds and early European land patents, including one of approximately 600 acres bearing the same name. Included in that grant were some of the most fertile maize lands of the Lenape. (Authors' collection.)

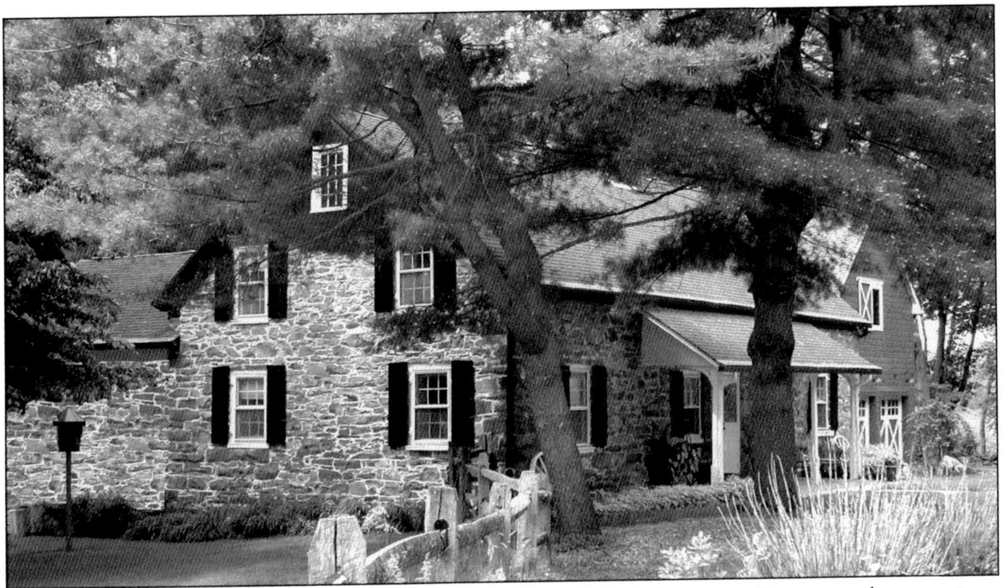

Built by Ysaak Van Wagenen in 1745, this is one of the earliest houses in Esopus, and generations of Van Wagenens are buried in the family cemetery on the farm. The farm was located in the Mogowasinck Patent, purchased from the Indians by Henry Beekman in 1682.[4] It adjoined Fischer's Patent, which was granted in 1681.[5] Ysaac's grandson Isaac D. Van Wagenen was a devout Quaker and helped Sojourner Truth to gain her freedom. (Authors' collection.)

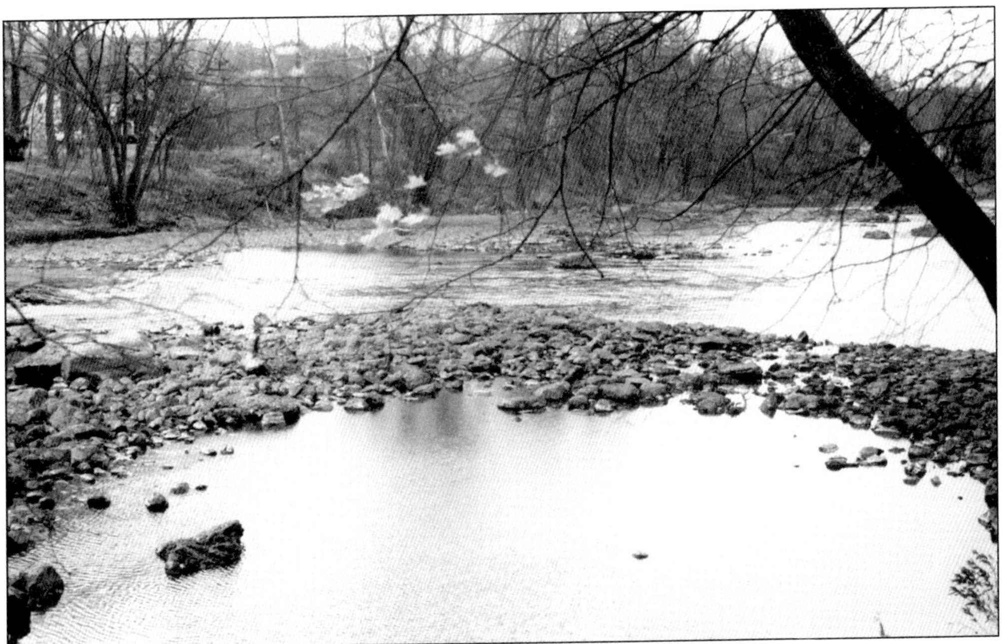

The drought of 1999 served at least one useful purpose. It allowed people to explore the old ford at Wagendal. This is what the ford looked like from the south. The expanse of open water was only about 15 feet wide and less than a foot deep. Early fords were made by placing large rocks in the riverbed and covering them with smaller ones to make the footing more even. Spring runoff would necessitate yearly repairs. (Photograph by the author.)

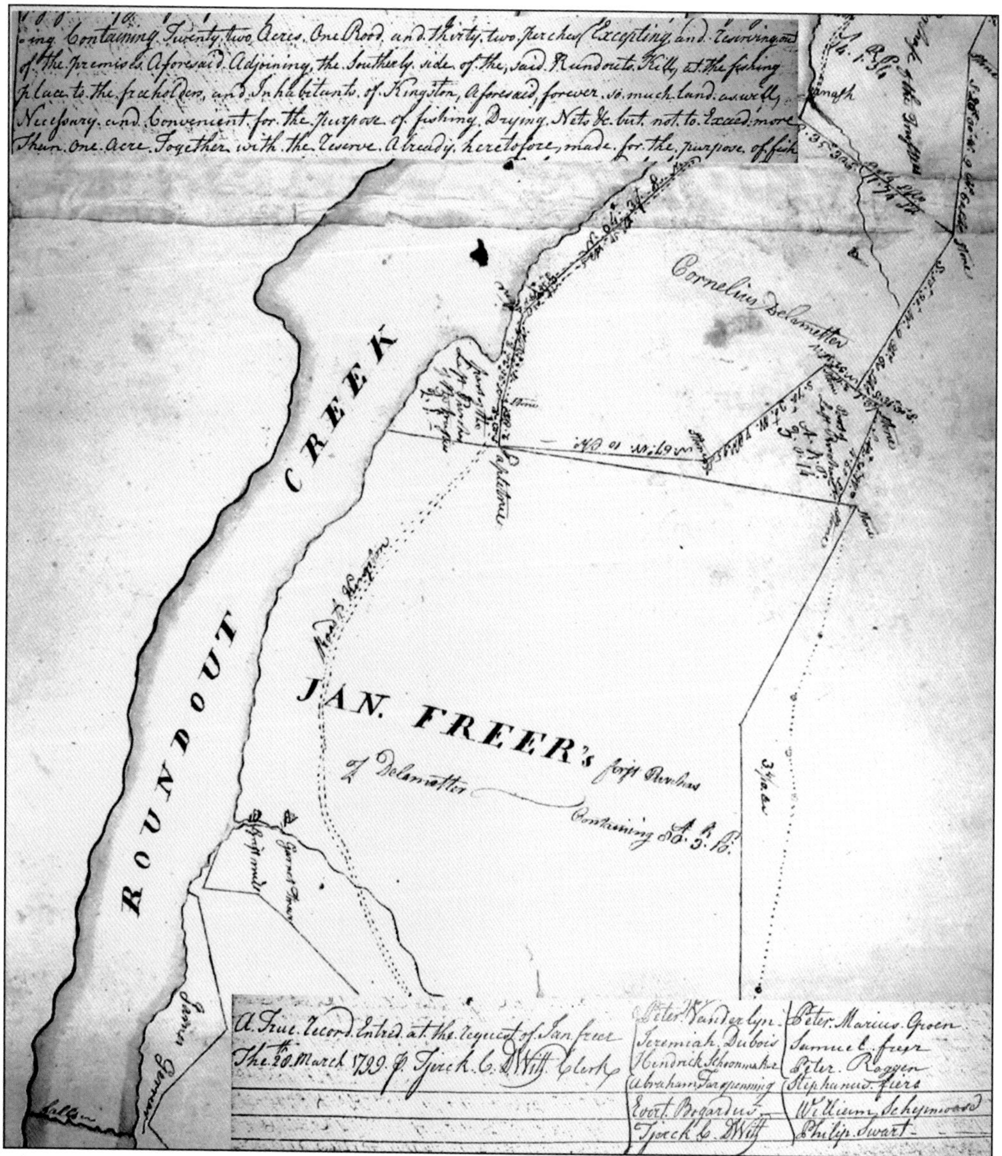

The traditional good sense and meticulousness of our Dutch forefathers shows through clearly in this 1799 map and its accompanying multi-page deed. These materials also illustrate the practical Dutch balance between individual and community rights. Most inhabitants of Esopus were freeholders, owning their land outright. These documents transfer title to four irregular pieces of land surrounding the Freer farm and gristmill from the "Trustees of Kingston" to Jan Freer. The land in the northwestern part of Esopus is now contiguous. The Van Wagenen, VanAken, Freer, and Delamater farms flow smoothly from each to the next with no unallocated land in between. What is especially interesting about this deed is the text inserted at the top of the image. A small parcel of land along the Rondout and near the mill is reserved for public use as a fishing place. From the language, it appears that this fishing place had been in long use. The deed also allows all freeholders access to the rest of the land for purposes of taking stone, wood, and trees "not in cultivation" for any reasonable use.

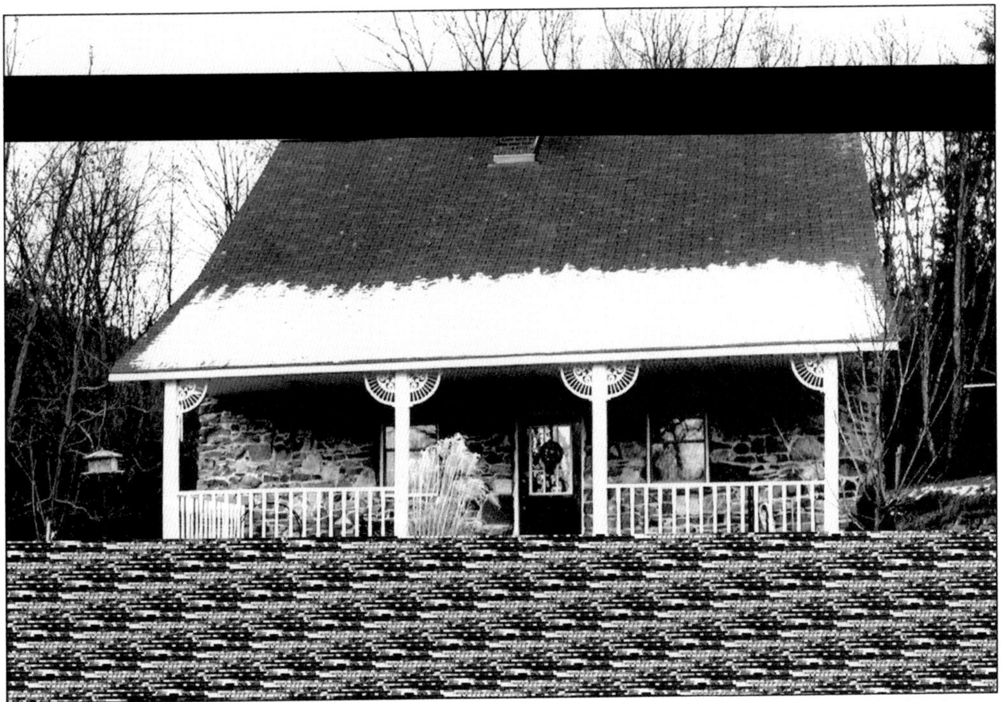

In 1745, when Ysaac Jr. and Sara Van Wagenen crossed the ford at Wagendal, they had a dream of starting a farm along the Rondout in the Mogowasinck Patent and at the foot of the trail to Hussey's Hill. The Van Wagenens had been in Wagendal since 1660, when grandfather Aert Jacobsen Van Wagenen settled there. In his will[6] (dated 1797), Ysaac passed the old stone house and farm along to his son David, and David to his son Isaac D. (Authors' collection.)

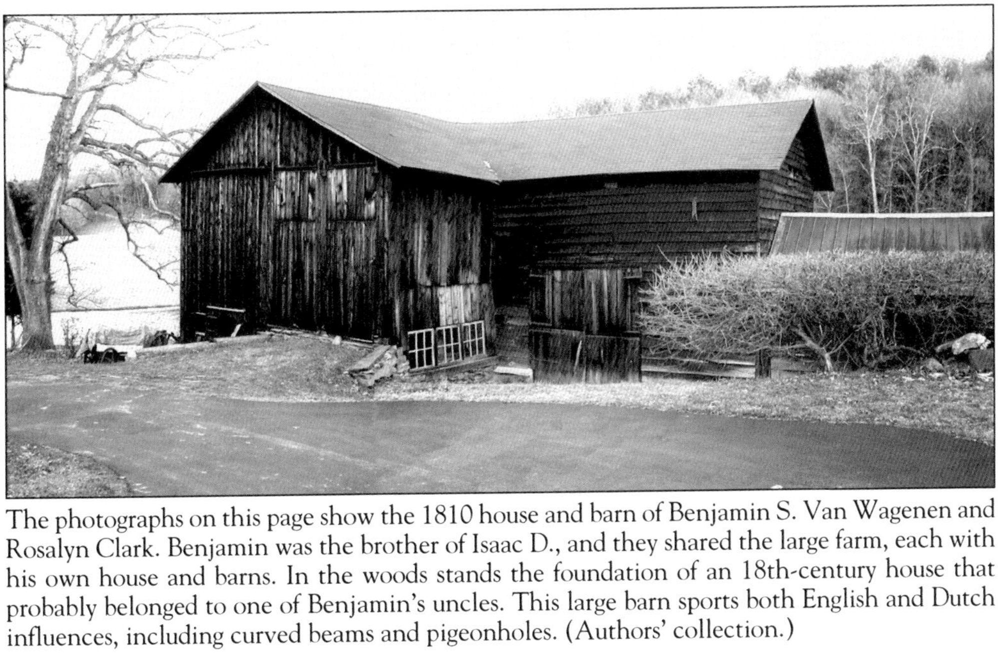

The photographs on this page show the 1810 house and barn of Benjamin S. Van Wagenen and Rosalyn Clark. Benjamin was the brother of Isaac D., and they shared the large farm, each with his own house and barns. In the woods stands the foundation of an 18th-century house that probably belonged to one of Benjamin's uncles. This large barn sports both English and Dutch influences, including curved beams and pigeonholes. (Authors' collection.)

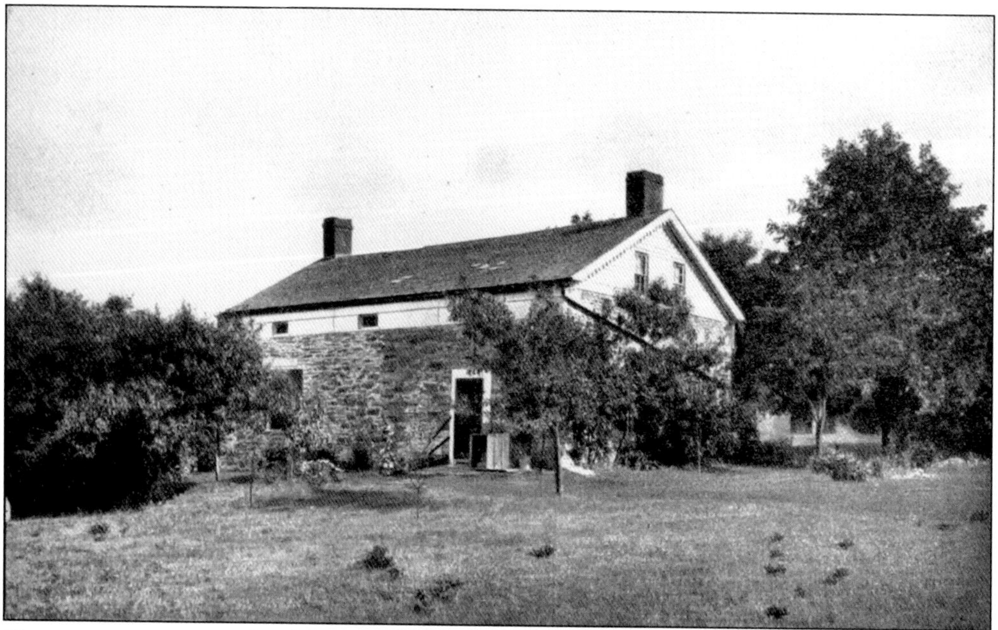

Here we see one example of the many old stone houses in the Port Ewen area. This is the Jug Tavern, built as a VanVliet home in 1767 and photographed *c.* 1900. In spite of the fun stories, it is unlikely that George Washington waited here during the battle of Kingston.[7] Jan VanVliet received a land grant from King William of Holland in 1652. The VanAkens settled in 1646. Two of their ancient houses (*c.* 1660 and 1690) still stand.

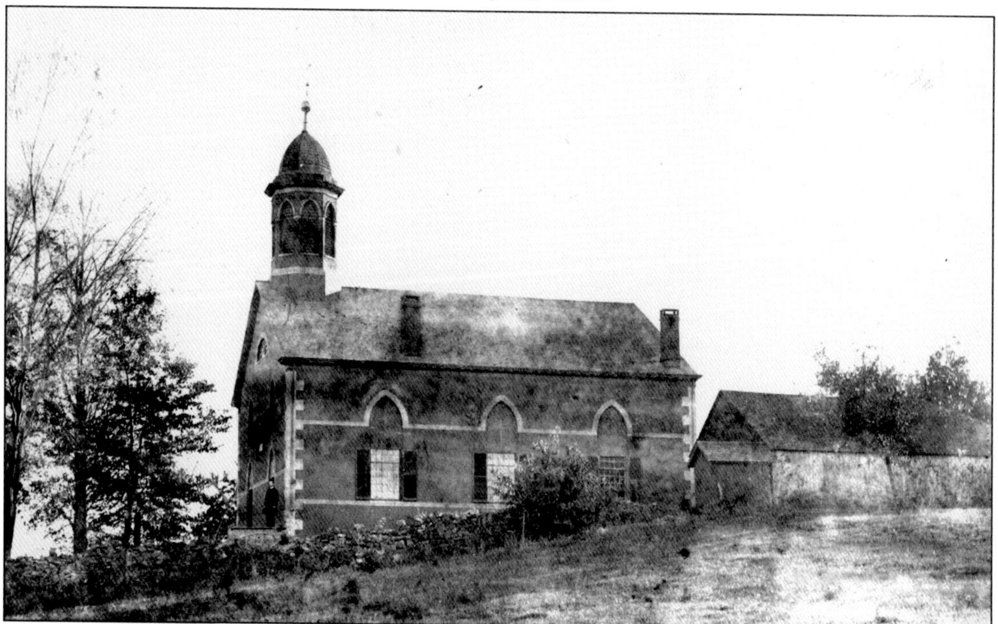

The Low Dutch Church of Klyne Esopus stands proudly on a small hill in Ulster Park. It was the first church in Esopus, established in 1791 near this location. The edifice in the photograph was constructed in 1827 and has recently been listed on the state and national historic registers through the efforts of Marian Sahler, Dorothy Dumond, the authors, and John Bonafide of the New York State Office of Parks, Recreation, and Historic Preservation. (Authors' collection.)

A 30-inch wampum belt of braided hemp and sewan accompanies this 1665 reaffirmation agreement made between Richard Nicholls, Esquire Governor, under his royal highness the Duke of York, and the Sachems and people called the Sopus Indyans.[8] Drafted during the transition to English rule, it was in part to confirm existing land titles. While the swan song of Netherlands governance occurred in 1674, the language tarried much longer, since many official documents were recorded in Dutch until 1710.

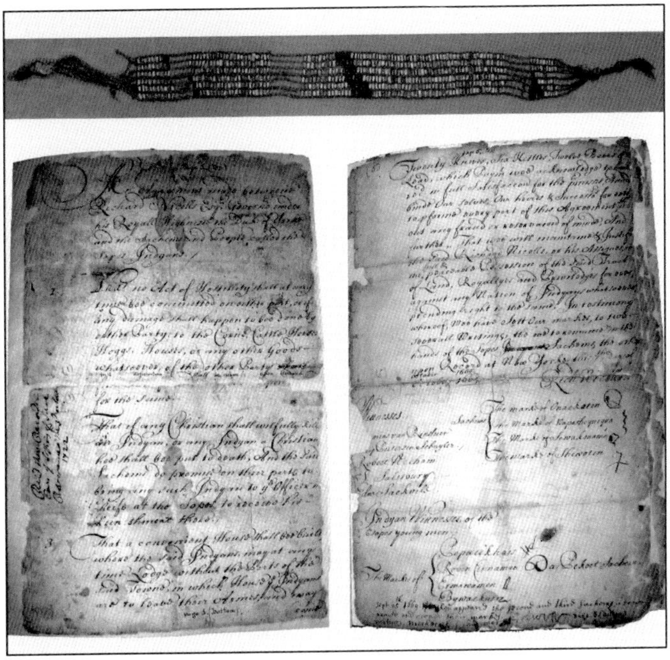

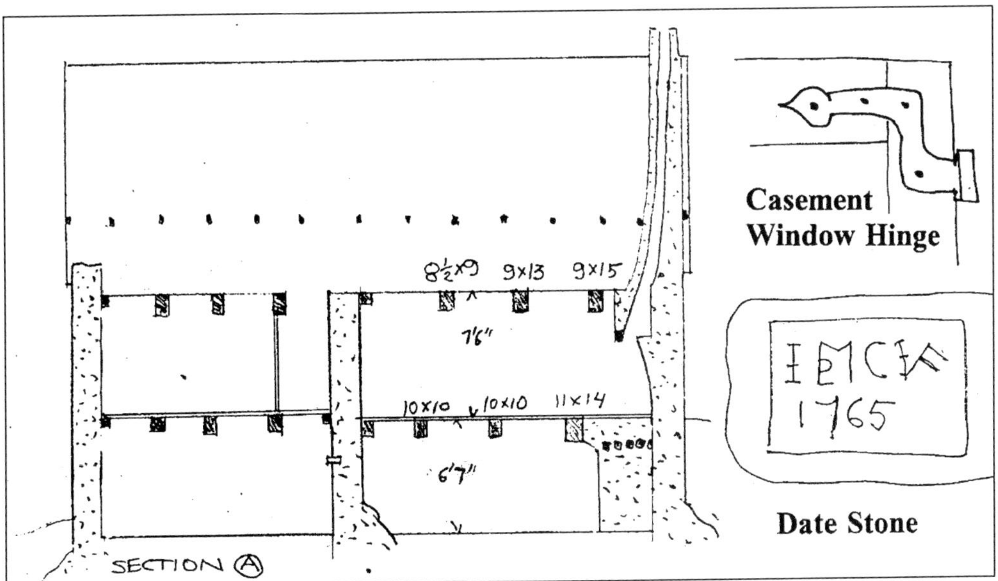

This is the floor plan of the Freer-Delamater millhouse as drawn by Peter Sinclair. Sinclair is the chief executive officer of Hudson Valley Vernacular Architecture, a group dedicated to the preservation of historic barns and homes. The floor plan shows the original house (c. 1745) at the left and the expansion at the right. The ancient, jambless fireplace and chimney have been replaced by a staircase (center). The house still contains a very early casement window and a barred basement window.

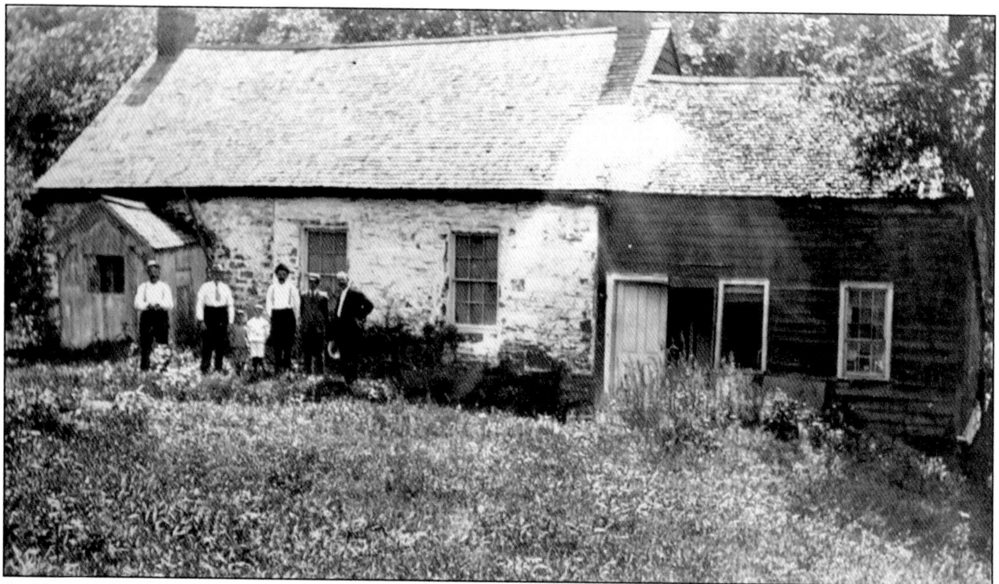

In Freerville stands the old farmhouse of Gerrit Isaac Freer. The section at the far right is a 19th-century addition. The center section bears a date stone reading, "GIF IDLM 1765." The left-hand portion is the original house and dates from no later than 1745. The fleeing crew of the *Martha Washington* is said to have sought refuge here after scuttling their ship west of Hamilton's Island during the burning of Kingston. (Authors' collection.)

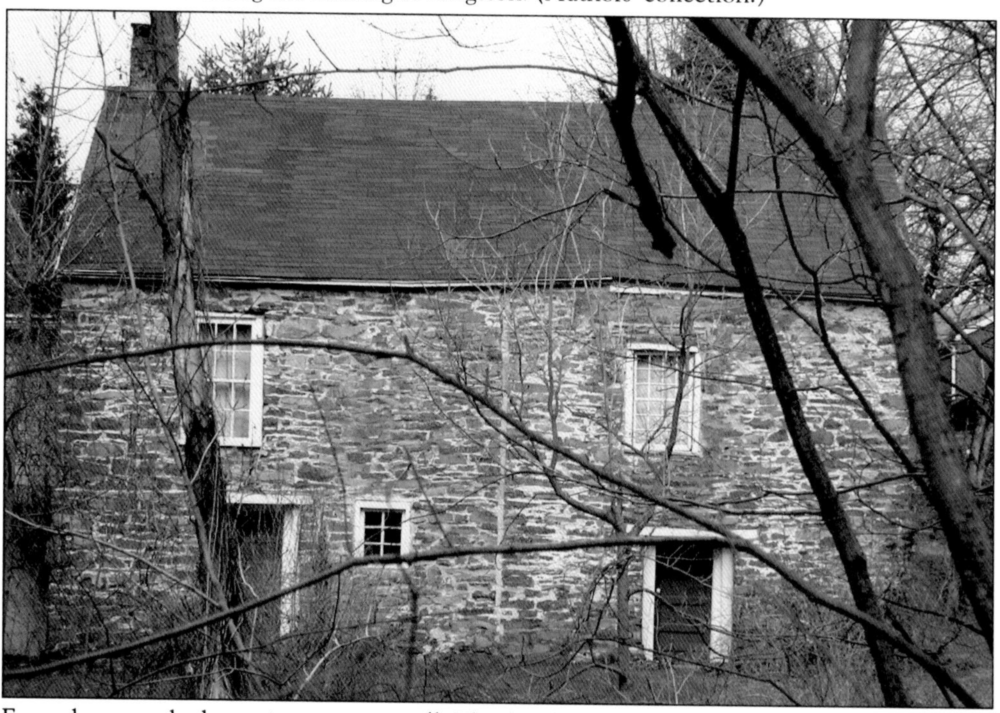

From the west, the house is two stories tall. The face has not changed since the late 1700s. The line at the center divides the two stages of early construction. Isaac DeLaMater and Gerrit I. Freer built and ran a gristmill on the Dwarfskill c. 1750. The millrace ran just in front of this view, and the mill was to the left near the Rondout Kill. (Authors' collection.)

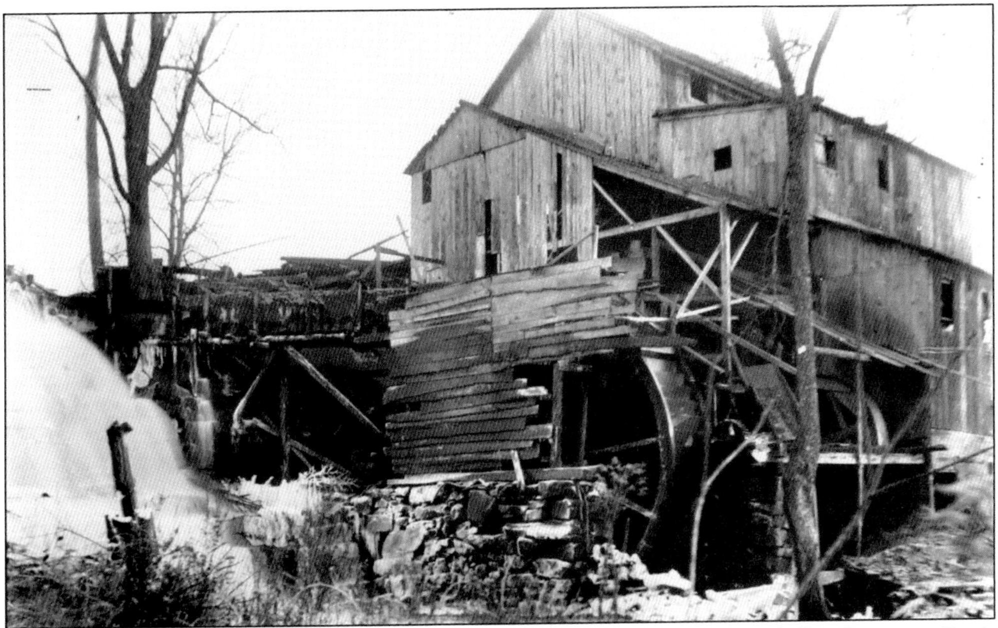

Depicted here are the ruins of a large mid-18th-century mill on the Swartekill at Sturgeon Pool. The mill had already been long neglected by the time this 1890s photograph was taken. The first known deed for this land[9] was to Arien Gerretse in March 1724 and granted him, among other lands, "four acres along the south side of the Swarte Kill by the two falls . . . and privilege to make two dams upon said falls."

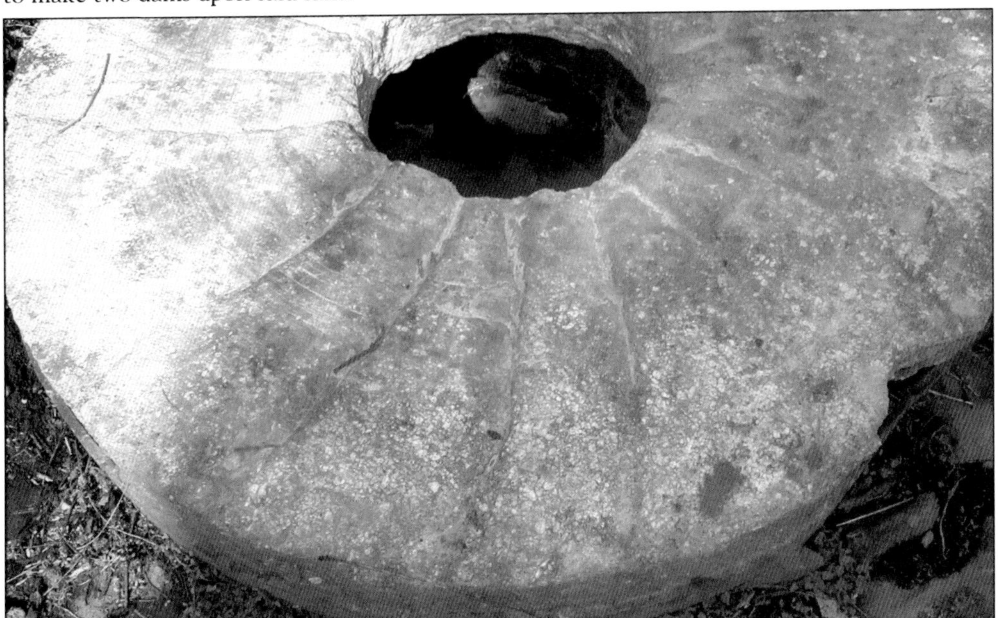

This is one of the original millstones from the Freer mill in New Salem. It appears to be a base stone and measures 53½ inches in diameter and 6 inches thick. It is banded with a welded iron ring two inches tall and half an inch thick. The center hole is 15 inches in diameter. This is a one-piece early Shawangunk millstone, but the banding is typical of that used on imported sectional stones. (Photograph by the author.)

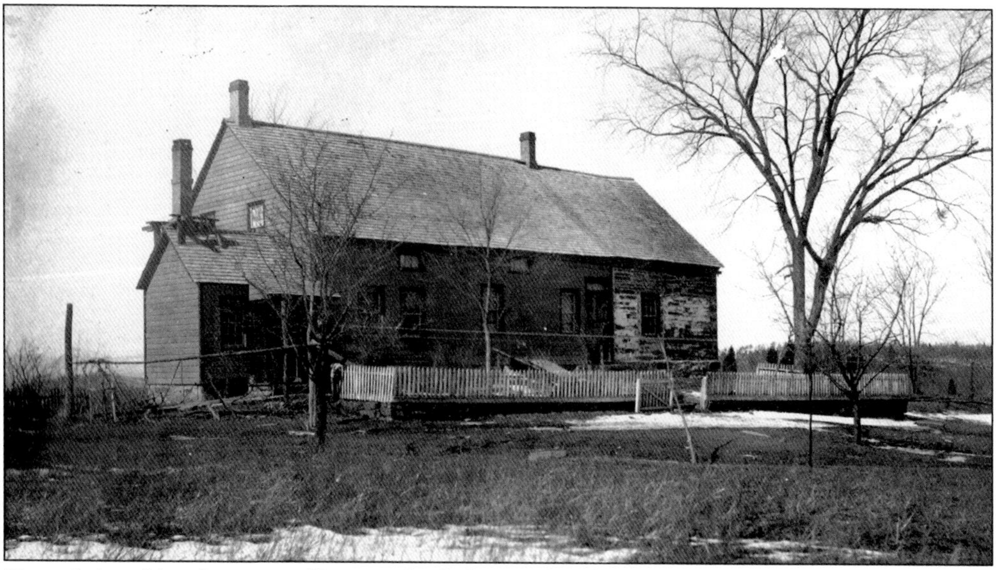

One of the oldest homes in Esopus, the lighter colored part on the right side was the 1709 cabin of Willem Smit, who came to work on the Hardenburg Patent in 1690. Later in the 18th century, the original ceiling was raised and a large addition added to the house. This is how it appeared during the 1890s, when it was owned by Luman Freer. The house is off Church Hill Road. (Beatrice and Martin Jordan collection.)

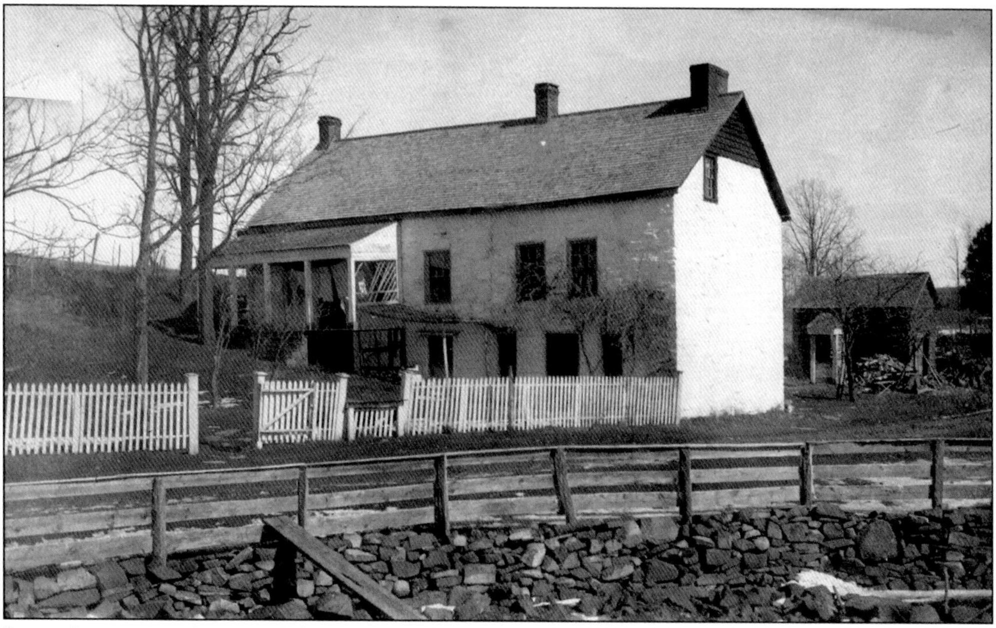

James Perrine was born on July 29, 1780, in France and immigrated to the United States to raise his eight sons and one daughter. His son John took over the family farm and businesses near Perrine's Bridge. James Perrine died in 1849. This 1750 stone house was home to the James (a grandson) and Helen Perrine family in the 1890s, when this photograph was taken. The view is to the northeast. (Beatrice and Martin Jordan collection.)

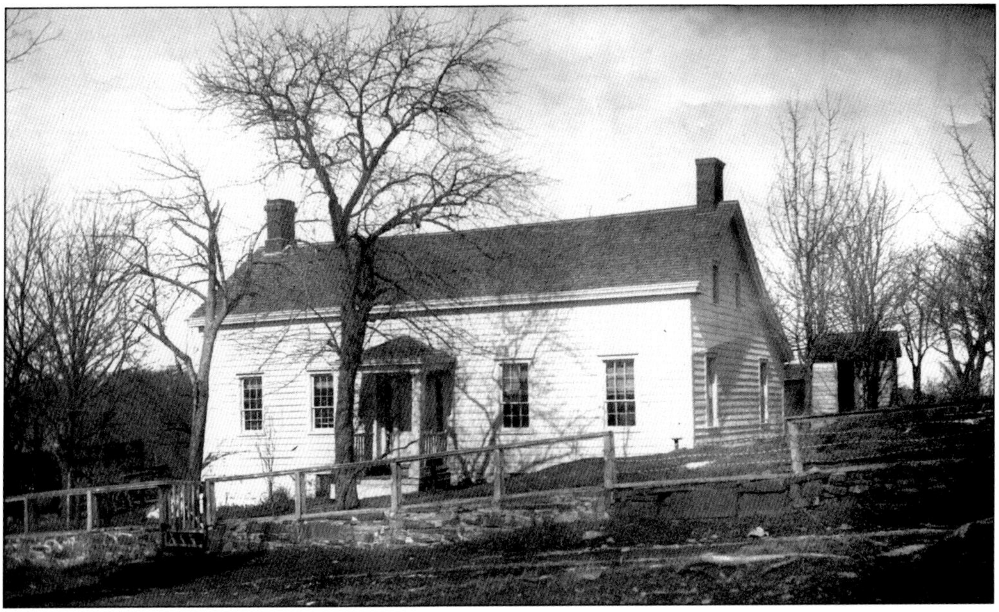

Shown are two 1890s views of the second Smith house in Rifton. The house is said to have been constructed in 1730 by a son of Willem Smit. Like his house, this one also stands on Church Hill Road. Barely visible at the left rear is part of the carriage house. The small building at the right rear is a toolshed, and the view is almost due north. (Beatrice and Martin Jordan collection.)

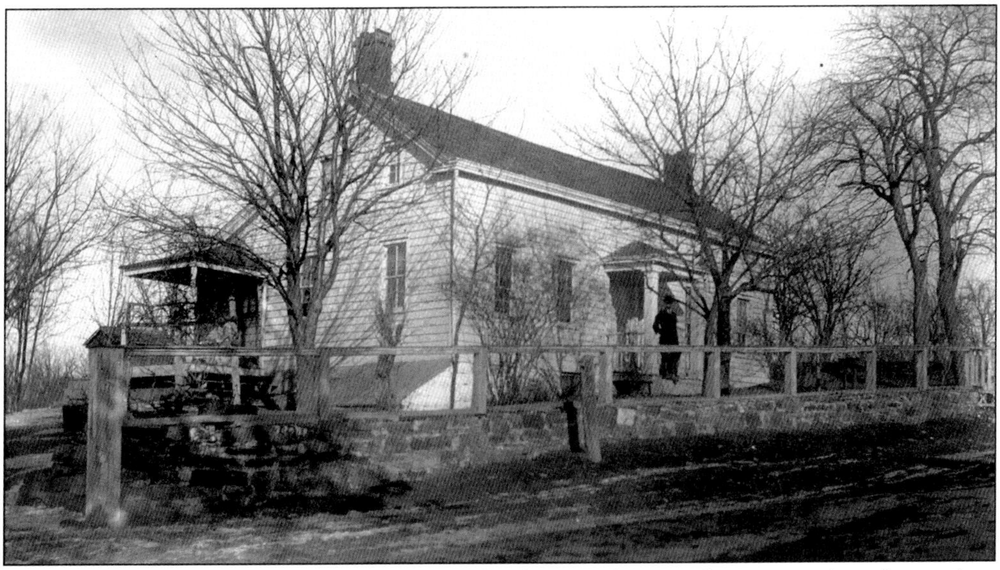

The view is toward the northeast and up the hill. The two photographs appear to have been taken at about the same time. Standing on the front porch is the owner, David Relyea. At the left side of the house are a cellar entrance in front and a back door to the kitchen at the rear. The rear saltbox portion of the house is an early-1800s addition. (Beatrice and Martin Jordan collection.)

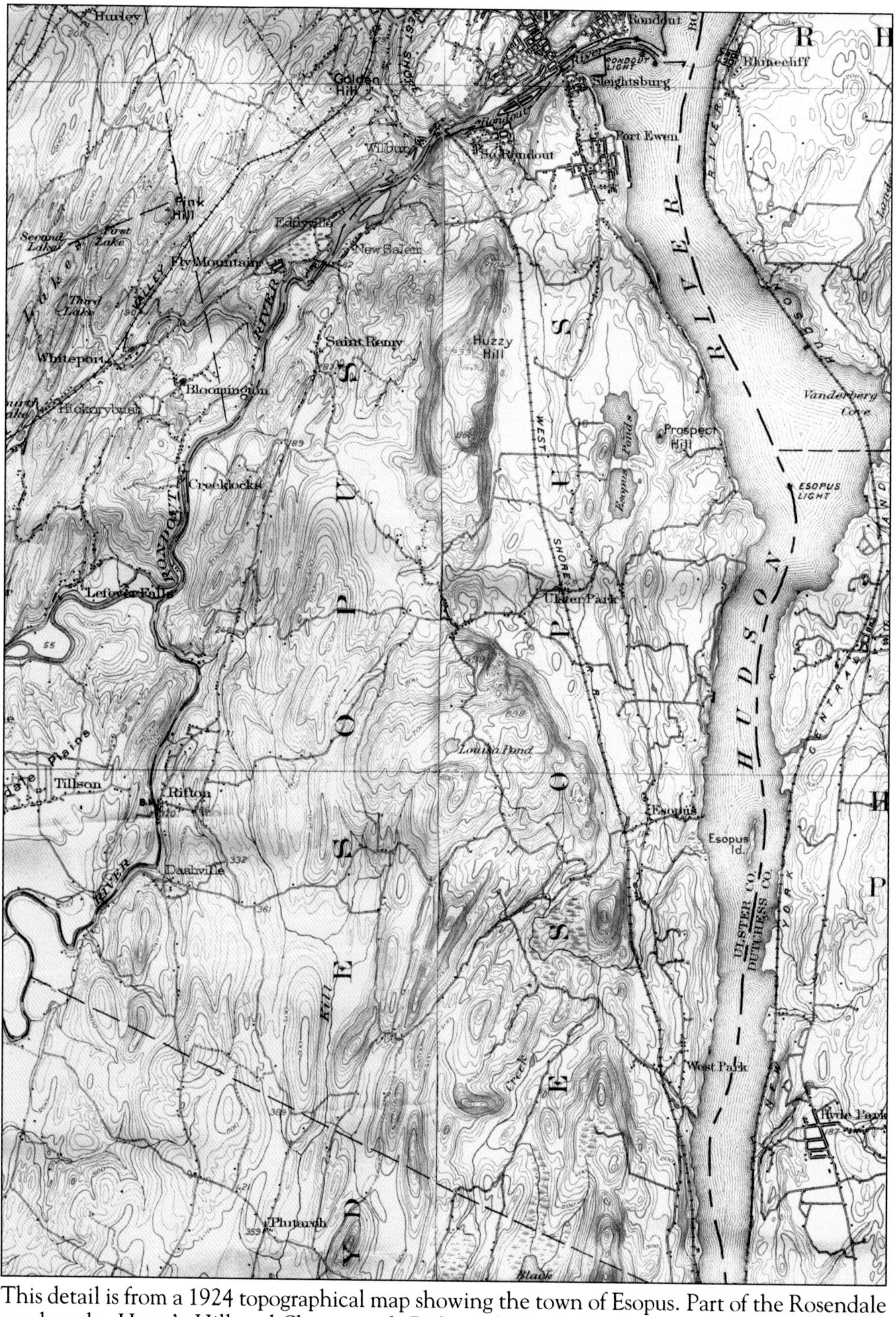

This detail is from a 1924 topographical map showing the town of Esopus. Part of the Rosendale quadrangle, Huzzy's Hill and Shawpeneak Ridge, which divide the town, are visible at the center of the map, as are the Rondout and Wallkill, which form Esopus's northern and western boundaries. (Authors' collection.)

Two

Bridging the Towns

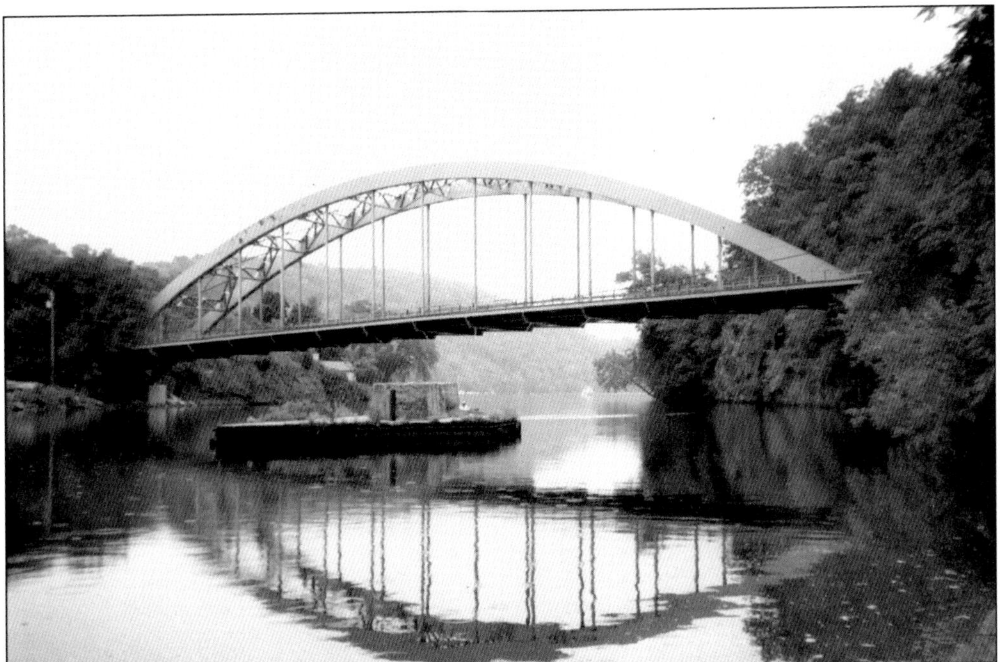

Esopus is bordered on three sides by water: the Hudson River to the east, the Rondout Creek to the north and northwest, and the Wallkill to the west. It is no wonder that its inhabitants devoted considerable time and effort to finding convenient ways to traverse those waters. In the earliest days, the inhabitants of Esopus and their neighbors crossed rivers at natural or man-made shallow places called fords. Some enterprising settlers soon discovered that ferry boats were a needed asset and a way to augment the family income. Benjamin VanAken had a ferry crossing the Rondout from St. Remy to Creek Locks before 1811. Other ferries were at Freerville (New Salem), Twalfskill, and Sleightsburg. A ford existed at Wagendal a century earlier. Eventually, bridges were built, but not necessarily where the reader might expect them. The first bridge over the Rondout on Route 9W was not constructed until 1922. We would like to take the reader on a journey across the earlier bridges of Esopus. This journey will begin in 1835. (Photograph of Eddyville–New Salem Bridge by Susan B. Wick.)

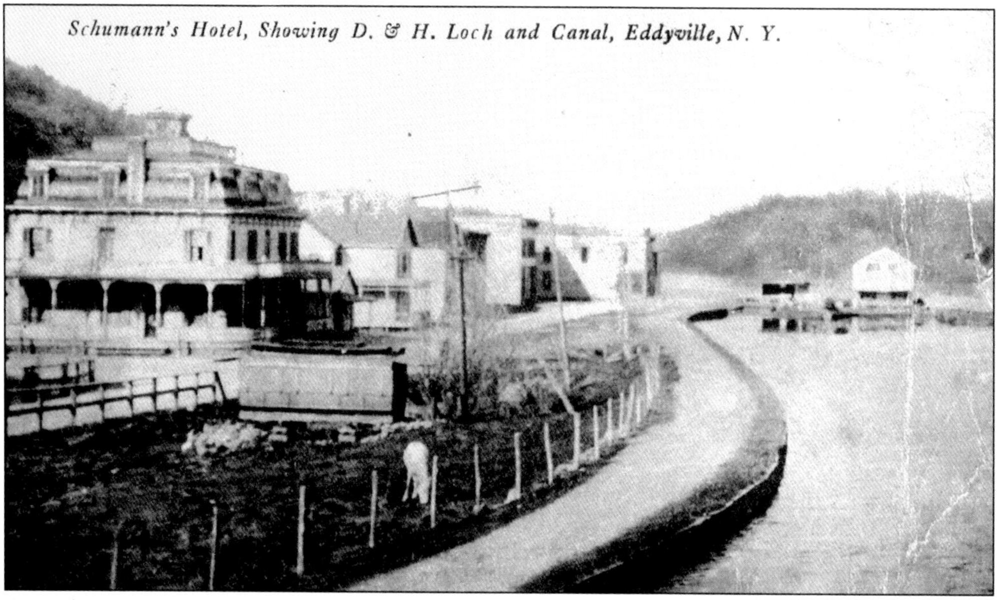

Directly across the Rondout from New Salem and St. Remy lies the hamlet of Eddyville. In early days, Eddyville had far closer ties to its Esopus sisters than it did to Kingston. In fact, until 1835, there was no road leading directly from Eddyville to Kingston. Instead, Eddyville, Freerville, and St. Remy were collectively called Fly Mountain. This name remained until the mid-1880s.

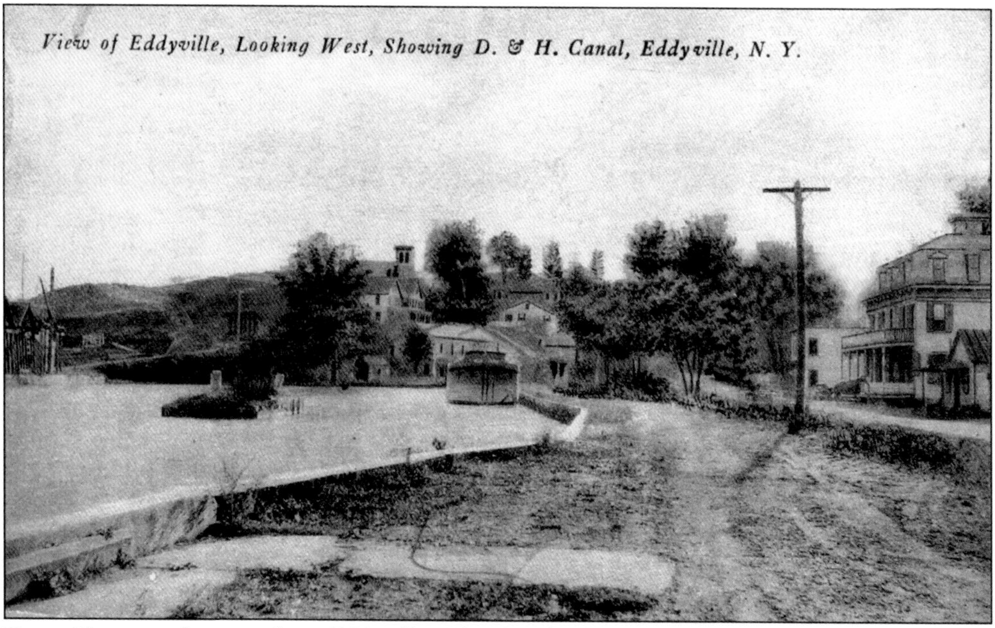

Two old postcard views show Eddyville. The first looks eastward toward Rondout, and the second looks westward toward the falls. Schumann's Hotel is visible in both pictures. Eddyville was a canal town and as such provided employment and entertainment to the residents of Fly Mountain on both sides of the creek, including Peter, the son of Sojourner Truth.[10] Freerville had extensive dockage, stores, housing, and the ferry of John Freer. (Authors' collection.)

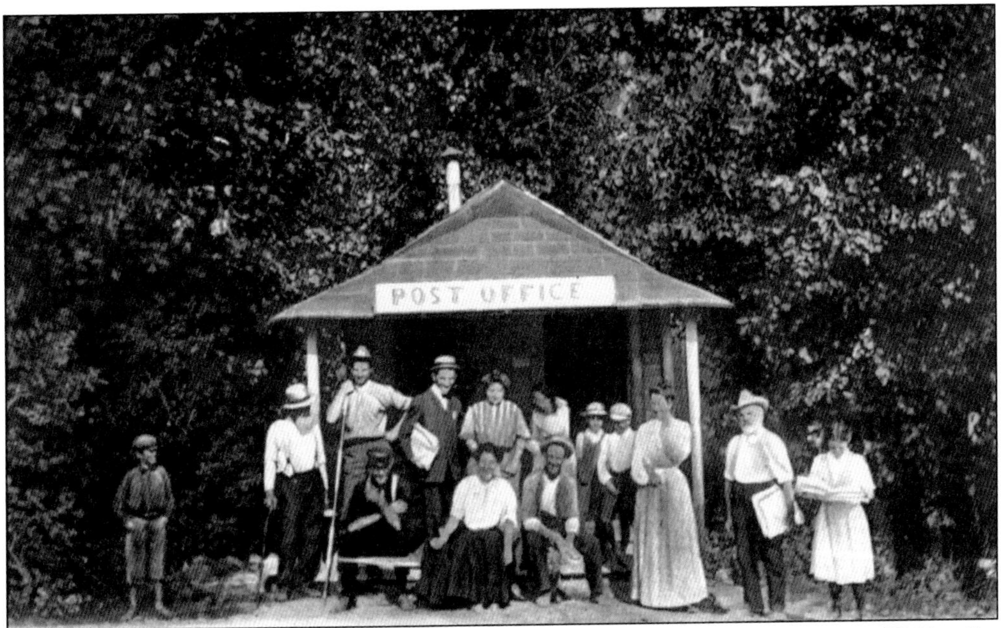

Until 1888, the Fly Mountain postal district served the residents and businesses of Eddyville, Greenkill, St. Remy, and New Salem. On January 6, 1887, Edgar Ellsworth applied to open a post office in St. Remy. One year later, in January 1888, Ellsworth is listed in U.S. Postal Service records as postmaster.[11] The man at the left (with white beard) is Peter M. Decker, who carried the mail to St. Remy. (Authors' collection.)

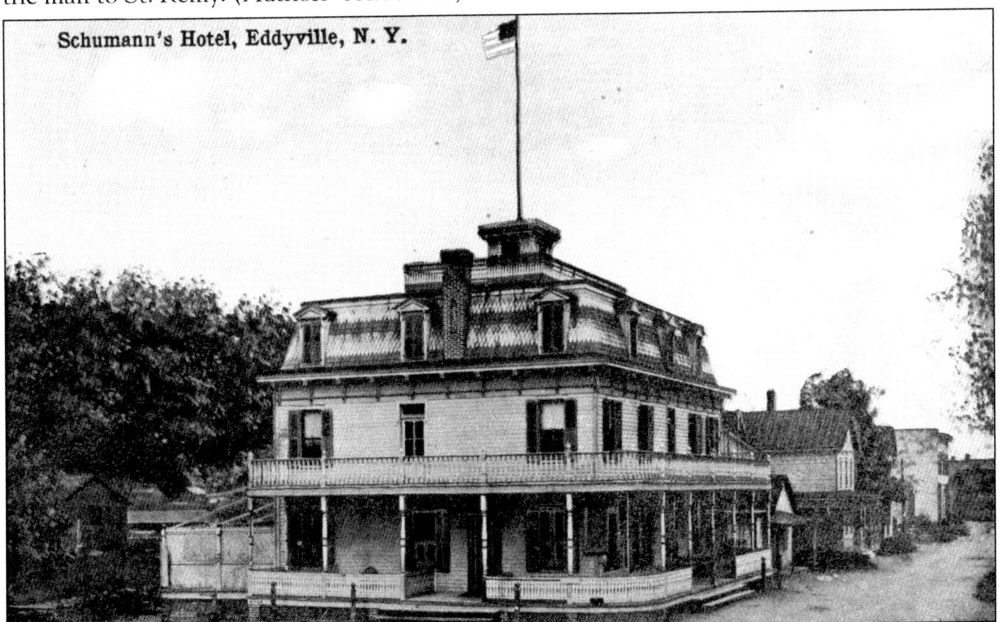

Here is a view of Schumann's Hotel, which was the common point in the photographs on the previous page. The hotel was razed when a new stretch of highway was constructed in 1959. The building at the end of the road is now the Anchorage restaurant. Before opening this hotel, Mr. Schumann was a teacher at District No. 5, across the Rondout and up the hill. (Authors' collection.)

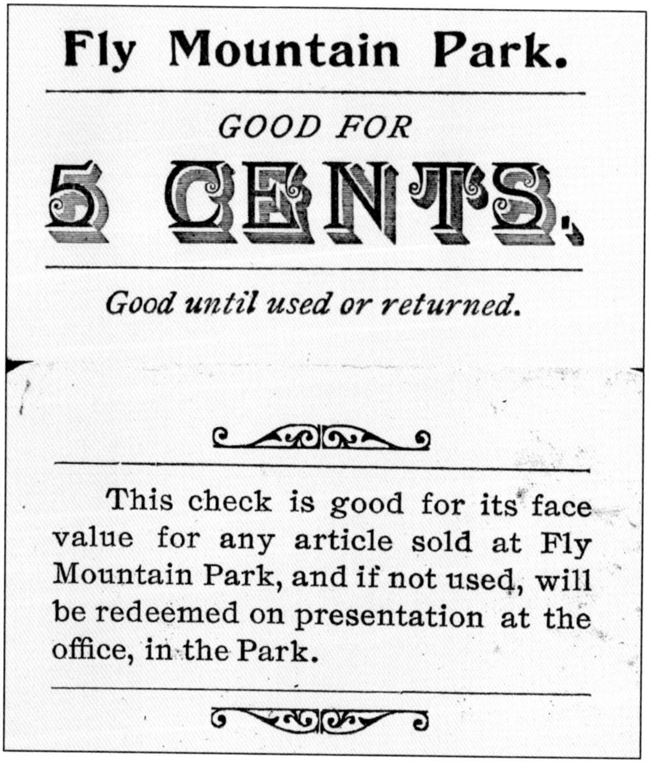
Fly Mountain Park.

GOOD FOR

5 CENTS.

Good until used or returned.

This check is good for its face value for any article sold at Fly Mountain Park, and if not used, will be redeemed on presentation at the office, in the Park.

Fly Mountain Park was located on Haber's Hill in New Salem. Haber's Hill is a high promontory overlooking the Rondout Creek, New Salem, and Eddyville. In the barn was a training facility for prizefighters. The large house is still home to the Haber family, who started the Haber Steamboat Company in 1886,[12] but most of the outbuildings associated with the amusement park are long gone. (Authors' collection, gift of Mrs. Haber.)

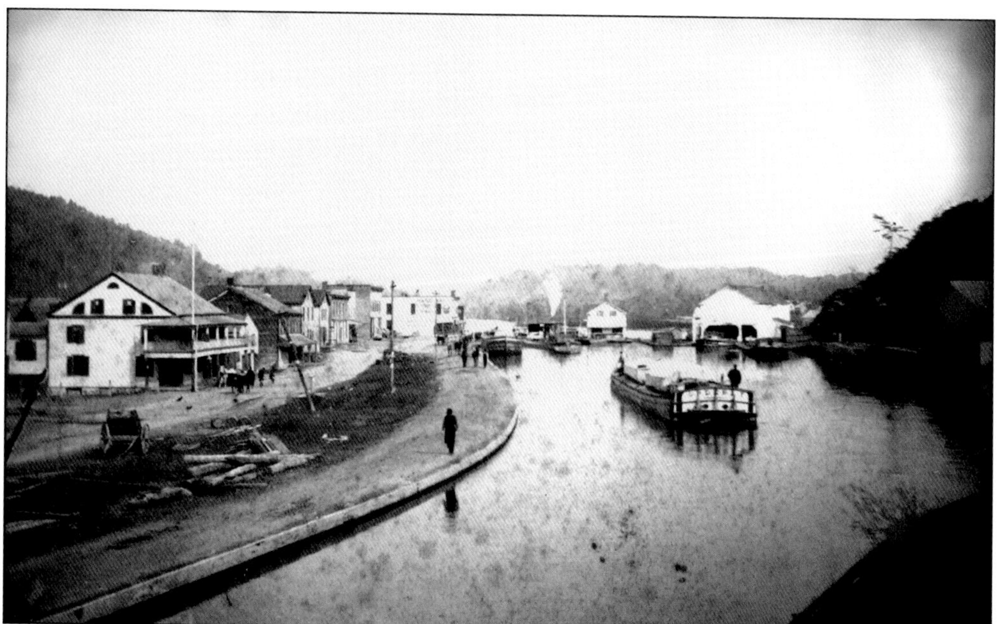

This photograph of the Delaware and Hudson Canal terminus at Eddyville was taken c. 1875 from one of many small bridges over the canal. This is where the canal entered tidewater and where canal boatmen stopped to rest and relax. Eddyville had many taverns. Three of them survived almost until the end of the 20th century. After 1857, opening a tavern required a petition. A petition for "Edyville" in 1868 was signed by 20 men.[13]

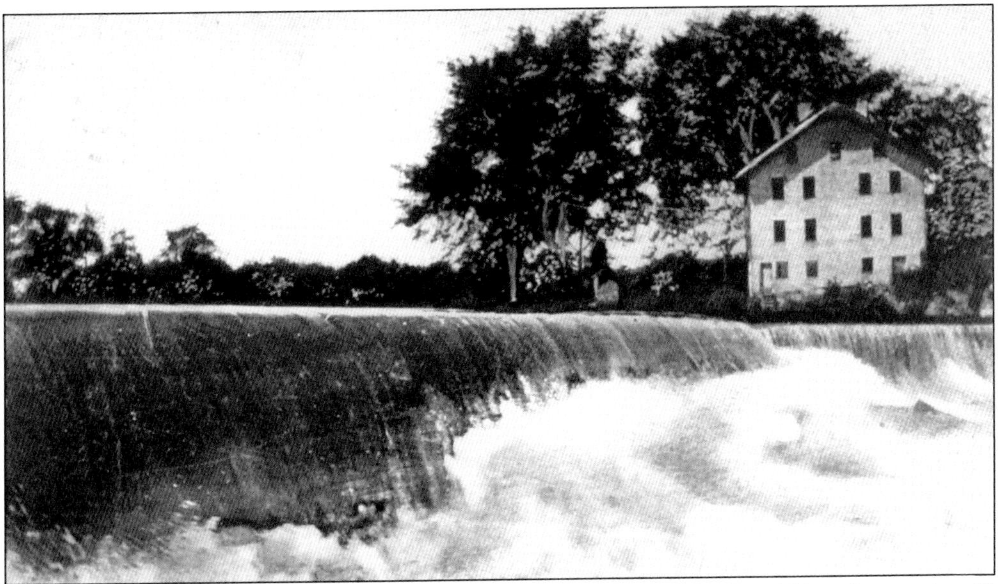

For the early settlers, water carried power, and power meant life. In 1911, a large gristmill house still stood at the Eddyville–St. Remy Falls. In ancient times, the technology to harness this amount of power was still in its infancy, but in 1796, a deed was given to partners John Armstrong and James Grier[14] to construct a splitting and rolling mill at the falls. (These types of mills worked metal into plates and split the plates into small rods for nails and other items.) (Authors' collection.)

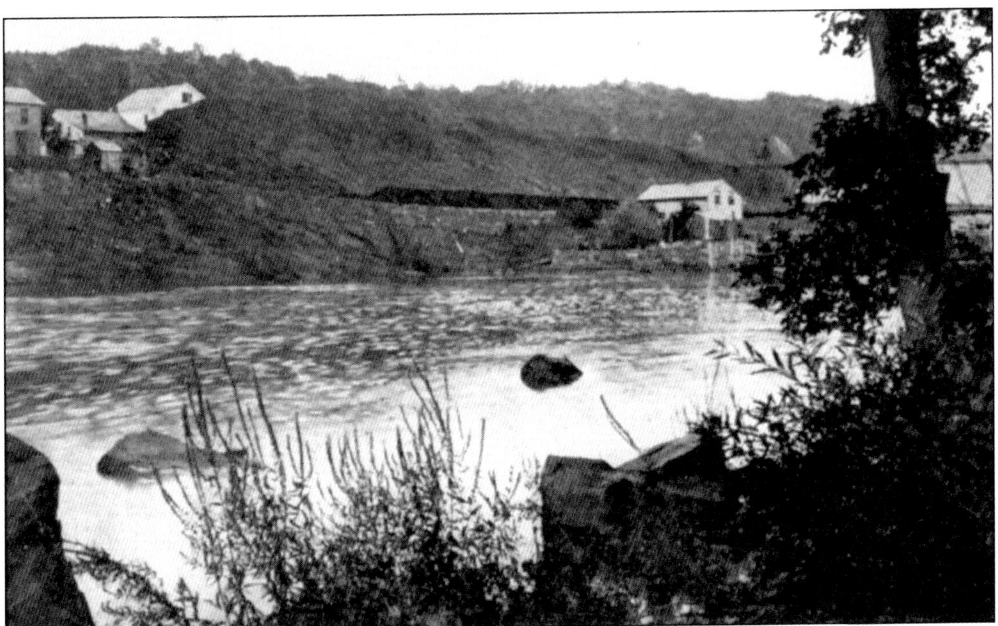

We do not know if the partners were successful, but in 1801, the falls, seven adjoining acres in St. Remy, and water rights for dockage and repair were sold outright to Thomas Tillotson for the sum of "one thousand, seven hundred and seven dollars and fifty cents"[15] to use as he saw fit. This was the first large-scale harnessing of the power of the falls. This 1905 photograph shows part of the 1867 iron bridge at the right. (Authors' collection.)

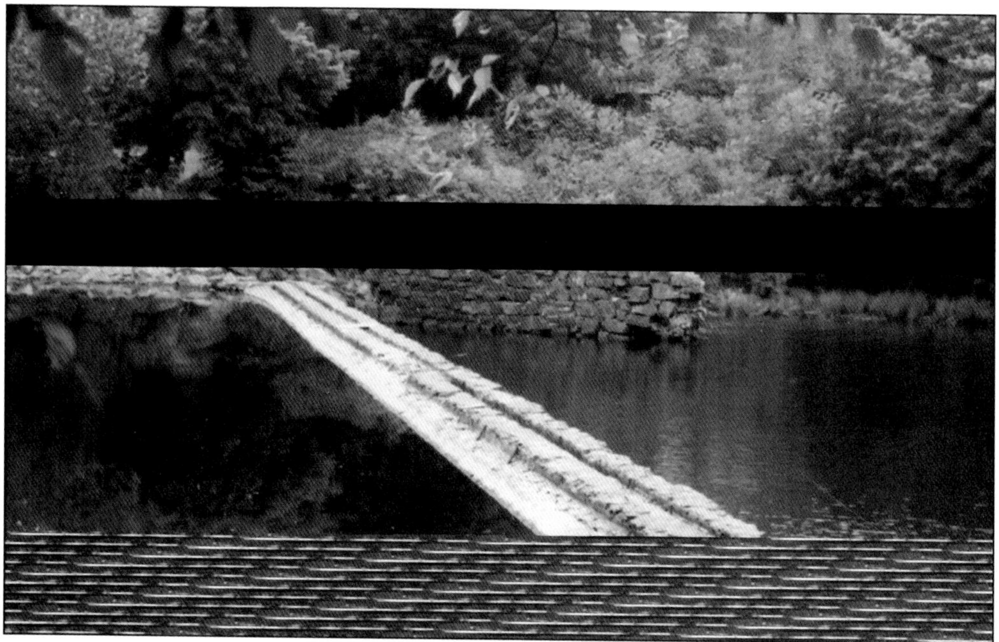

During the drought of August 1999, the falls were essentially stilled. The top of the dam is about four feet wide and has three full-length indentations where massive timbers are spiked to the stone-and-concrete structure. The iron spikes are at least two feet long and a full inch in diameter. At the far end of the 200-foot-long dam stands the remains of the sluiceway, where the mill wheel turned. (Photograph by the author.)

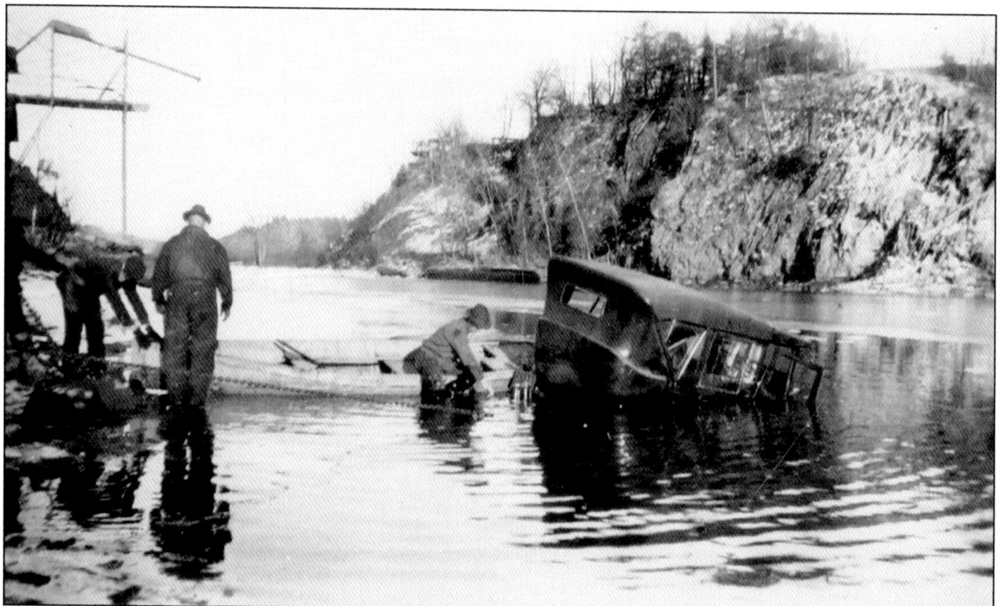

It is said that Harry Houdini himself practiced his water escapes near the Rondout Falls when visiting his good friend and biographer Walter Gibson[16] (creator of *The Shadow*) on Cutler Hill. Let us hope that the occupants of this car managed to exercise Houdini-like skills in 1929, when they drove into the creek under the bridge. The workmen are using rigging from the Roosa sawmill to bring the vehicle back to dry land. (Martin Jordan collection.)

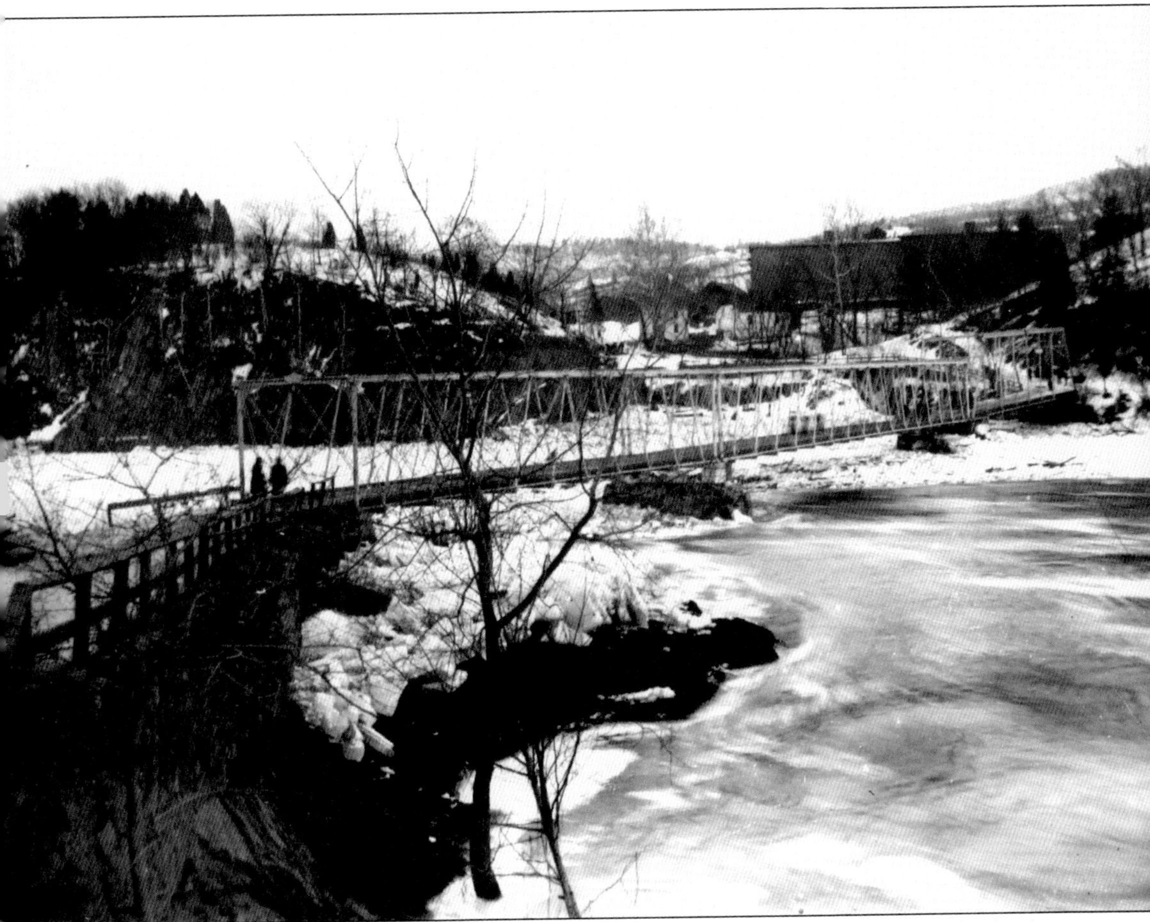

The great flood of January 1910 was unkind to the Eddyville–New Salem Bridge. The bridge itself was constructed *c.* 1867 and looks rather fragile.[17] The lightweight truss construction was state of the art for the era—spindly, light in weight, and quite strong. However, it was designed to carry only foot, horse, and carriage traffic. The spring runoff during the year this photograph was taken was very heavy, and although the structure had already survived the great floods of 1869 and 1878,[18] it was torn from its piers by this freshet. The very large structure in the background is Dimond's[19] icehouse, and the smaller structure in front and to the left of the icehouse is the *c.* 1745 Freer house. This photograph comes from an original glass-plate negative. Many people believe that the bridge shown above was the first bridge between New Salem and Eddyville. They are only half correct. It was the first *iron* bridge. Turn to the next page for newly discovered information. (Florence Prehn collection.)

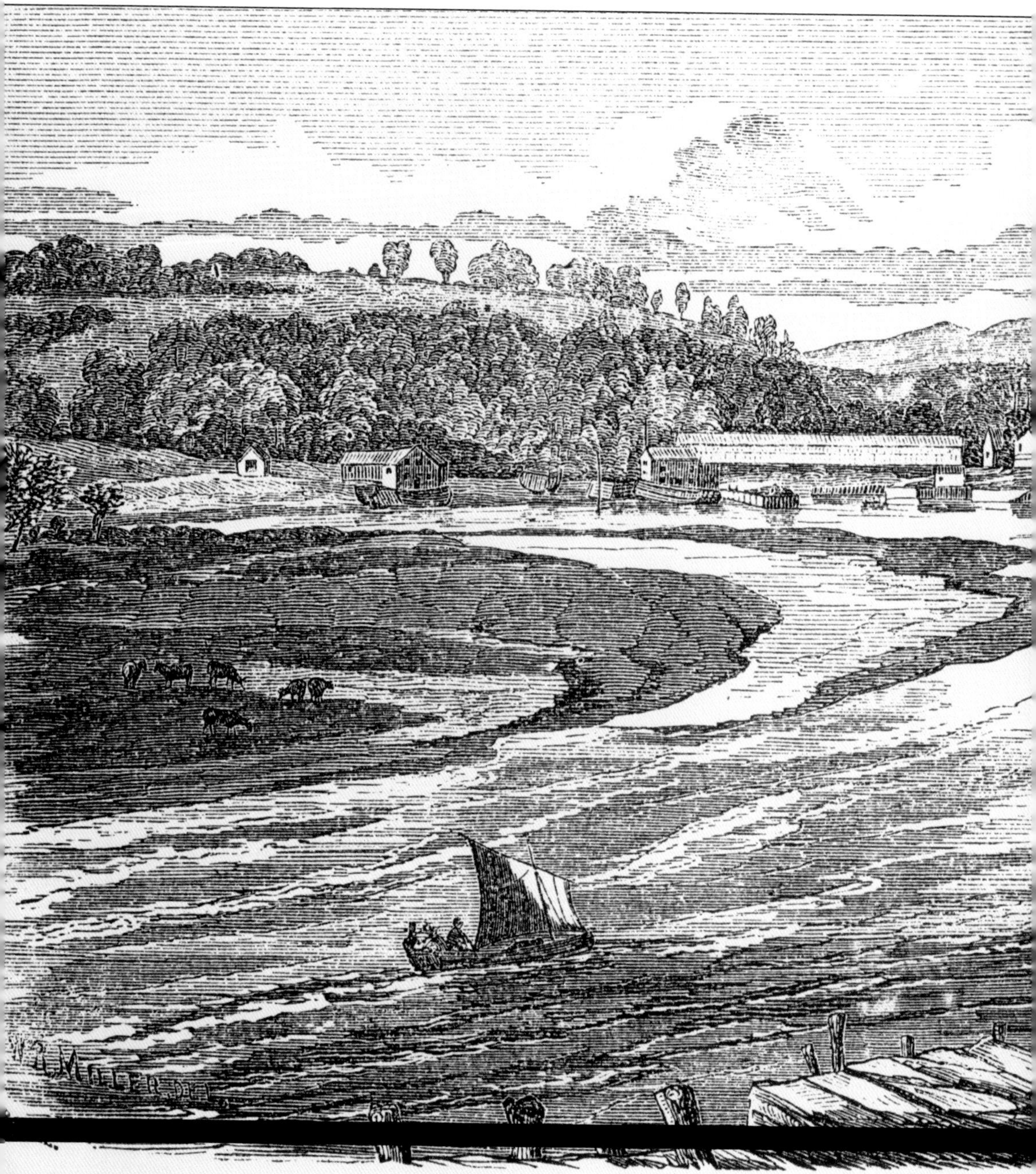

EDIEVILLE, ON THE RO

This outstanding woodcut print was published in *Gleason's Pictorial Drawing Room Companion* on September 9, 1854. The accompanying text read, "VILLAGE OF EDIEVILLE [*sic*], N.Y. This pleasant little village is situated on the Rondout Creek, a small but pretty river of New York State, which rises in Sullivan county, flows west [*sic*] through Ulster County, and enters the Hudson near Rondout village. The appearance of the town is of a charming character, and the

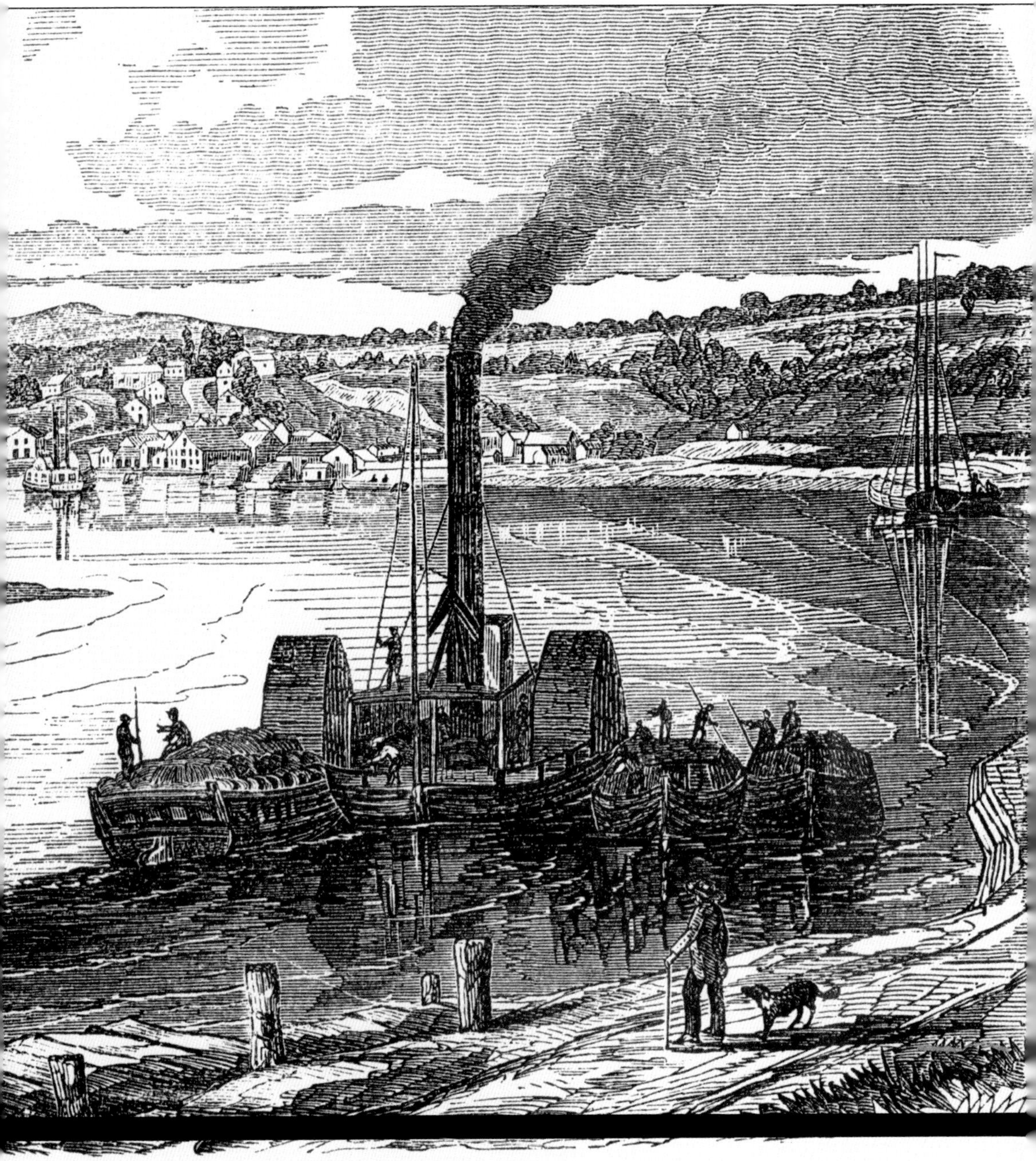

T CREEK, NEW YORK.

surrounding scenery is quite picturesque." In this view, we see a steam-powered tugboat in the foreground, towing laden canal boats to Rondout, and Eddyville in the background. On the left is a small sailing vessel, and livestock are grazing on Hamilton's Island (now Gumaer's Island). The background shows something marvelous. Below Haber's Hill and spanning the creek is a long covered bridge. (Courtesy of Gary W. Ewer.)

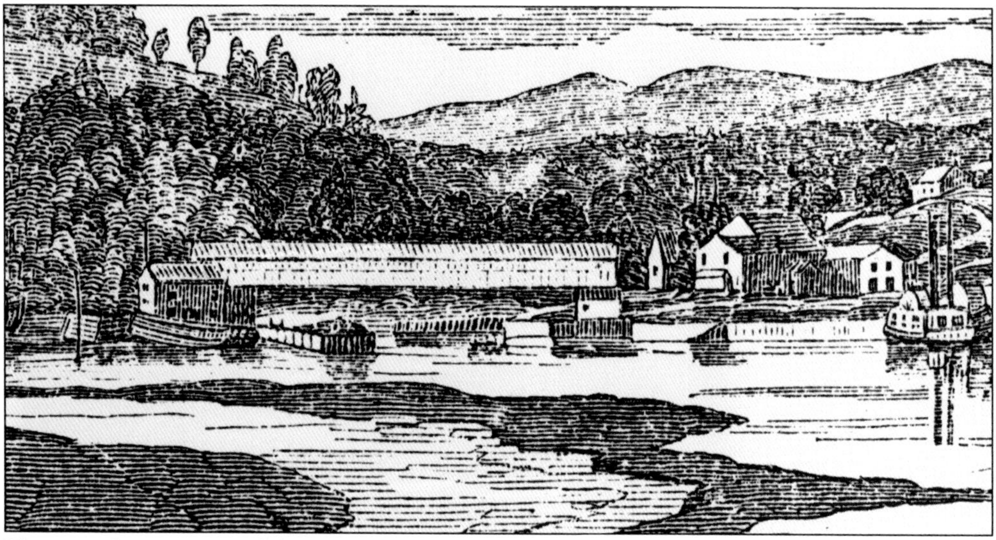

This is a closeup view of the covered bridge linking Freerville (New Salem) and Eddyville. It appears to be of Town Lattice style[20] and about 165 feet long. The bridge connected Water Street in Freerville with Canal Street in Eddyville. The Eddy Ville Bridge Company filed a site plan for this bridge on July 8, 1844.[21] The northern abutment was located 75 feet west of the old one on higher ground.

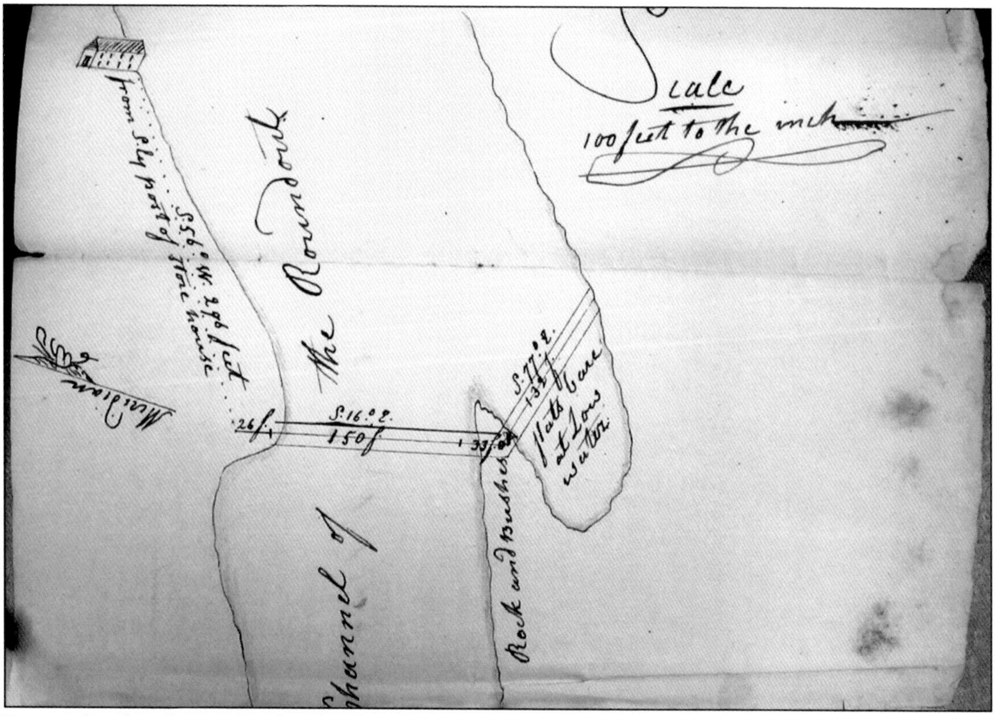

Papers for the above plat for the first bridge were filed by the Eddy Ville Bridge Company on June 3, 1835.[22] The bridge was constructed shortly thereafter but was seemingly too close to the water. A freshet washed it away in January 1839. Prior to the construction of this bridge,[23] John G. Freer of Freerville ran a ferry across the creek. Unfortunately, the original sketch is too fragile to unfold fully for scanning or copying.

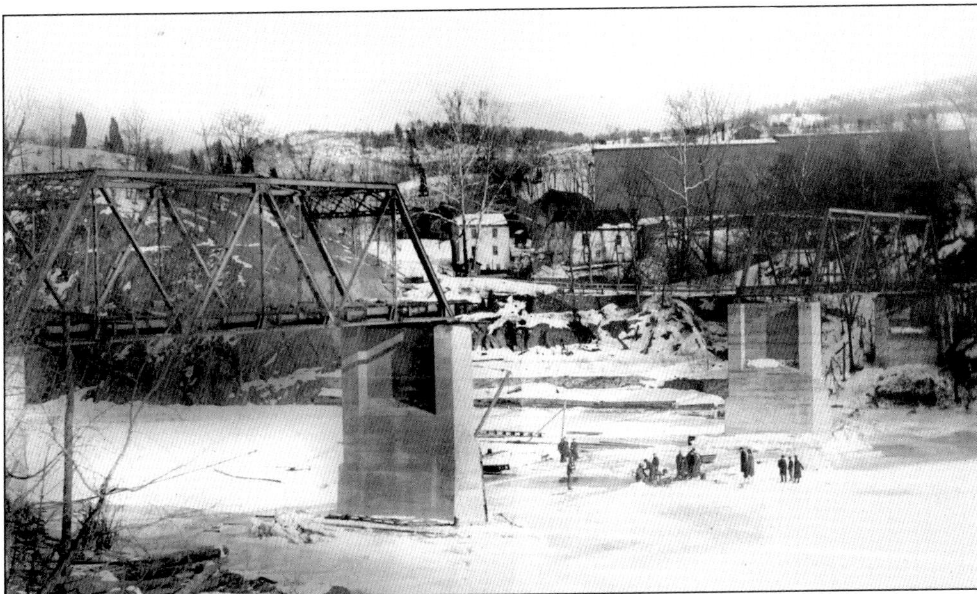

Shown is the Eddyville-Freerville Bridge after removal of the 1867 iron bridge and during construction of the fourth bridge, which was the second iron bridge. It is the winter of 1912, and the bridge is two-thirds complete. Notice how much higher the piers seem than in the photograph earlier in the chapter. We can also see many local residents enjoying a day on the ice under the bridge and Dimond's icehouse to the rear. (Beatrice Jordan collection.).

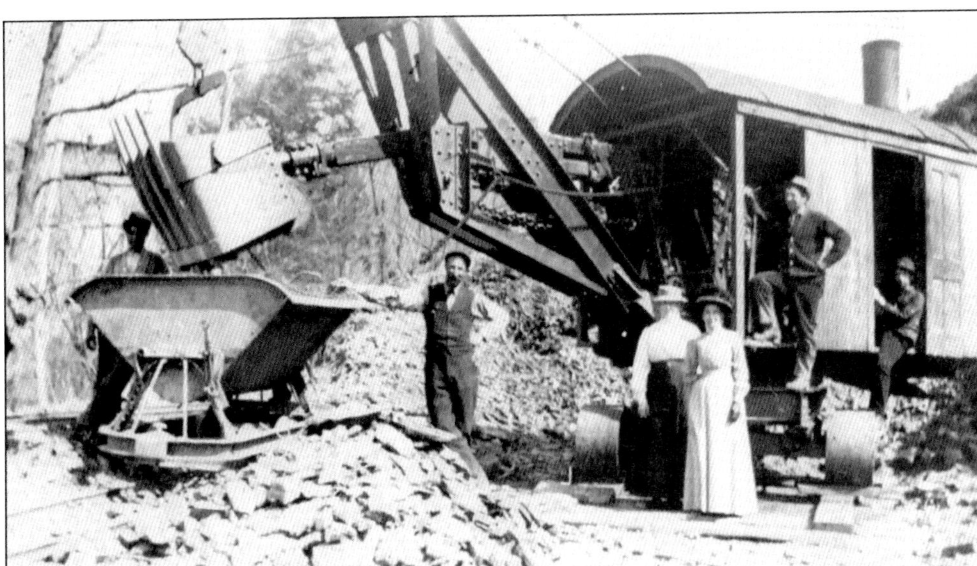

In order to build the new and improved bridge of 1912, the crew had to cut through a large amount of rock on the southern side of the creek. Here we see the proud workmen with their state-of-the-art Merrihew steam shovel. The reverse of this photograph is inscribed, "From Elizabeth Freer to Aimee [Mrs. Alfred VanAken] 1912." (Raymond Krom collection.)

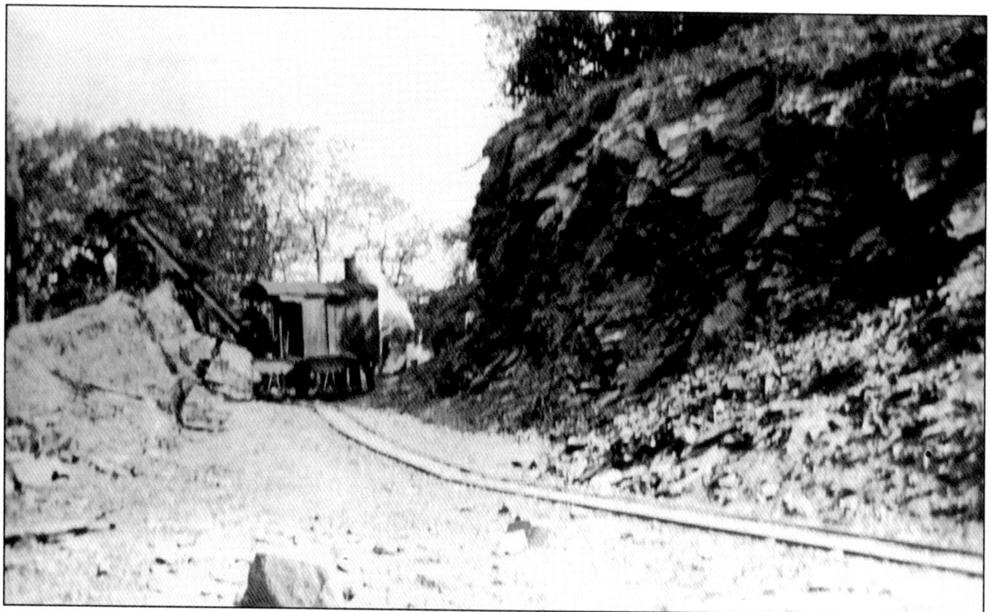

This is another 1912 photograph of the steam shovel, which is cutting through the hard rock between the east end of the bridge and the icehouse. The road made a 90-degree turn after the bridge, hugged the side of the hill, and proceeded northward for one-tenth of a mile before joining the road from Freerville to St. Remy.

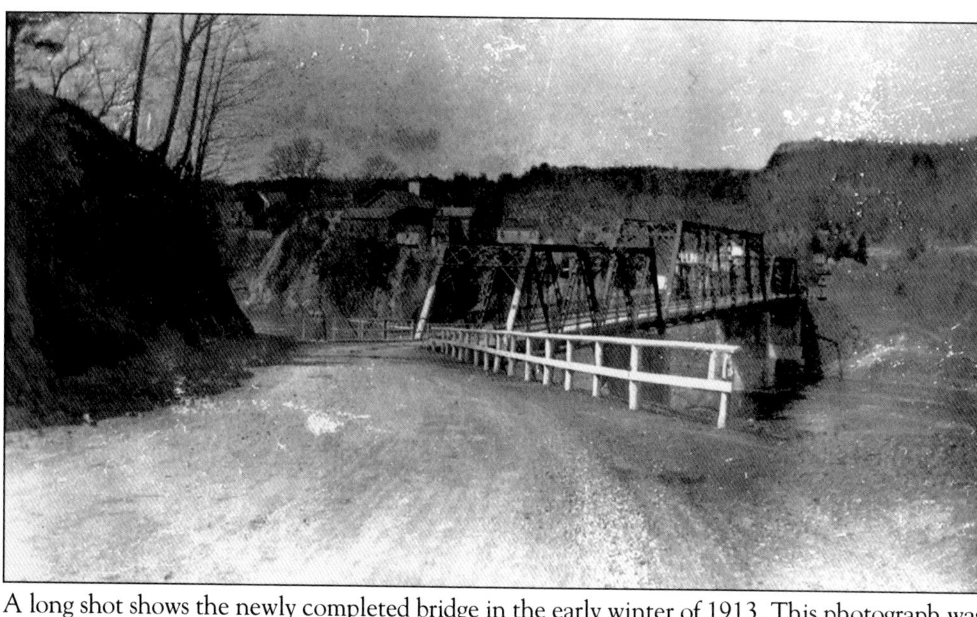

A long shot shows the newly completed bridge in the early winter of 1913. This photograph was taken from the Freerville end, and the sharp turn at the exit of the bridge is clearly visible. Upon close inspection, the ghostly figure of a man can be seen standing at the end of the bridge. Rumor has it that the man is Isaac F. Freer, but that remains unproven. (Raymond Krom collection.)

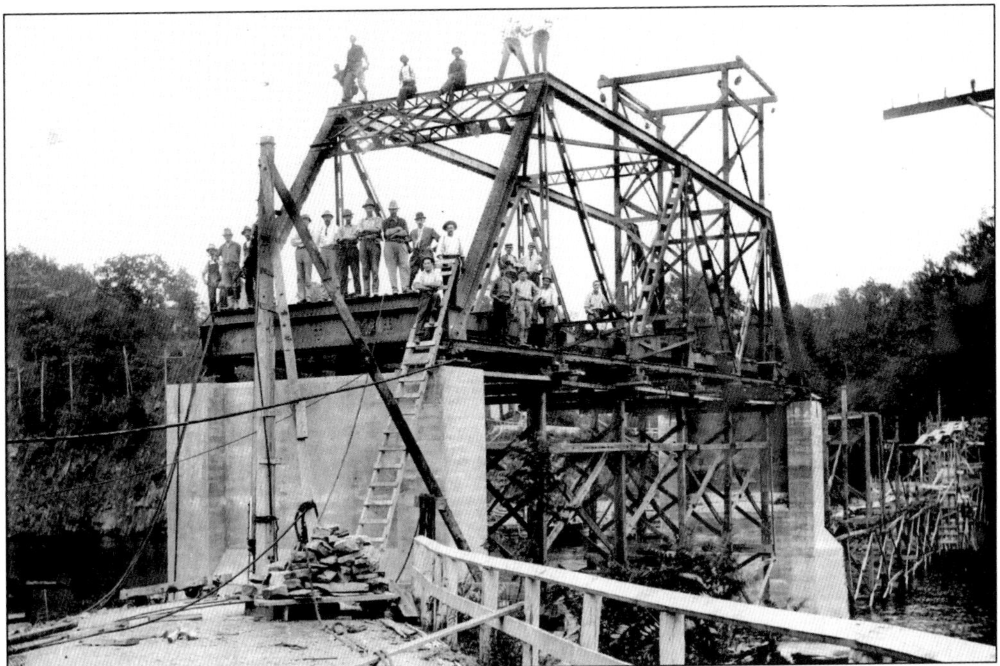

On this page, we see two group portraits of the crew that assembled the bridge of 1912. In the photograph above, they are working on the first section at the northern end. The falsework is visible for the full width of the creek, and it looks as if the first section has just been completed. Notice the crude wooden ladder and the workmen atop the highest truss.

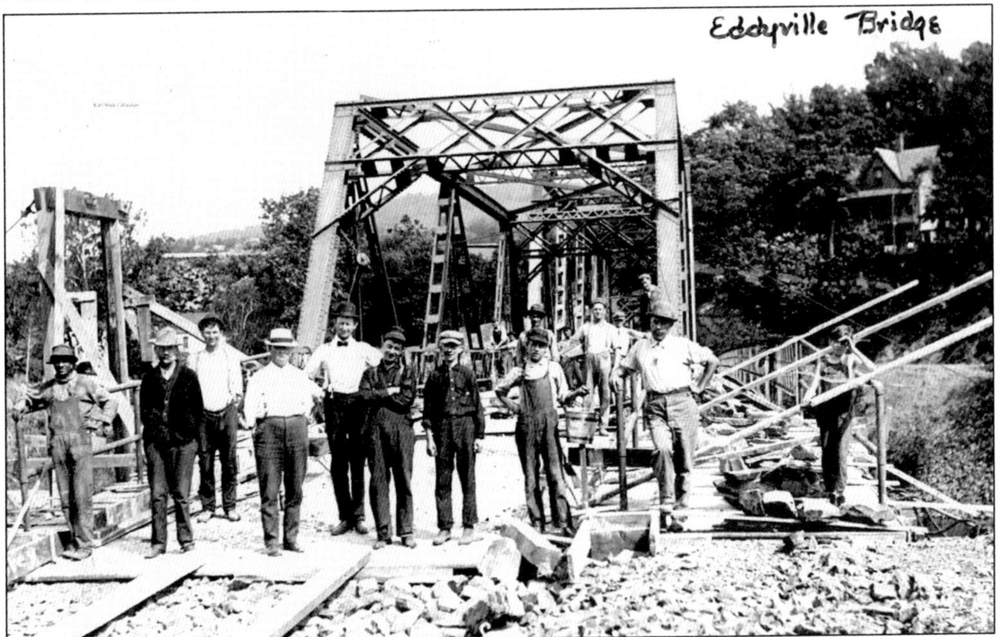

Now all three sections are complete, and grading is in progress at the northern approach. It appears that the men fourth and fifth from the left are foremen or agents. Next to them are three teenage boys. Teenage boys often worked to augment the family income. Construction projects such as these were blessings to those with mechanical ability and strong backs.

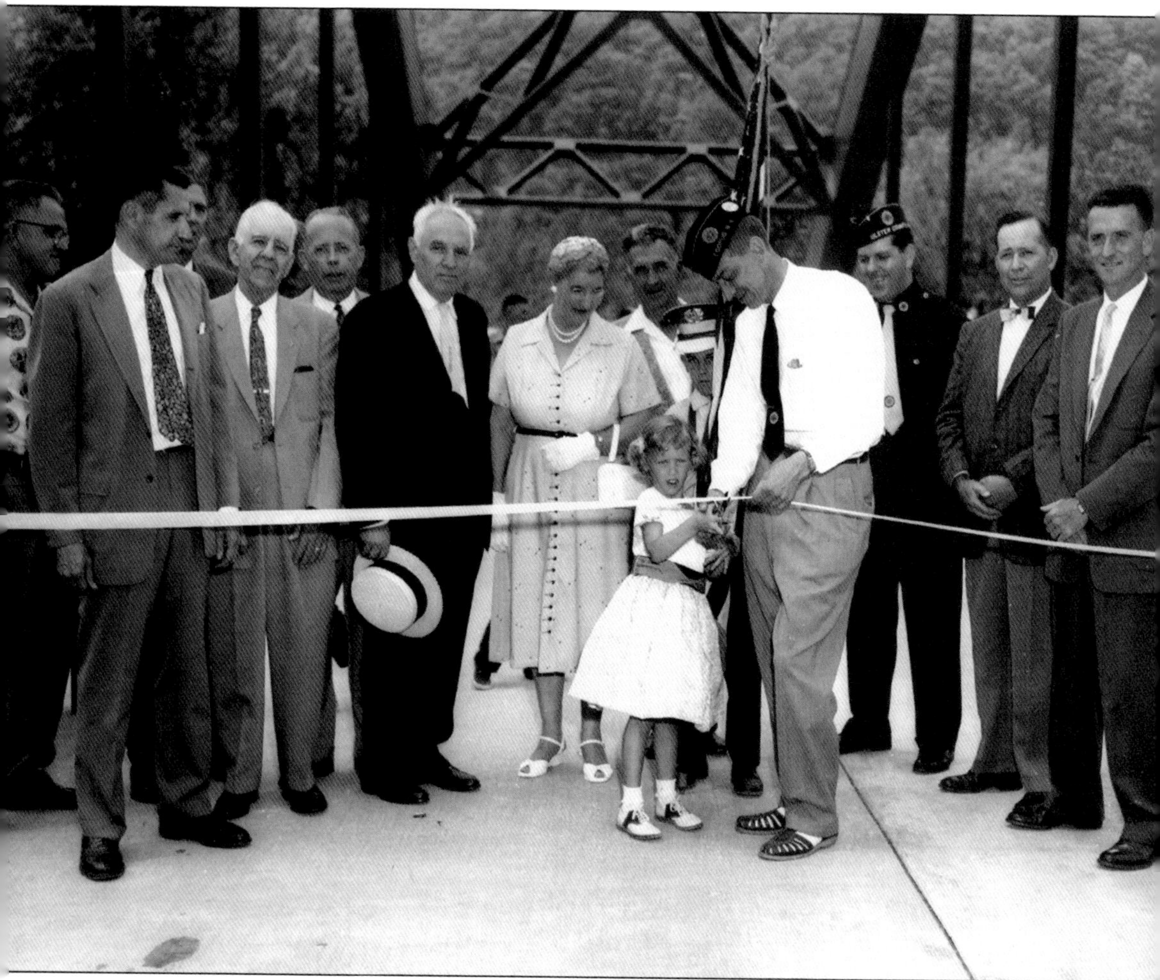

Even the workmanship of 1912 could not stand forever. By 1954, the center supporting pier under the now "old" bridge was severely undermined. Fishermen reported seeing the entire pier rattle and shake when heavy trucks crossed the bridge. Finally, on June 8, 1959, and at a cost of $736,000, a new single-span bridge was opened.

"G. Knute Beichert commander of Town of Esopus Post 1298, American Legion assists Jean Slater, daughter of Mr. and Mrs. Ralph L. Slater of New Salem in cutting ribbon officially opening the Eddyville Bridge Saturday afternoon. Witnessing the event are (l-r) front row Supervisor Roger W. Mabie, Town of Esopus; Pratt Boice, guest speaker Town of Ulster; Supreme Court Justice Roscoe V. Elsworth, guest speaker Town of Esopus; Mrs. Elizabeth Acker councilman, Town of Ulster, Marc Eckert color bearer, Anna Devine 4-H Drum Corps; Edgar Maurer, Legion county commander who led the Pledge of Allegiance; Justice of the Peace Milard Davis and Councilman Edgar Elliott, both of Town of Ulster; back row, Justice of the Peace John O. Beaver, and Councilman E. Stirling Potter, both Town of Esopus Justice of the Peace Arthur A. Reilly, Town of Ulster, and Justice of the Peace Allan Dargie Town of Esopus." —The *Kingston Freeman*.

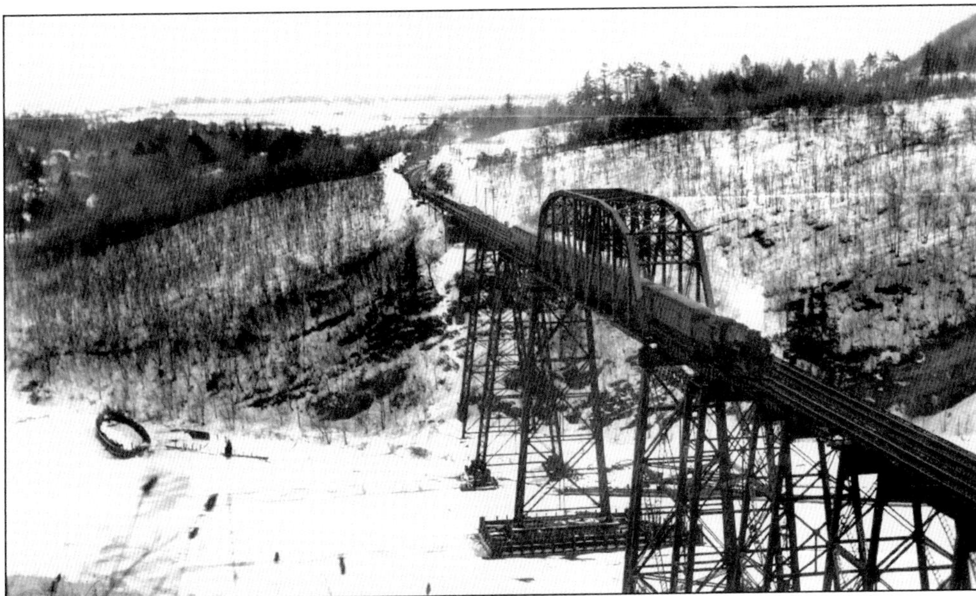

The West Shore Railroad trestle is one of the most important bridges leading into Esopus and is an impressive example of engineering. The trestle was constructed in 1898, replacing an older version. This photograph probably dates from the 1930s or 1940s. The single engine pulls five passenger cars on the double-track line and makes its way over the trestle, 180 feet above the Rondout Creek.[24] Passenger service was discontinued in 1958, and one track was removed in 1960. (Authors' collection.)

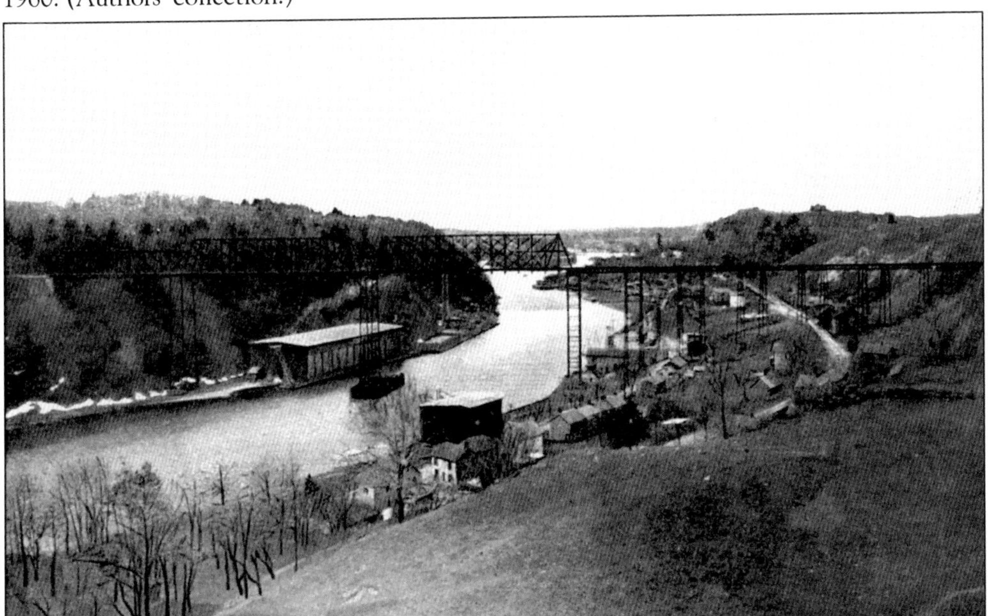

This is a rare shot of the "old" West Shore Railroad bridge, which was constructed in 1883. Notice that the shape of the main truss section is trapezoidal instead of curved. Below the trestle stands an icehouse of Ganson & Son.[25] This is one of many along the river and creek. This one was replaced by the Wallkill Portland Cement Company factory that same year.[26] (Authors' collection.)

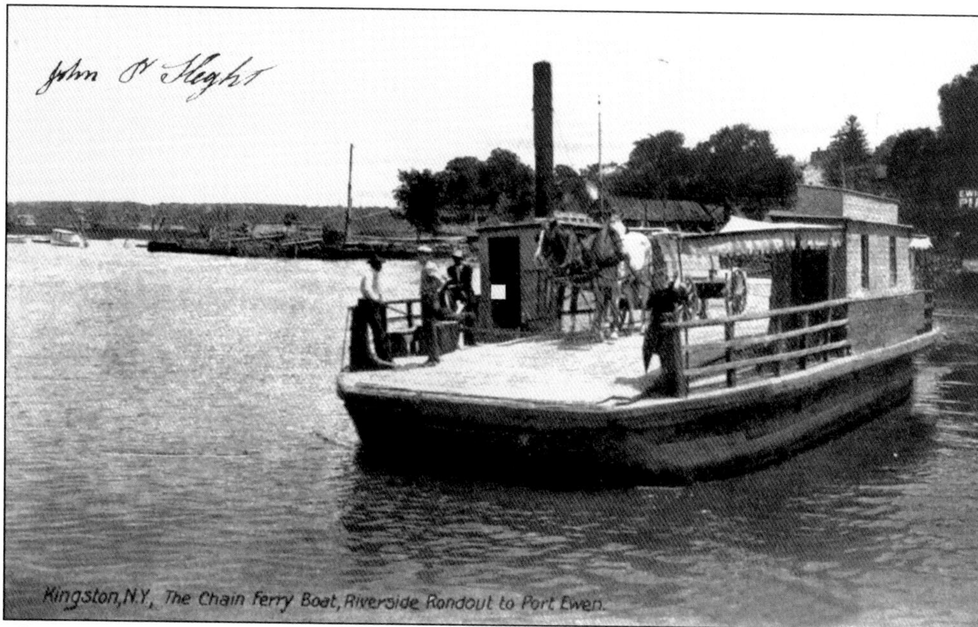

There was a long tradition of ferries across the Rondout. Our earliest references are William Swart in 1798 and John P. Sleght (original signature inserted above) in 1799 running ferries from Connelly and Sleightsburg to Rondout. Isaac D. Sleght (*sic*) held the license for this ferry in 1864.[27] This is the skilly putt, or pod. The skilly putt was pulled along a large chain back and forth across the creek. (Authors' collection.)

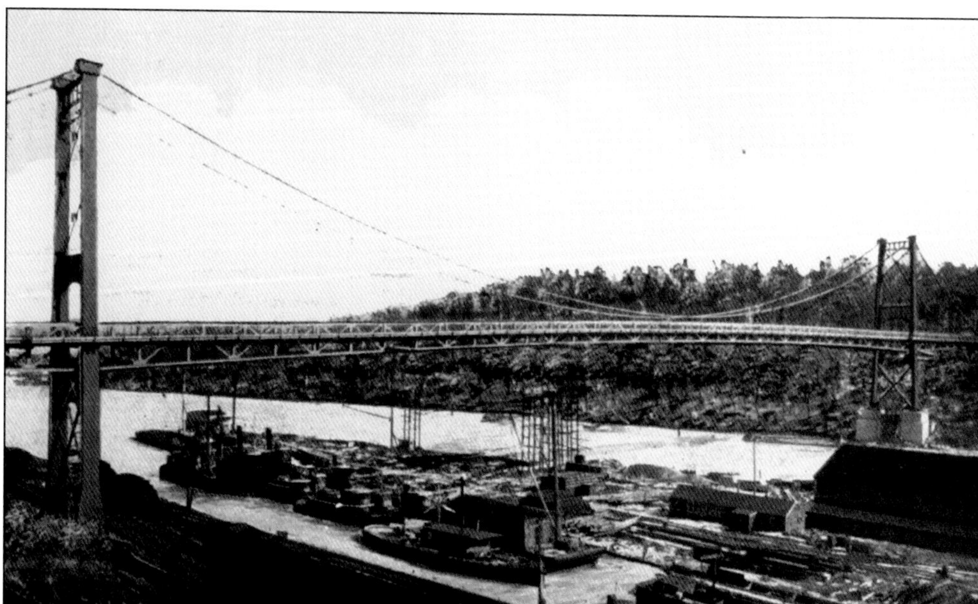
Finally, in 1921, almost a full century after bridges at the other corners of town were laid out and built, a bridge linking Port Ewen with Rondout was built. This was a most impressive structure, measuring 1,145 feet in length and costing $700,000. The builder was the Tench and Tench Company. The cornerstone was laid on September 18, 1920, and the formal opening was held on November 29, 1921. (Authors' collection.)

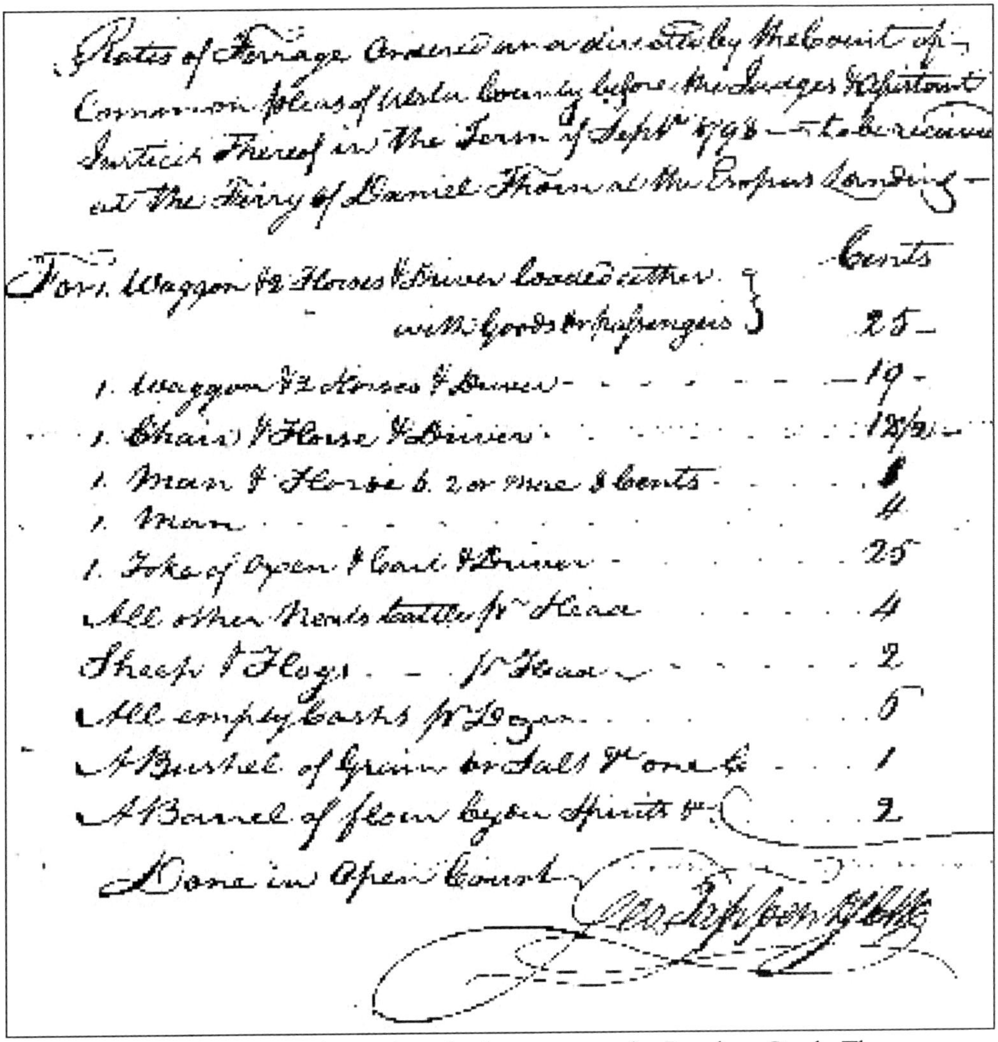
Rates of Ferriage Ordered and directed by the Court of Common Pleas of Ulster County before the Judges & Justices Thereof in the Term of Septr 1798 — to be received at the Ferry of Daniel Thorn at the Esopus Landing —

	Cents
For 1 Waggon & 2 Horses & Driver loaded either with Goods or passengers	25
1 Waggon & 2 Horses & Driver	19
1 Chair & Horse & Driver	12½
1 Man & Horse 6. 2 or more 5 cents	[illegible]
1 Man	4
1 Yoke of Oxen & Cart & Driver	25
All other Neat Cattle pr Head	4
Sheep & Hogs pr Head	2
All empty Carts pr Wagon	6
A Bushel of Grain or Salt & [illegible]	1
A Barrel of flour beer Spirits &c	2

Done in Open Court

[illegible] Clerk

This is a copy of the approved rate chart for ferries across the Rondout Creek. The rates were identical for all ferries, and it cost $100 annually to hold a ferryman's license. The annual cost remained constant from the 1790s until the 1860s.[28] Daniel Thorn was one of a small group of licensed ferrymen at Esopus. The court was very strict about enforcing uniform rates throughout the county and fined the licensee heavily if he or she failed to post the proper rates or charged a premium. The cost did vary somewhat in neighboring counties. In Ulster, for example, a man cost 4¢, and sheep and hogs were 2¢ apiece. In the neighboring Greene County town of Catskill, a live sheep cost 3¢, but a dead one was 4¢.

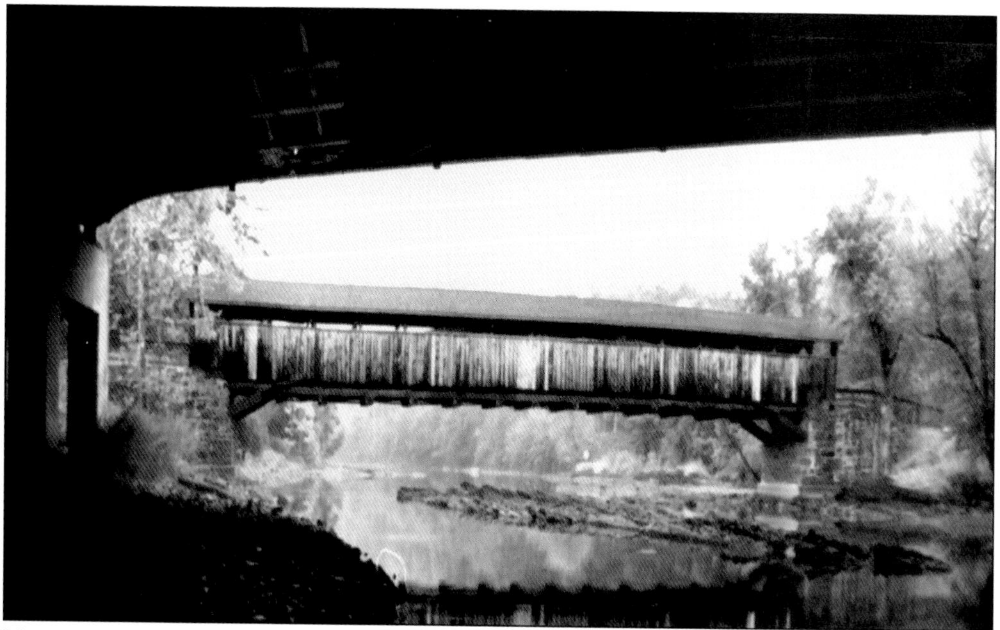

Upstream from the New Salem covered bridge and at the Dashville corner of the town is Perrine's Bridge. This bridge was commissioned in 1834 and constructed by Benjamin Wood (not West). The county invested $1,500 and the state $700 in its construction. This early bridge linked the Esopus community around Perrine's Bridge with Tillson in the Hurley Patent. Tillson is now in the town of Rosendale. (Authors' collection.)

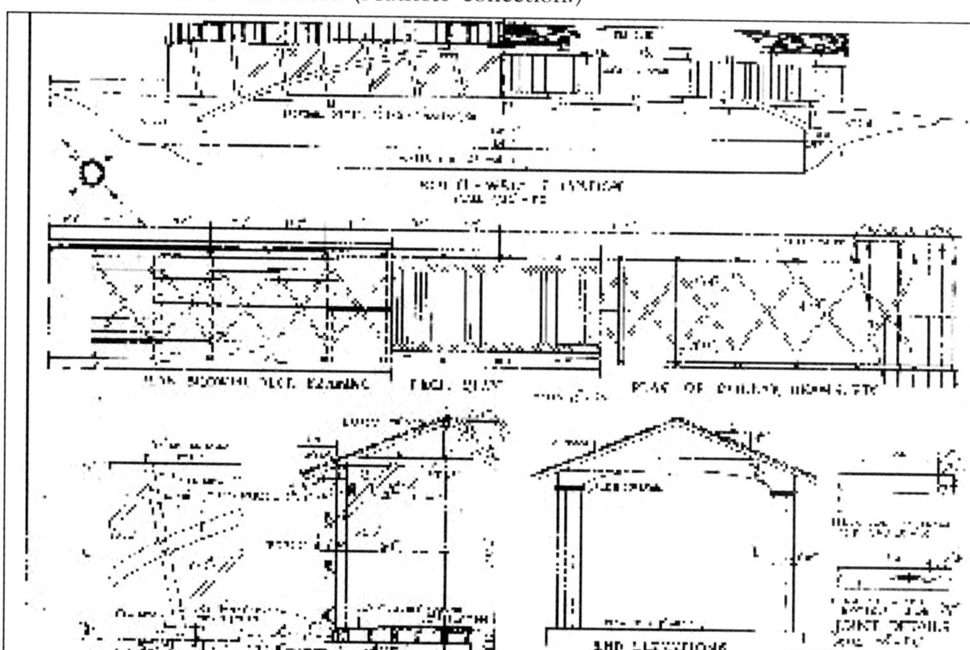

On April 2, 1934, the U.S. Department of the Interior completed this architectural blueprint drawing of Perrine's Bridge for its Historic American Buildings Survey. The blueprint shows complete construction details with measurements and is available for study at the Library of Congress. The bridge spans 138 feet 3 inches from pier to pier.

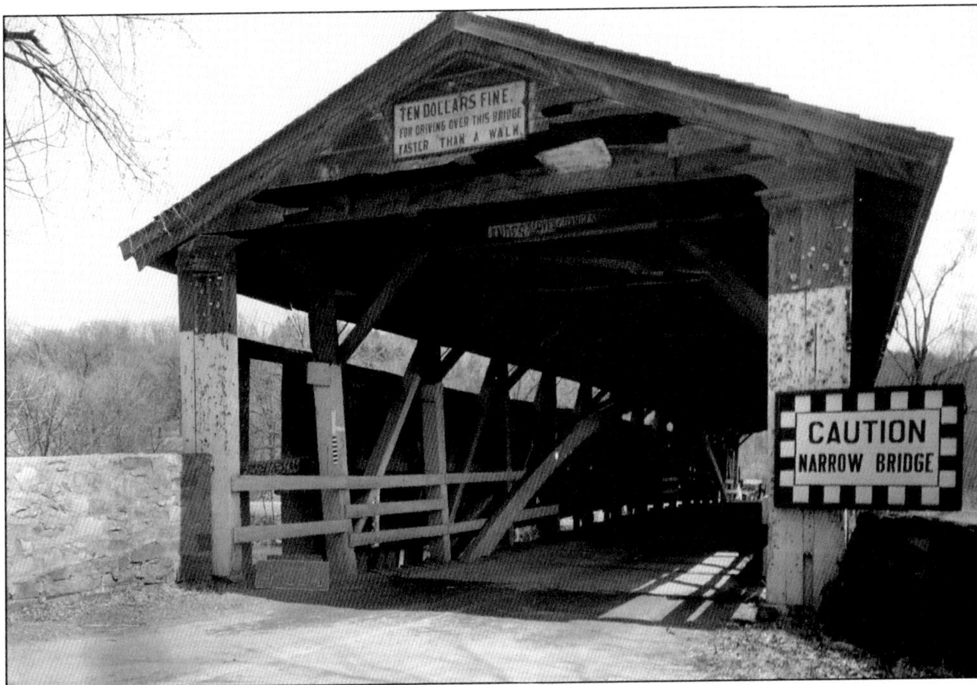

The hamlet of Perrine's Bridge had a hotel and tavern[29] owned by the Perrine family, a school, a cemetery, and a blacksmith shop. It was less than a mile from Dashville Falls and Arnoldton, where mills were in operation as early as 1827.[30] The bridge provided a way for workers from Rosendale to commute to the mills and for travelers to traverse the Wallkill on their way to New Paltz or Kingston.

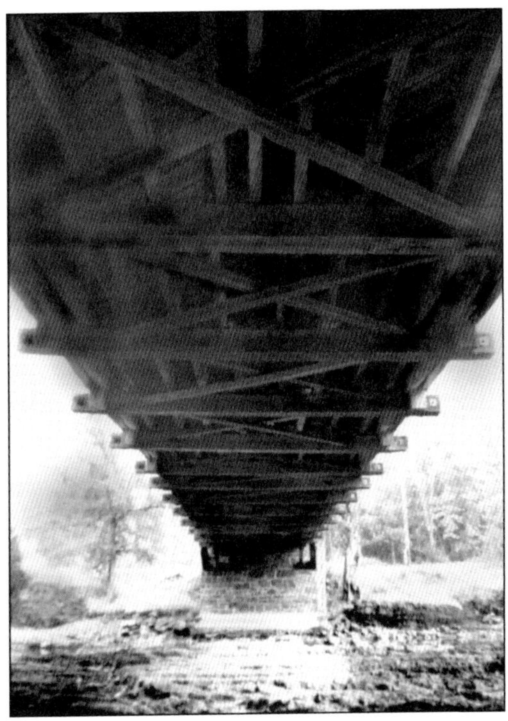

Prior to 1835, the only way to cross the Wallkill was via a ford near the current location of the Route 32 bridge. The previous photograph was taken sometime around the bridge's 100th anniversary in 1935, and this one was taken by the author. This photograph gives a nice impression of the mass of the bridge hanging suspended by the Burr Arch trusses above. (Authors' collection.)

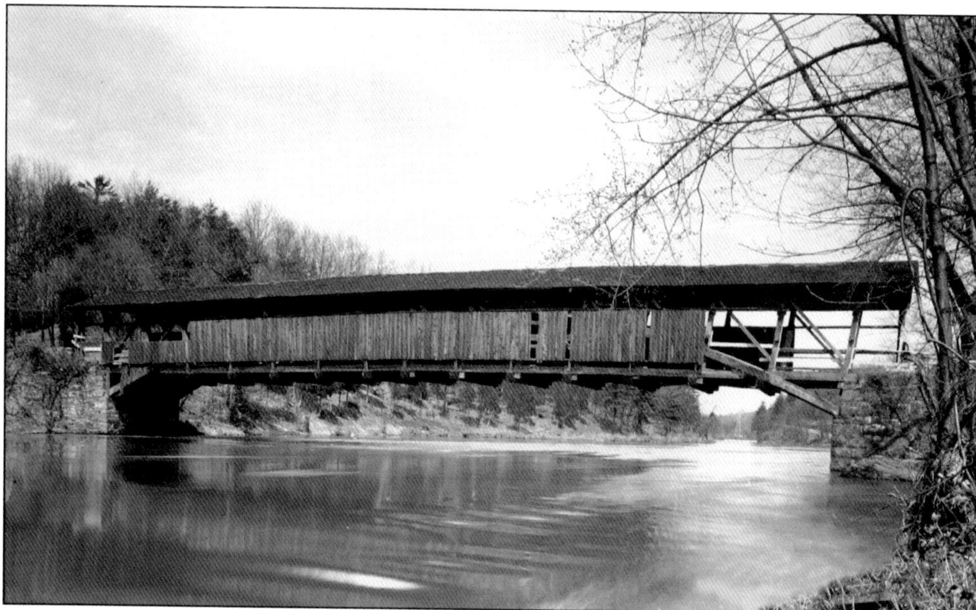

By 1946, the bridge was beginning to deteriorate. Many of the sheathing boards had fallen off or had been kicked off by children looking for good fishing spots. The purpose of the sheathing was to protect the beams and joints from the weather. With the covering gone, the skeleton of the bridge was now in danger. It was closed to traffic in 1946. (Library of Congress.)

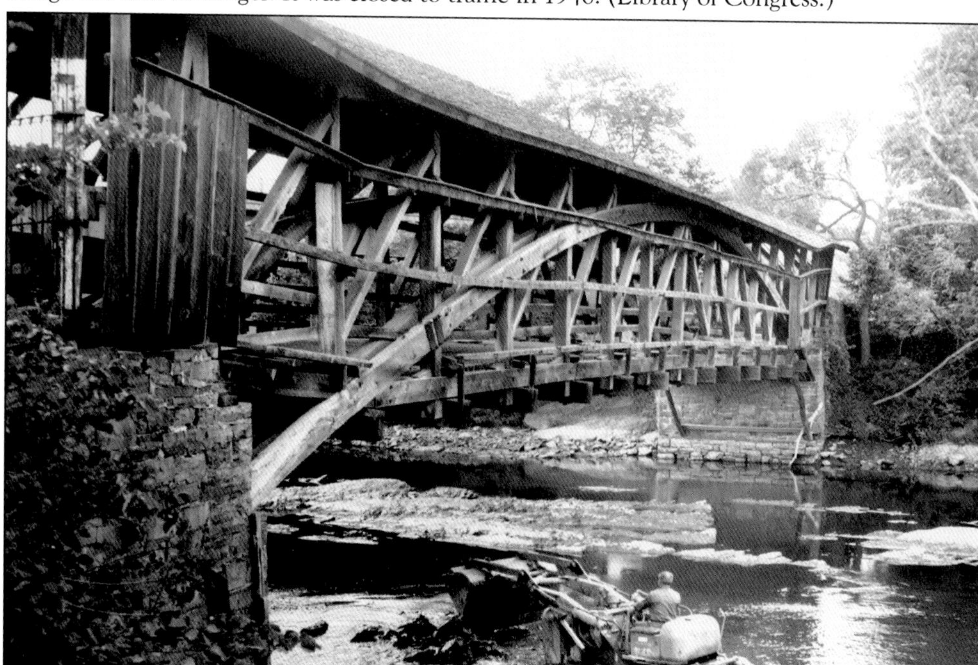

In 1966, Perrine's Bridge was declared a New York State Historic Site, and local groups led by John Grady of Rifton sought funding for restoration. Other individuals wanted to have the bridge torn down. Luckily, funding was available and restoration work began. Here the reader can plainly see the old chestnut beams of the Burr Arch truss, distorted at both ends but still trying to bear the weight of the bridge.

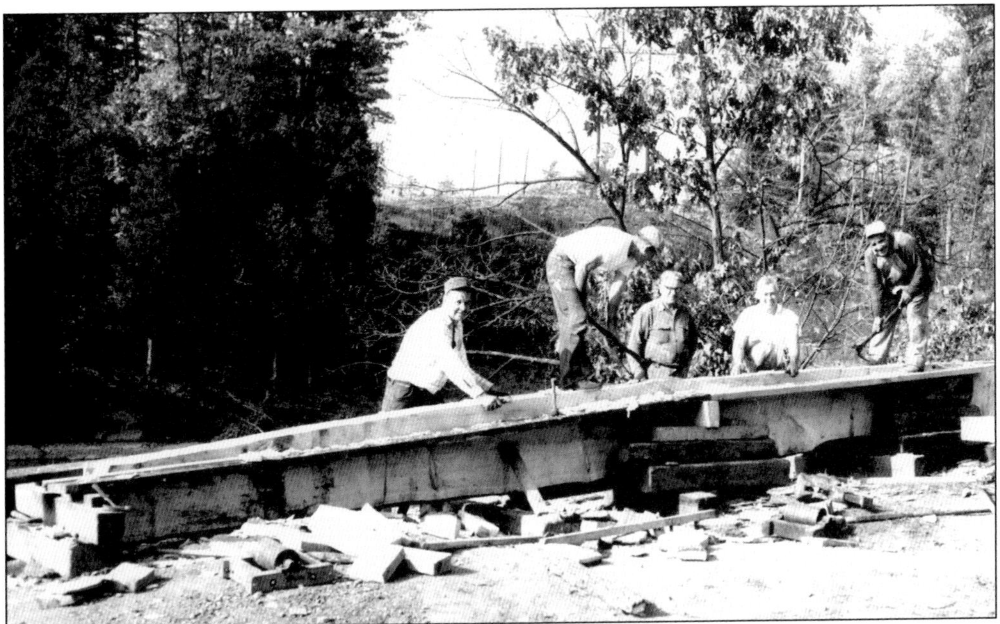

The last real repair to the bridge had been in 1917 at a cost of $3,000. Our intrepid workmen had a difficult task ahead of them. They performed marvelously. Here they are using old methods to size and smooth a huge curved beam. From left to right are Henry Winkky, Sal Russo, Clark Bonesteel, George Cole, and Ray Bonestell.

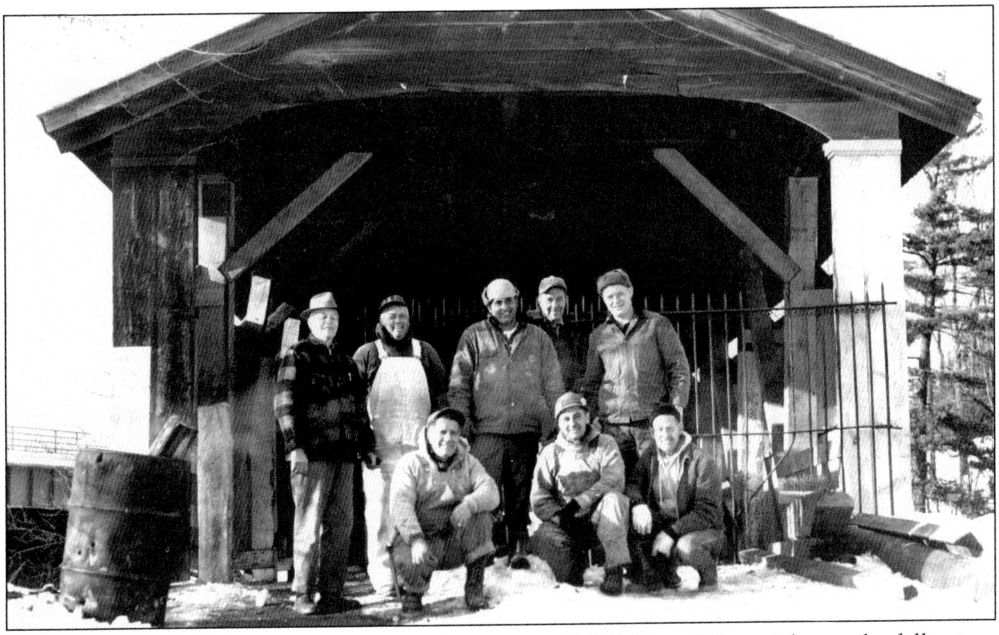

This is the entire restoration crew during the winter of 1968. From left to right are the following: (front row) Sal Russo (roofer), Vince Monteleone (roofer), and Ray Bonestell; (back row) John Grady, George Cole, unidentified, Henry Winkky, and unidentified. These specialists did a terrific job, but the county failed to maintain the bridge. This led to the need for yet another restoration in 1997, at a cost of $195,000. Let us hope that no more renovations will be necessary.

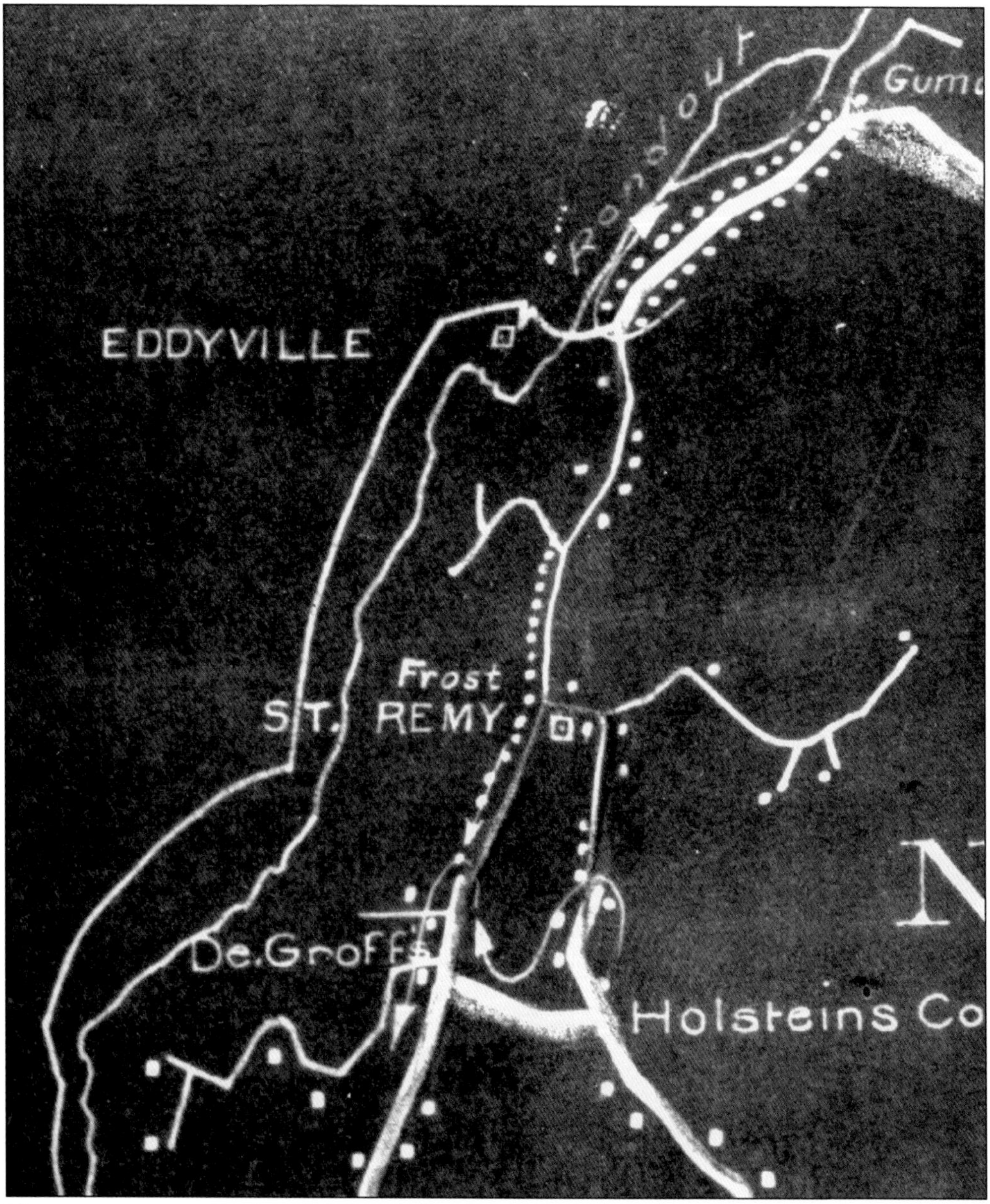

Here we see a portion of a 1905 Post Office Department map showing the route that the rural delivery drivers took to deliver mail out of the Ulster Park Post Office. The hamlet of St. Remy had its own post office from January 1888 until June 30, 1954. The location is shown by the square box near the center of the map. The areas to the south were served by a rural carrier. Edgar Ellsworth was the first postmaster, and Robert A. Hoffman was the last.[31] In 1954, the St. Remy Post Office became a branch of the Kingston Post Office and remained open until at least 1978.[32] Samuel Haines Carman was the last clerk in charge. It was his great-grandfather Peter M. Decker (see page 23) who carried mailbags from the Fly Mountain post office to St. Remy during its first decades of service. (Authors' collection.)

Three

St. Remy

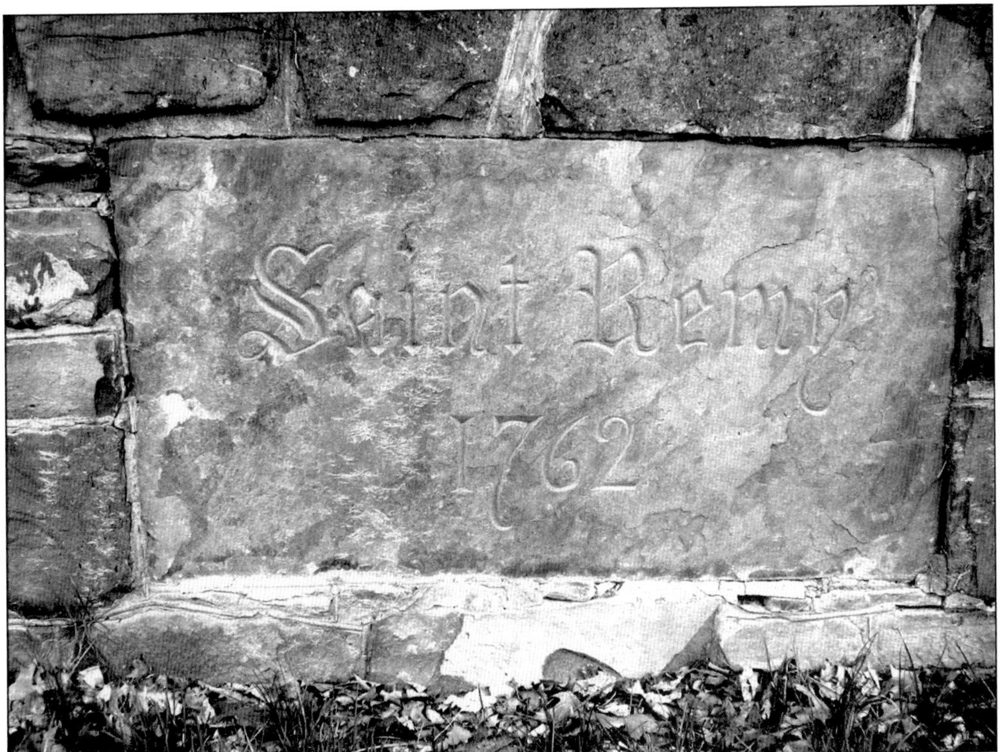

St. Remy was first settled in 1745 by Isaac Van Wagenen Jr. of Wagendal. During that period, the area was called "Greenkill." Van Wagenen crossed the ford near the old Indian fishing weirs of Mogowasinck and started his farm on the wide steps overlooking the Rondout Kill. At about the same time, Garret I. Freer and Isaac Delamater built a gristmill and stone house at the other end of town on the Dwarfs Kill near its confluence with the Rondout. These two early settlements along Swartekill Road are the anchor points for this chapter. In 1762, the three first settlers were joined by brothers Jan and Gideon VanAken, who came over Hussey's Hill seeking their fortunes. Jan brought his wife, Grietjen DeGraff, six sons, and five daughters. Gideon brought his wife, Maria Ploeg, two daughters, and five sons. Of the four early houses built by these pioneers, the three stone versions still proudly shelter their owners two and one-half centuries later. Gideon's home of mud wattle on post and beam was recycled in the mid-1800s (see the house on page 78). (Authors' collection.)

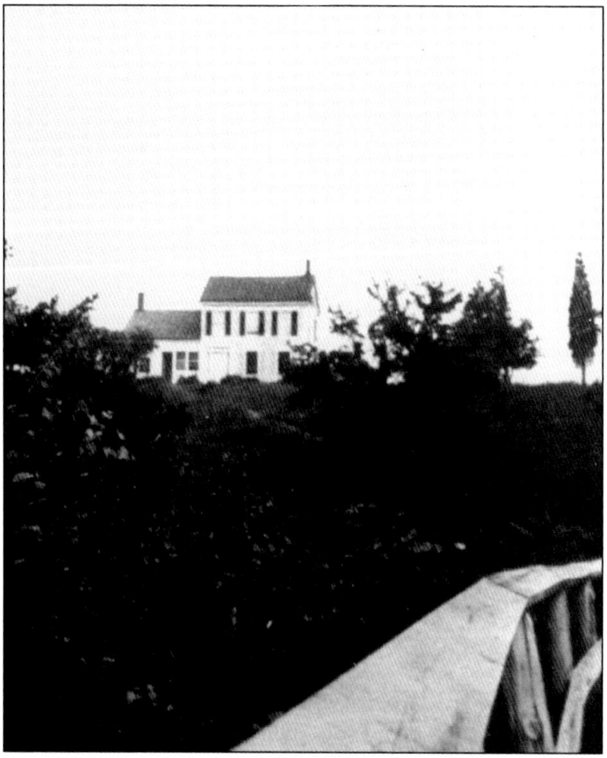

At the top of the hill leading into St. Remy stands the Emberson-Rennie house. Like a sentinel, it overlooks the old slave graveyard and Dimond's Pond. This, like most early houses, was constructed in parts. The two sections are quite obvious from this vantage. The complete house dates from c. 1850, built by a member of the Freer family. In the foreground is a wooden guardrail. This style of protection was the norm in 1922, when the photograph was taken. (Beatrice Jordan collection.)

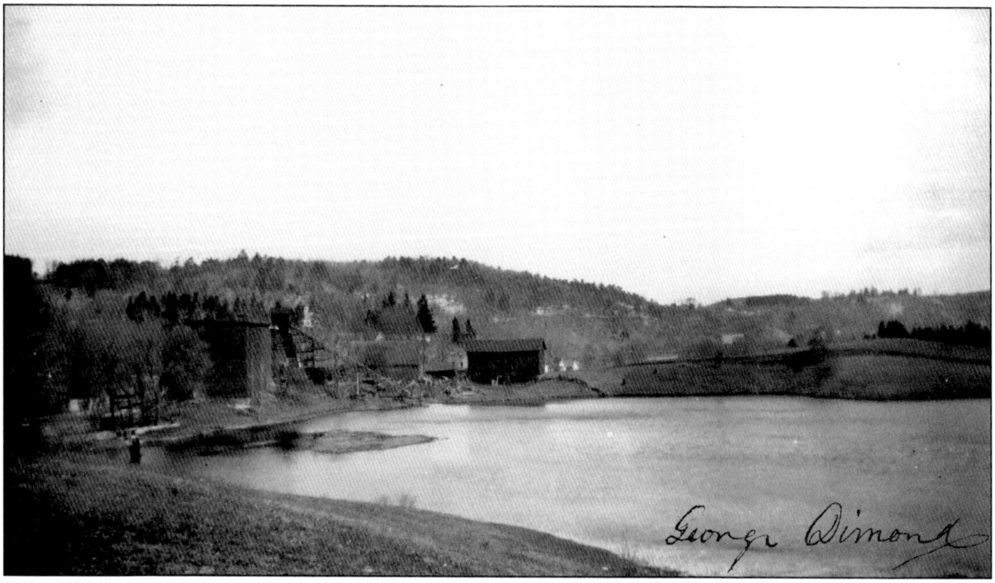

When the residents of the Emberson-Rennie house looked out their northern windows, they would have looked down upon this scene. This is the western end of Dimond's Pond. The buildings are far larger than they appear. In fact, the one at the left is an icehouse several hundred feet in length. A side view of the same building is in chapter 2. The signature is that of George Dimond. (Beatrice Jordan collection.)

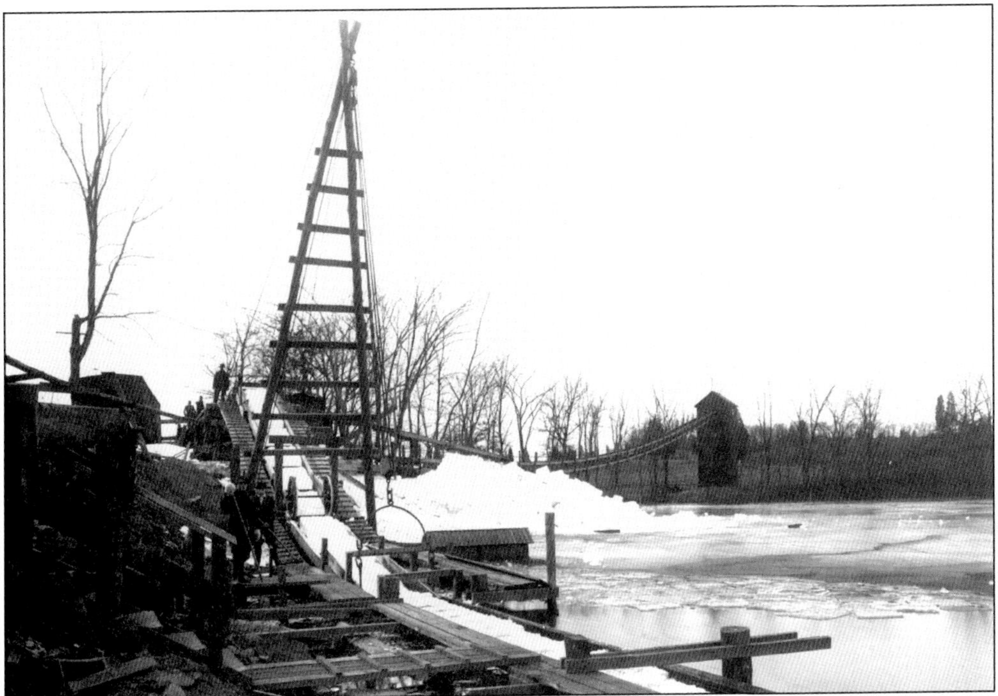

This is what ice harvesting would have looked like on Dimond's Pond in the 1870s. In the foreground, next to open water, is a wooden chute used as a pathway for the large blocks of ice. The ladderlike device is an A-frame used to hold a pulley. Ropes keep it vertical or at another desired angle. A rope through the pulley attaches to a set of tongs used to lift the blocks. (Haber collection.)

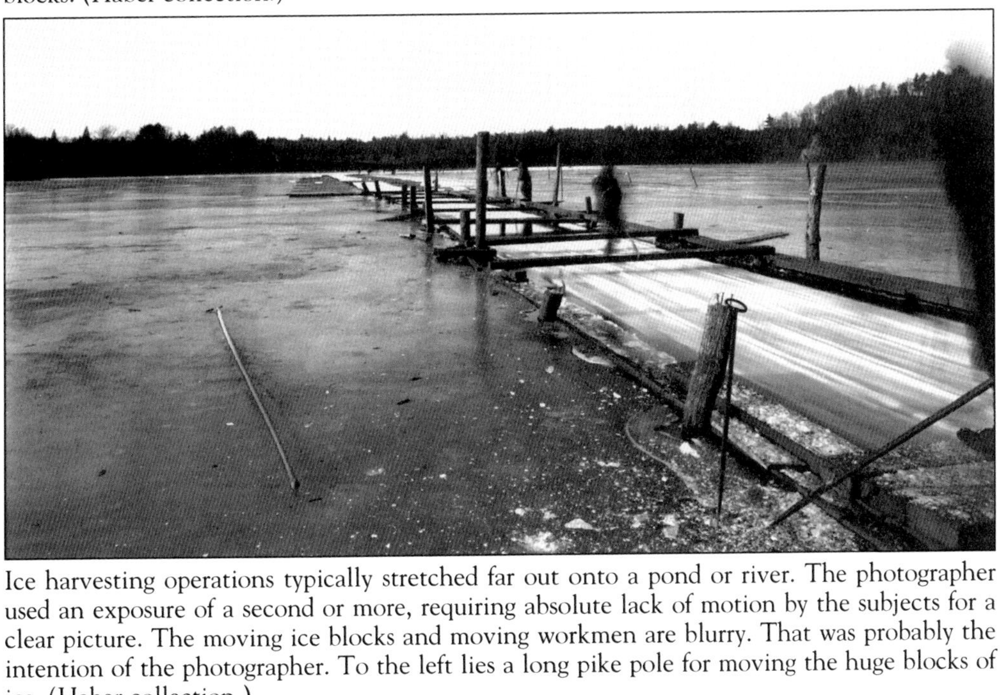

Ice harvesting operations typically stretched far out onto a pond or river. The photographer used an exposure of a second or more, requiring absolute lack of motion by the subjects for a clear picture. The moving ice blocks and moving workmen are blurry. That was probably the intention of the photographer. To the left lies a long pike pole for moving the huge blocks of ice. (Haber collection.)

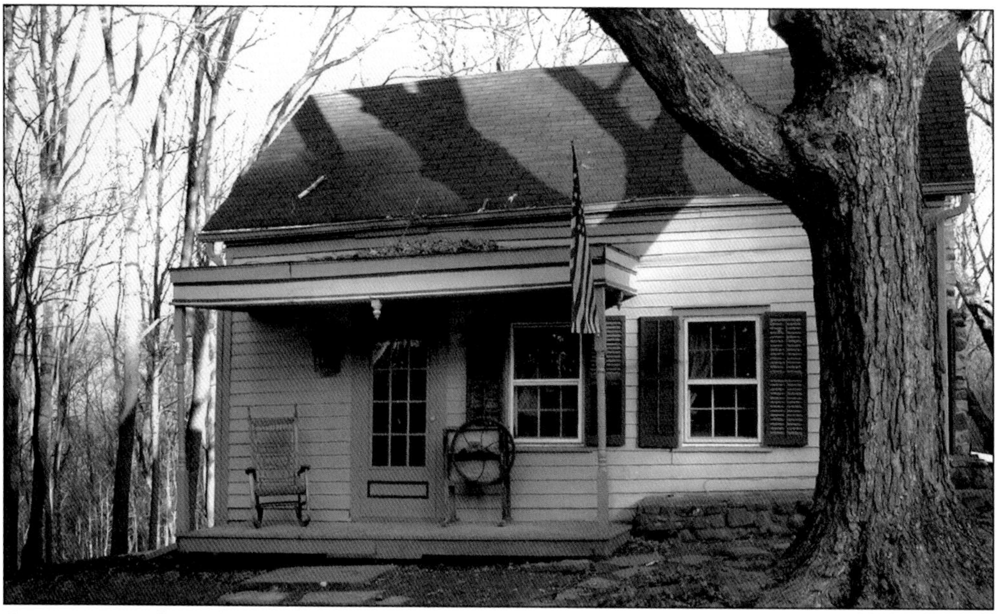

As we proceed southward on Main Street, we come first to a small but interesting wood-framed house belonging to Mrs. VanAken, according to an 1853 map.[33] She was probably Catharine T. VanAken, the widow of Abraham P. VanAken. Abraham was a grandson of Jan VanAken, who first settled in the hamlet. The tiny house is an excellent example of a post–Revolutionary War wood-framed house. (Authors' collection.)

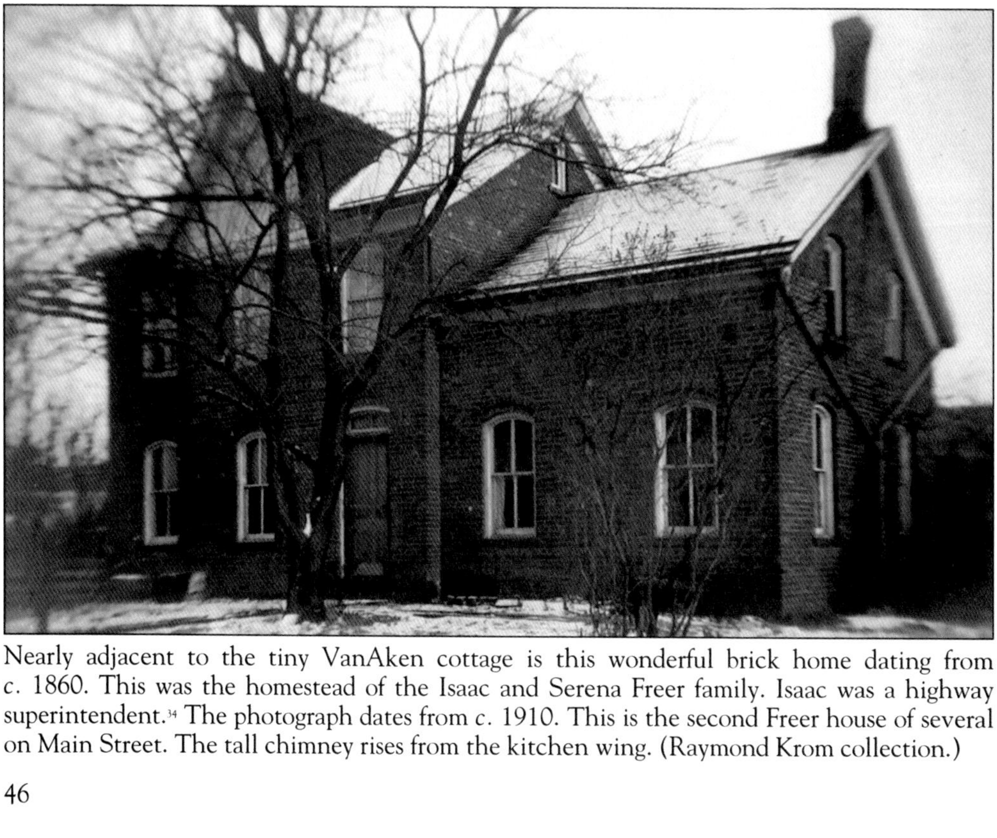

Nearly adjacent to the tiny VanAken cottage is this wonderful brick home dating from *c.* 1860. This was the homestead of the Isaac and Serena Freer family. Isaac was a highway superintendent.[34] The photograph dates from *c.* 1910. This is the second Freer house of several on Main Street. The tall chimney rises from the kitchen wing. (Raymond Krom collection.)

Elsie (left) and Ruth Freer grew up in the Isaac Freer house, and Ruth later settled there. It is believed that Ruth and Elsie were daughters of Isaac. Freer had a daughter named Elizabeth, born in 1893, and this photograph dates from c. 1902. Compare this photograph of Elsie with the adult photograph of Ruth Freer on the next page. (Authors' collection.)

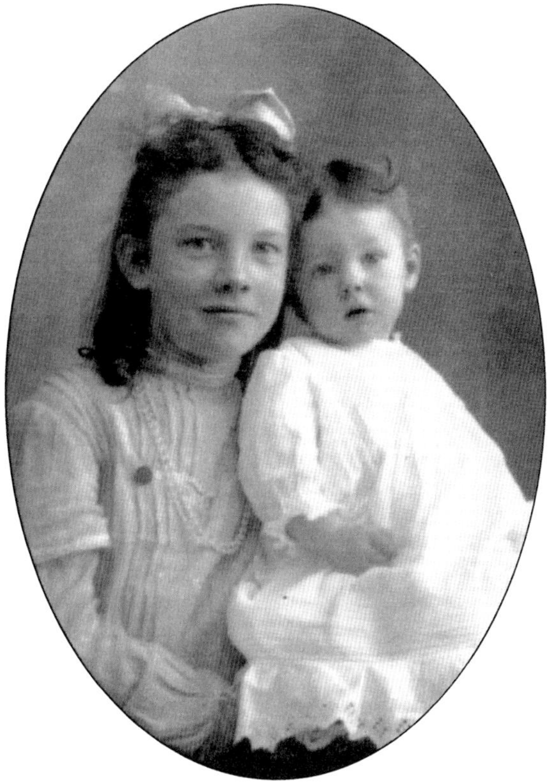

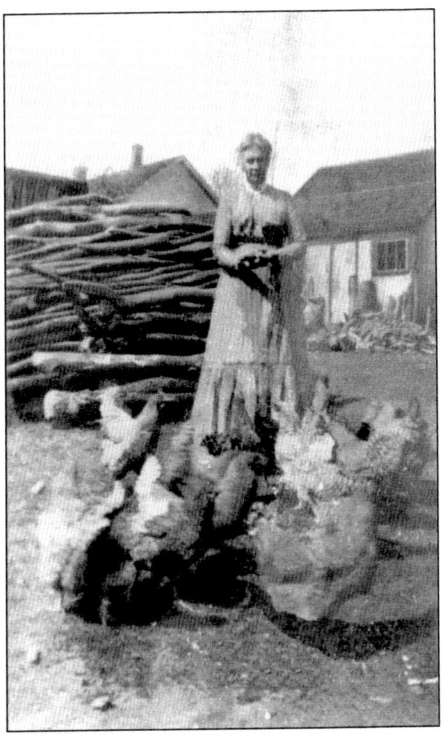

The woman in this picture is Ada DuBois, or Grandma DuBois, as Ruth Freer affectionately named her on the back of the photograph. This scene is typical of life in Esopus. Many residents raised chickens and other fowl for fresh eggs and meat. The eggs from these free-roaming hens must have tasted wonderful. Notice also the large stack of kindling wood. (Authors' collection.)

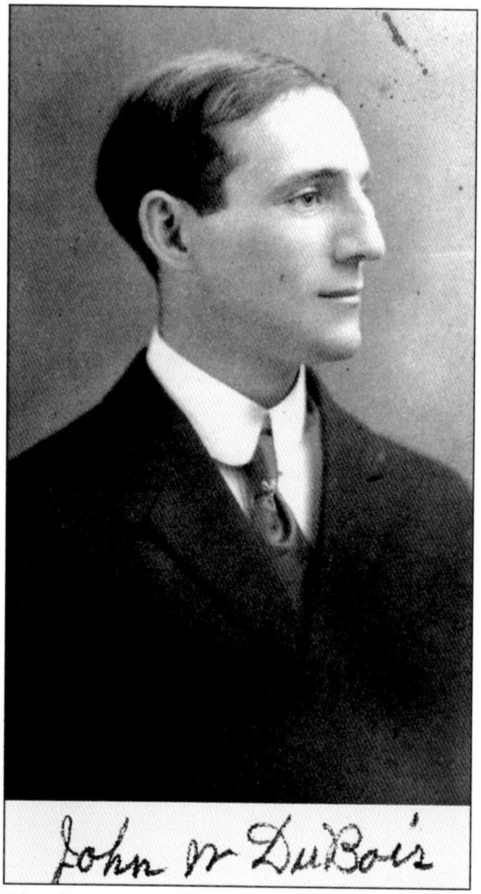

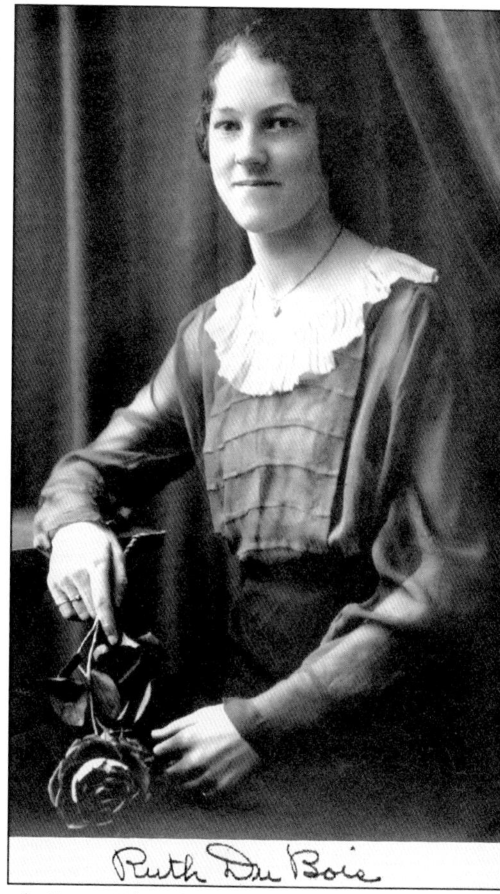

This happy couple is John W. DuBois and Ruth Freer. The photographs date from *c.* 1920. Several in Ruth Freer's collection contained the signatures of the subject. There are many photographs of Ada DuBois among the Freer mementos. (Authors' collection.)

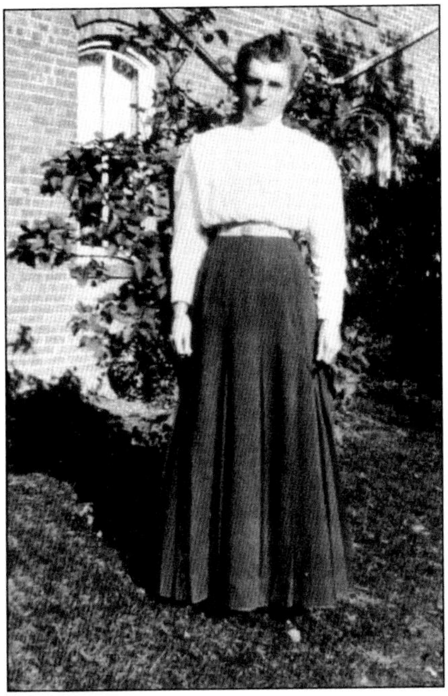

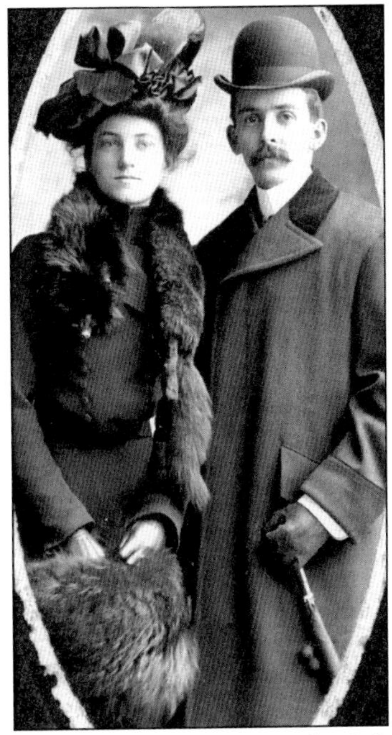

These are two more photographs from Ruth Freer's collection. The photograph on the left shows Ada DuBois and the south face of the brick house that Ruth Freer grew up in. On the right are Minnie and Will Fallman.

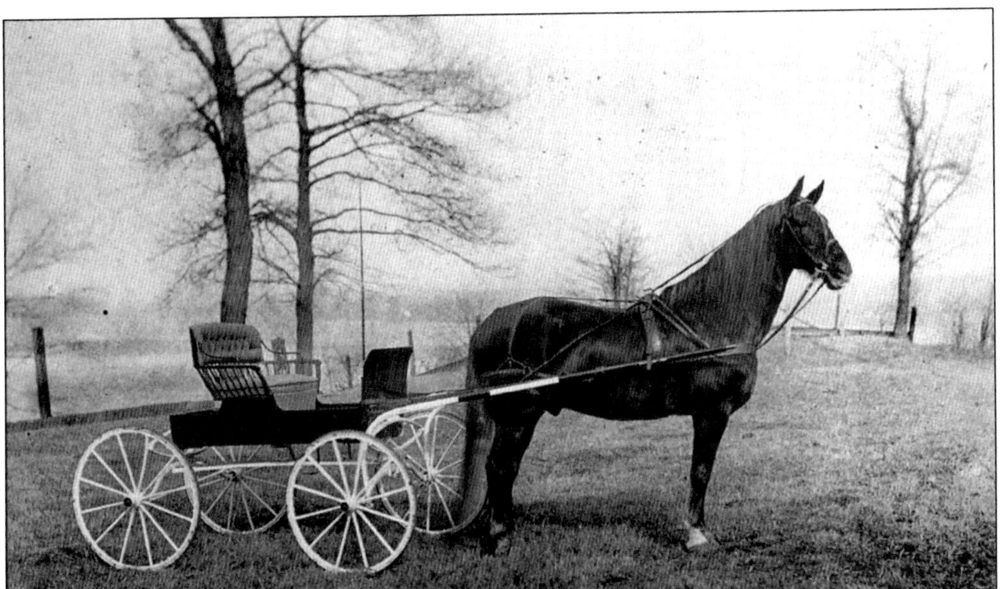

This carriage, with its white-and-black motif, was the pride of its owner, Ezra Dubois. The inscription on the reverse of this 1906 photograph reads, "To Mrs. Elizabeth Freer, Uncle Ezra DuBois with his horse." Perhaps Uncle Ezra is behind the camera. (Raymond Krom collection.)

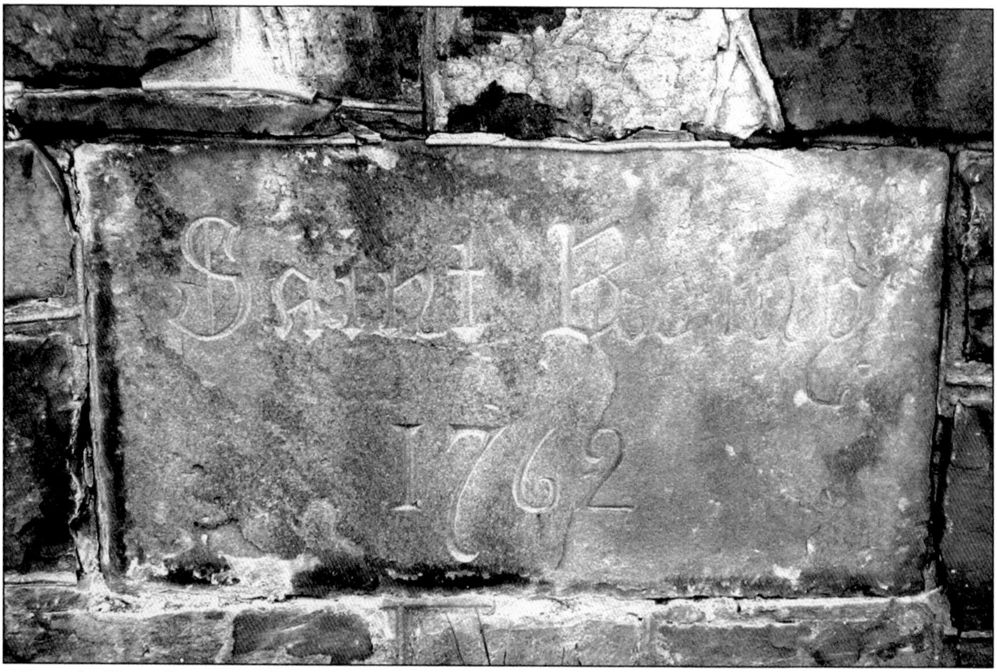

About halfway between the Isaac Freer home and the John Freer home, and on the opposite side of road, stands a large stone-walled entranceway with twin date stones. This impressive entry was constructed by Abram B. Hasbrouck *c.* 1840, when he named the hamlet after a favorite town in France. The left-hand stone appears here, and the other is at the opening of this chapter. (Authors' collection.)

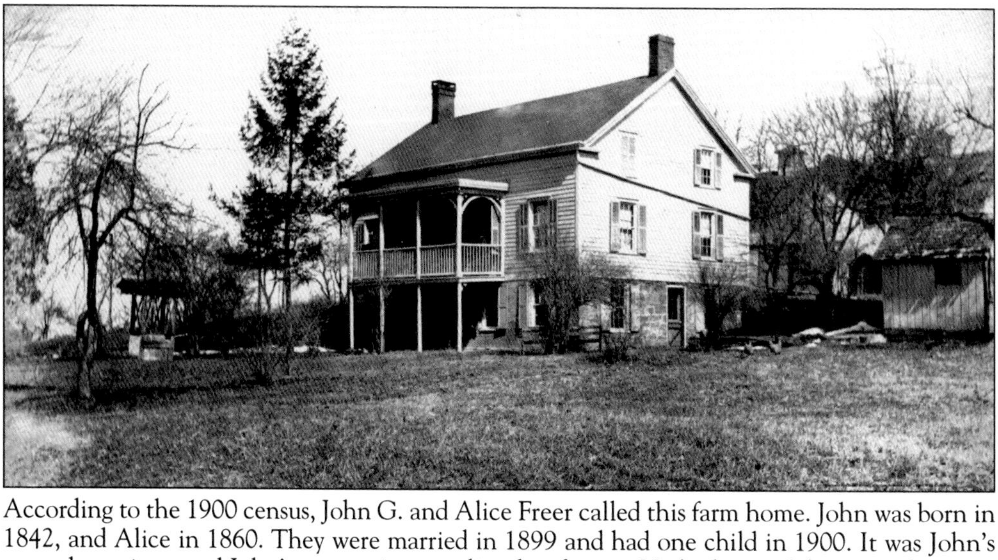

According to the 1900 census, John G. and Alice Freer called this farm home. John was born in 1842, and Alice in 1860. They were married in 1899 and had one child in 1900. It was John's second marriage, and John's occupation was listed as farmer. He had one of the nicest barns in the town of Esopus. It is partially visible behind the house. (Raymond Krom collection.)

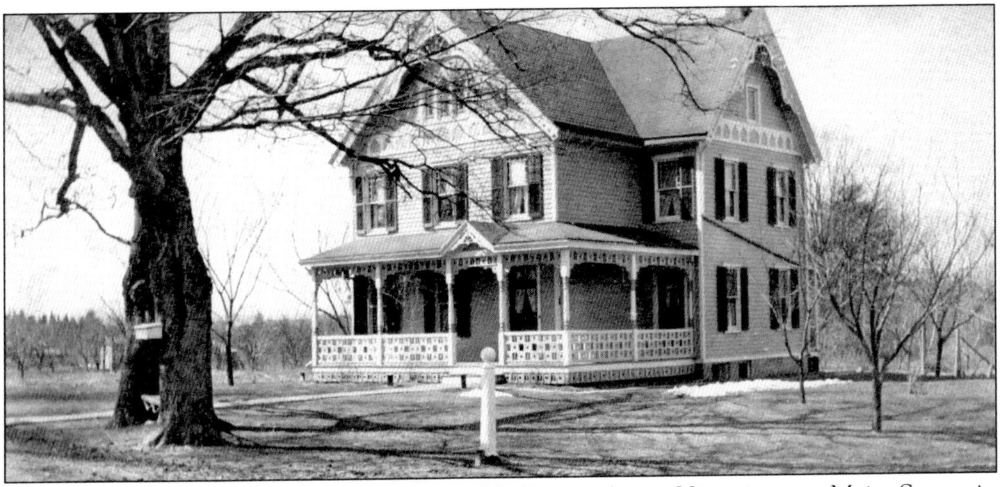

In 1893, Edgar Ellsworth built this beautiful Queen Anne Victorian on Main Street in St. Remy. Ellsworth was extremely active in local organizations, as a charter member of the Order of Red Men Pokonoie tribe and a founder of the St. Remy Fire Department. He was an officer and active member in each organization. (Beatrice Jordan collection.)

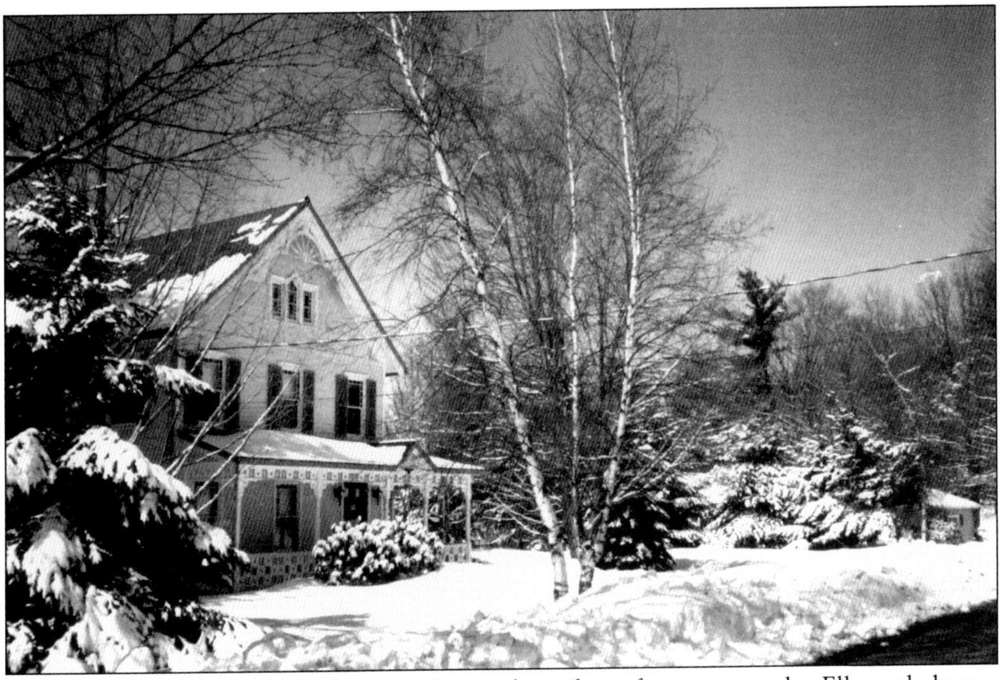

The blizzard of March 1993 dropped almost three feet of snow onto the Ellsworth house. It is now owned by Mr. and Mrs. Martin Jordan. Mrs. Jordan is the granddaughter of Edgar Ellsworth and has kept the house in excellent condition. The trim is original both inside and out. Behind the house was a medium-sized barn that was burned down by teenagers in the 1970s. (Authors' collection.)

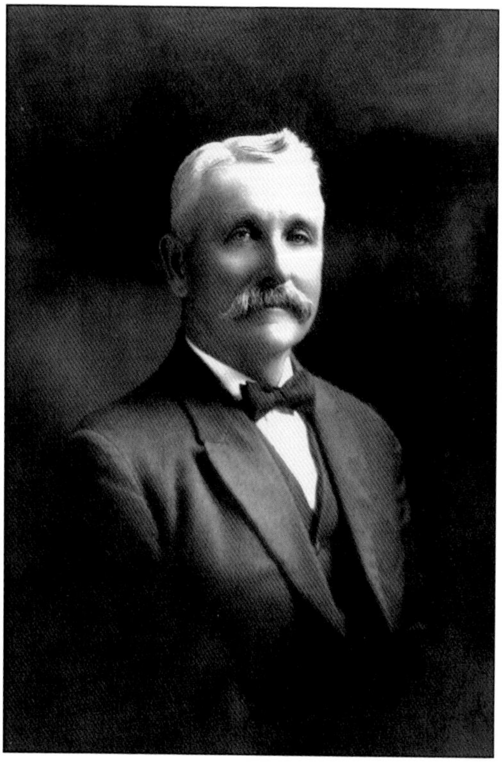

This is Edgar Ellsworth, who built the Victorian house on the previous page. He was born in 1858 in Rifton and lived in one of a pair of Carpenter Gothic houses that still stand near Pendergast Point Road. (Martin Jordan collection.)

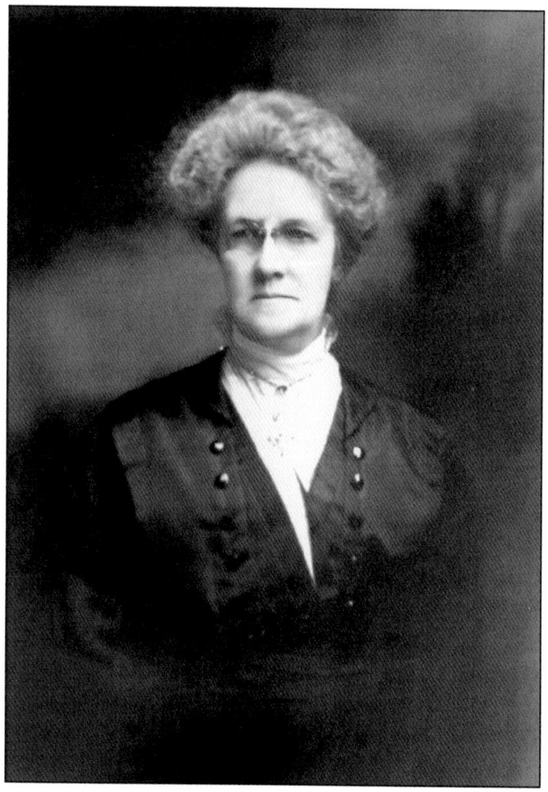

Elmira Smith Ellsworth was the wife of Edgar Ellsworth. She was a direct descendant of William Smith, who was the first settler of Swartekill (now Rifton). She was born in 1858, as was her husband, and died in 1953, outliving him by 33 years. (Martin Jordan collection.)

Depicted here is a true museum piece. These are but two pages from an entire book handmade by Ophelia Roosa. This book is simply incredible! Each page contains a lock of hair from a friend or relative of Roosa, and each lock is sculpted into a pattern and adorned with ribbons, bows, and ink vignettes. This is the opening page and contains Roosa's own hair.

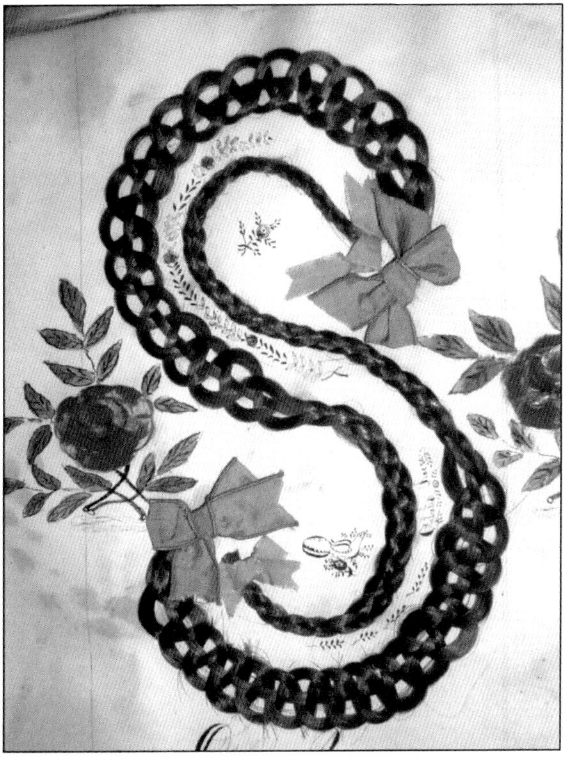

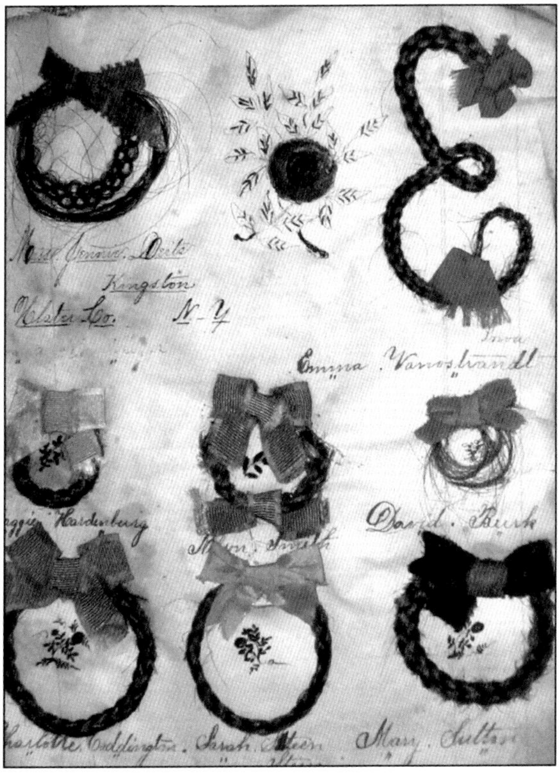

This is one of about 40 additional pages. Beautifully preserved, each hair retains its original color and texture. Every resident of Ulster County with old family roots (no pun intended) will find an ancestor here. The names on this one page are Jennie Diets, Kingston, New York; Emma Vanostrand; Maggie Hardenburg; Nelson Smith; David Burk; Charlotte Coddington; Sarah Steen; and Mary Sutton.

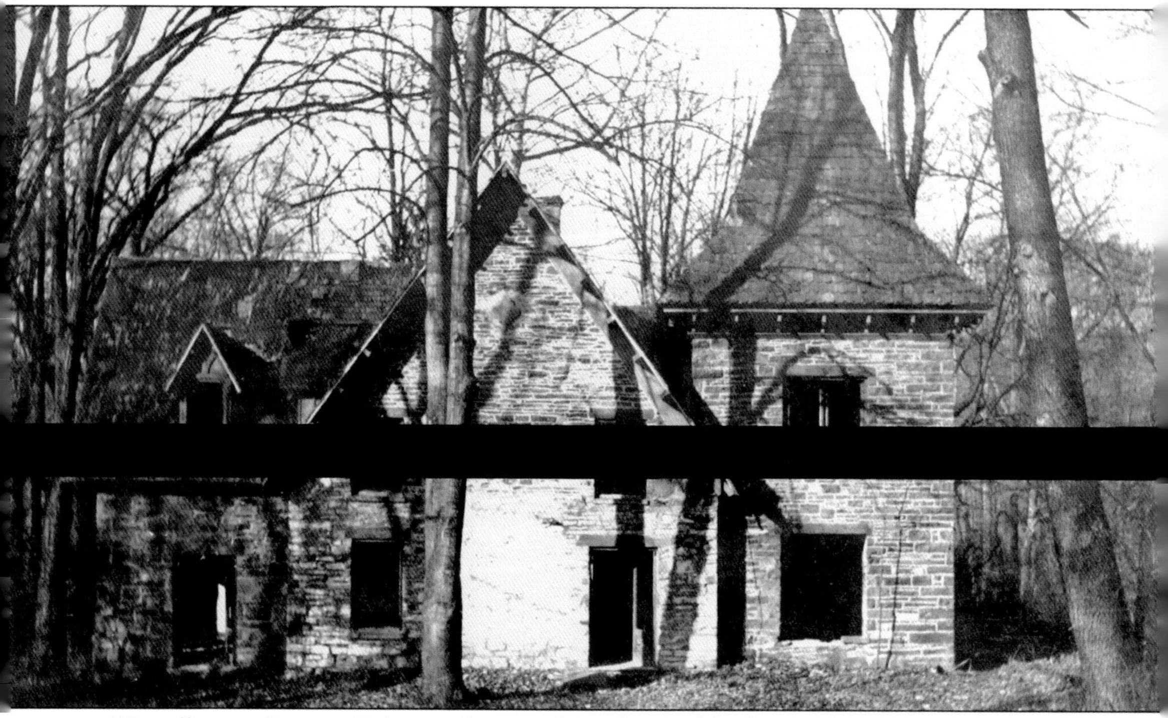

We will now take a small detour along a side road, a road leading to the estate of Mr. Mainetti. This is where the lane between the stone gateposts led until the "new" part of St. Remy (called St. Remy Park) was built over it. In this *c.* 1900 photograph, a vacant old stone mansion is seen. This house is the centerpiece of St. Remy history, for amidst the tower and additions stands the house of Jan VanAken, who with brother Gideon settled the hamlet in 1762. After Jan's death in 1787, ownership passed to his youngest son, Benjamin.[35] Benjamin owned and operated a ferryboat across the Rondout Kill from the foot of Greenkill Road in St. Remy to near the mouth of the Greenkill (stream) in Creeklocks.[36] In 1840–1842, Abram Bruyn Hasbrouck purchased the old farm and began to enlarge and improve the house. Abram was president of Rutgers and the founder of the Ulster County Historical Society. St. Remy became his country home and showplace. He entertained President Grant here. After his death in 1879, the house became the property of his daughter Mary Timpson.[37] This photograph was probably taken after her death. (Authors' collection.)

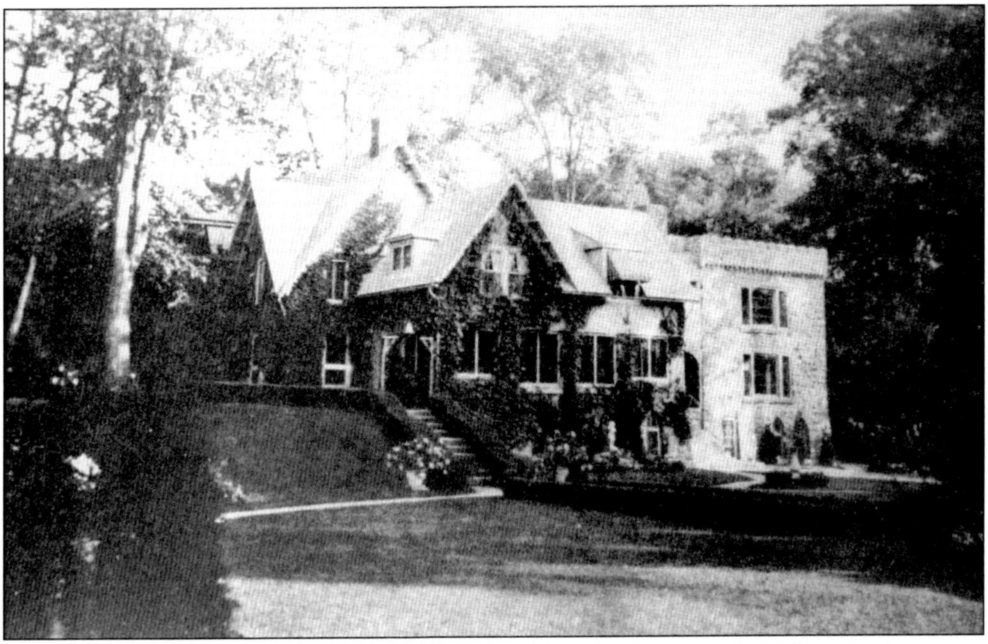

A 1929 photograph shows the house fully restored by Mrs. Herman A. Kelly, who began restoring it c. 1912. A date stone in the southeast gable has her and Herman A. Kelly's initials. Mrs. Kelly featured the house in the New York State Historical Association's "Historical Tour of Ulster County" in 1935 (below).[38] Directly below is a quote from her obituary with spelling errors as in original.[39]

"Mrs. Hermon A. Kelley of St. Remy, Ulster County, died at Kingston on March 26, 1946, after a prolonged illness.

"She was a native of Cleveland, Ohio, where she resided until she came to St. Remy, many years ago. At St. Remy she bought the estate of the late Hon. A. Bruyn Hasbrouck. She was intensively interested in horticulture, and developed the estate along original, artistic lines until her gardens were acknowledged to be among the most beautiful in Eastern New York. As a member of the Ulster Garden Club she gave great impetus to principles and achievements. She was a hostess of charming qualities and entertained graciously.

"Besides being a member of The Ulster County Historical Society, she was a member of the New York State Historical Association and a trustee of the Senate House Association of Kingston. A son, Kendall Kelley, of Cleveland, survives her."

Historical Tour of Ulster County
Stop C 4 Miles–

No. 18 MRS. HERMAN A. KELLY,
St. Remy, for tea

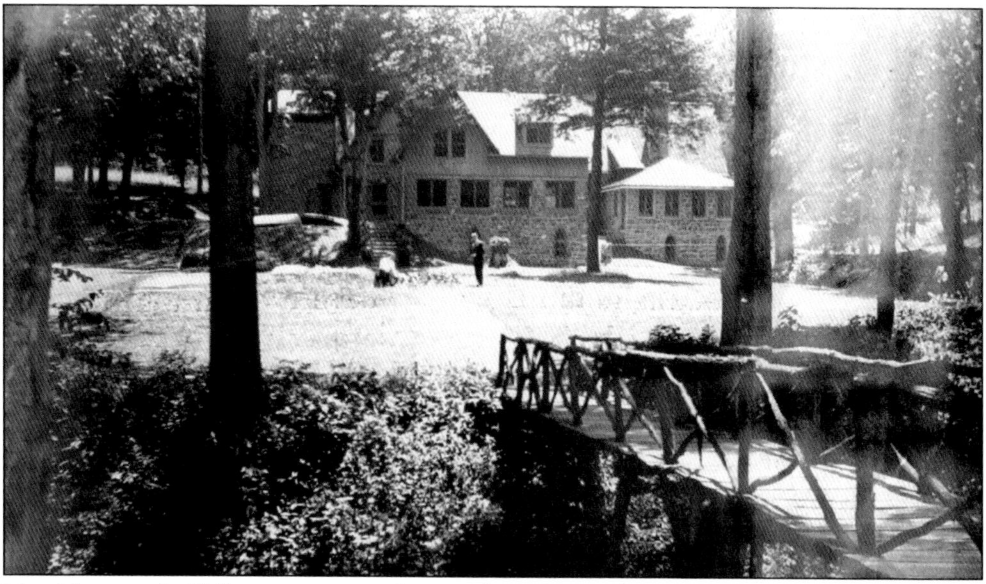

Mrs. Herman A. Kelly was interested not only in horticulture but also in the young people of the hamlet. The grounds of her estate were always open for informal entertainment, and she encouraged visits by locals and travelers alike. This 1929 view of the back lawn shows a wonderful rustic bridge spanning a small ravine. The grounds and gardens were carefully planned and executed. (Authors' collection.)

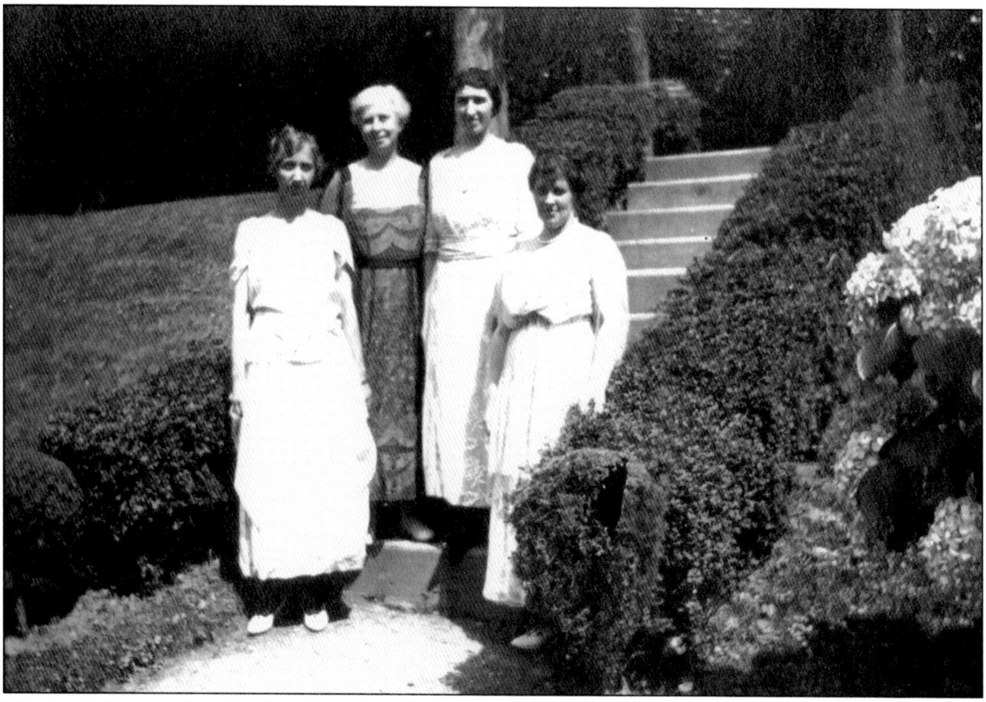

Elizabeth Ryan, a local girl with six brothers, spent many an afternoon at the estate. It must have been a special place for her to get away from the boys. Here we see Mrs. Herman Kelly (second from the left) entertaining (from left to right) Elizabeth, Della Grady, and an unidentified visitor among the late-spring blooms *c.* 1920. (Authors' collection.)

The western border of the old farm and of the estate was the center of the Rondout Creek.[40] There was a boat launch on the grounds, and there were always boats on the creek during the summer months. Not only did Mrs. Herman Kelly encourage others to enjoy "Kelly's Lake," she also enjoyed participating. This photograph was taken one summer in the early 1920s from one of several rowboats carrying guests. (Authors' collection.)

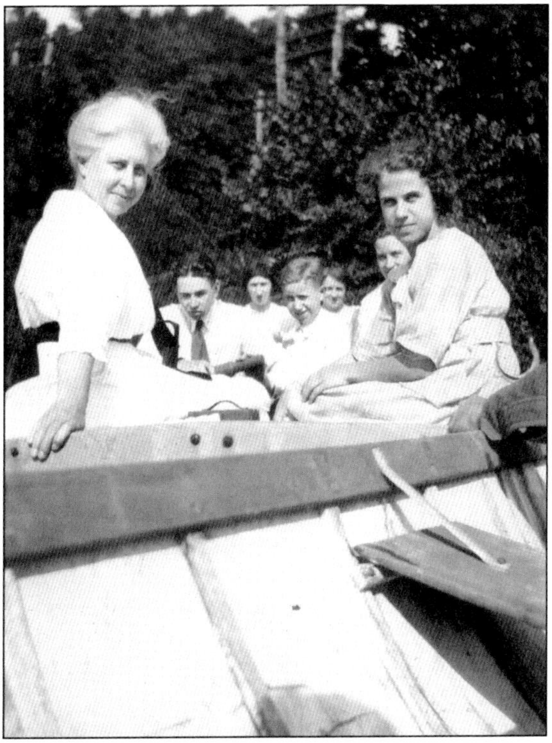

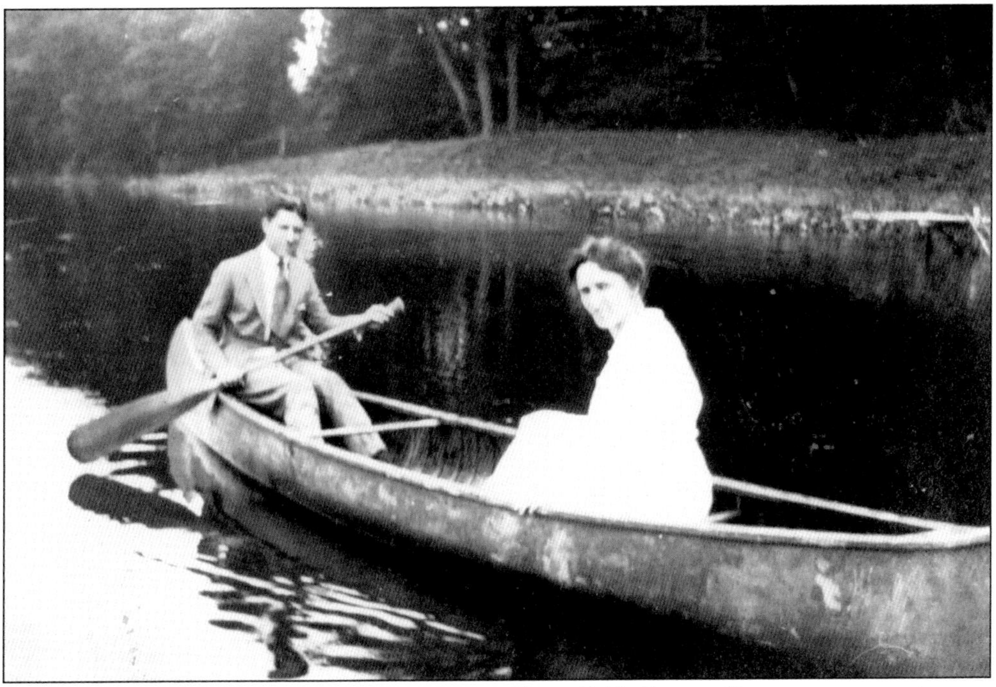

This scene depicts a more intimate moment in June 1919. Eugene Ryan is trying to impress Della Grady with his nautical skills. He must have done a good job of it. The two were an item for many years. Those who have paddled a canoe know that it is no simple matter, especially while wearing a suit and tie. (Authors' collection.)

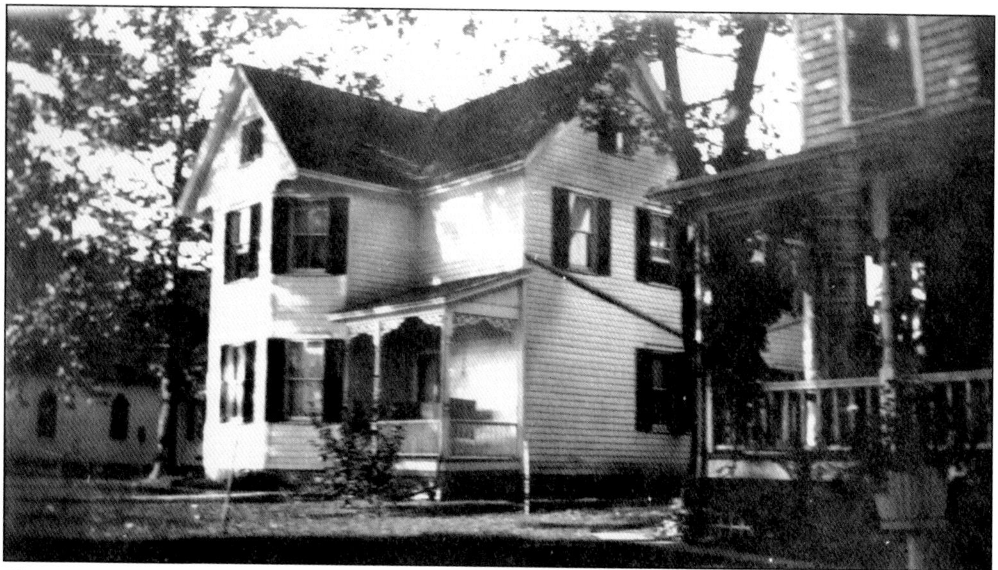

Shown is one of several Krom houses in September 1922. This is one of a row of late-Victorian houses on Main Street. The first part of the house dates from 1885–1890, with an addition in 1909 and a kitchen wing added in 1929. To the left is the St. Remy Chapel. Old Hawley Krom was a fixture around St. Remy in the 1960s. He dug graves, cleaned the firehouse, and always smelled of cigars. (Beatrice Jordon collection.)

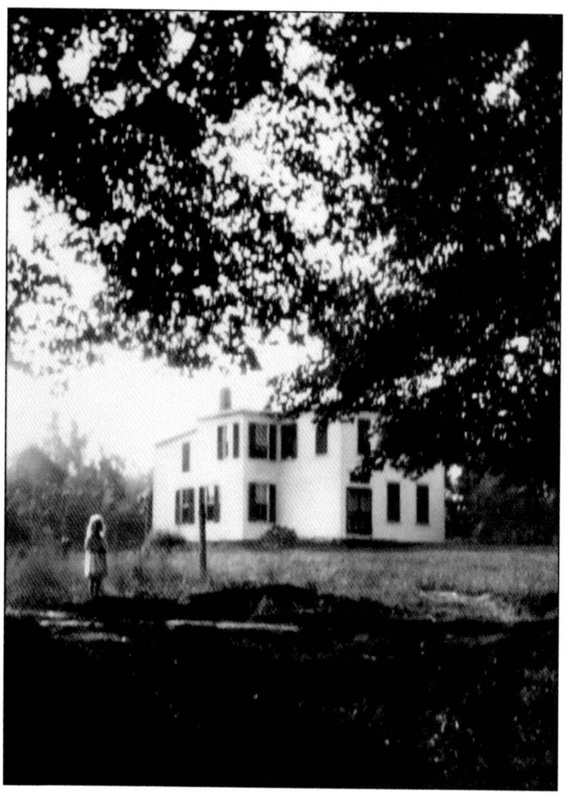

This is the Lorenzo E. Terpening residence in August 1922. The farm was one of many in Esopus that supplied fruit to city dwellers. Lorenzo Sr. left the farm to his sons Lorenzo and Harvey. Lorenzo never married. Harvey and his wife, Elizabeth Freer, raised their family here. When the new highway was built in 1960, it cut through the farm. Terpening strung a chain across the roadway the night before it was due to open. (Beatrice Jordon collection.)

Carlos Terpening is shown in a 1924 photograph. He was the son of Harvey Terpening and was born in 1920. He had an older brother named Harvey Jr. and younger sisters named Harriet and Olga. Like so many Esopus children, he eventually moved away from the family farm to seek his fortune in the more populated city of Kingston. (Raymond Krom collection.)

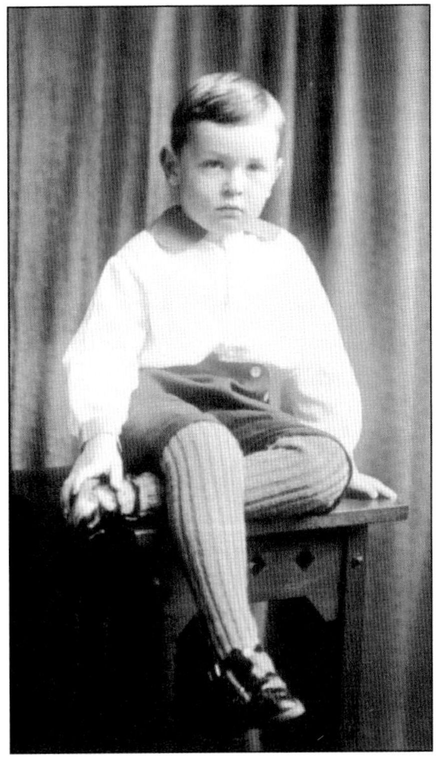

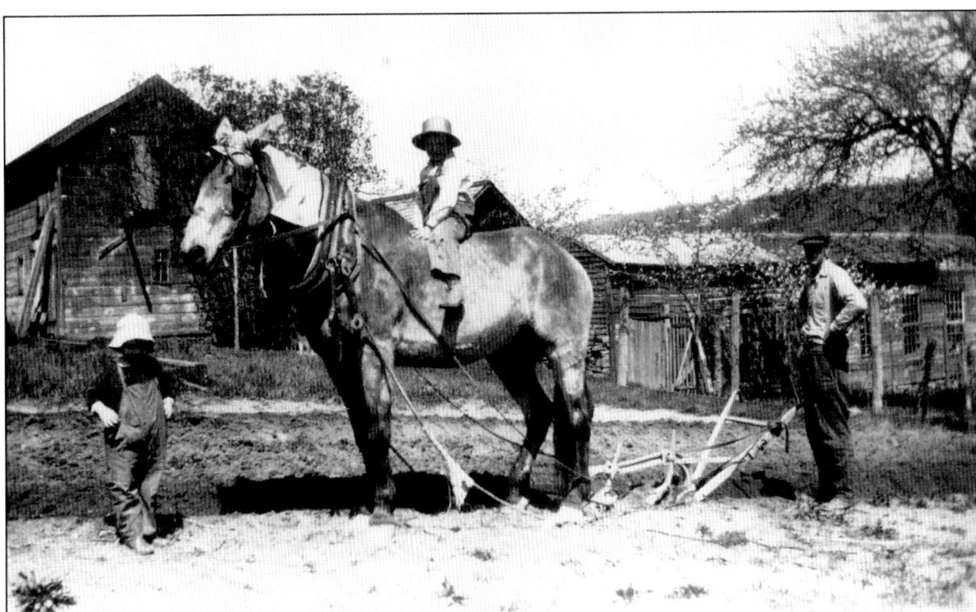

It is c. 1923, and brothers Carlos Terpening and Harvey Terpening Jr. are helping their uncle Lorenzo plow the gardens. Mules were often used for farm tasks and transportation. While draft, or "heavy," horses were stronger, mules were far less expensive and more versatile. Having a mule allowed the smaller farmer to make due without both a draft horse and a carriage horse. (Raymond Krom collection.)

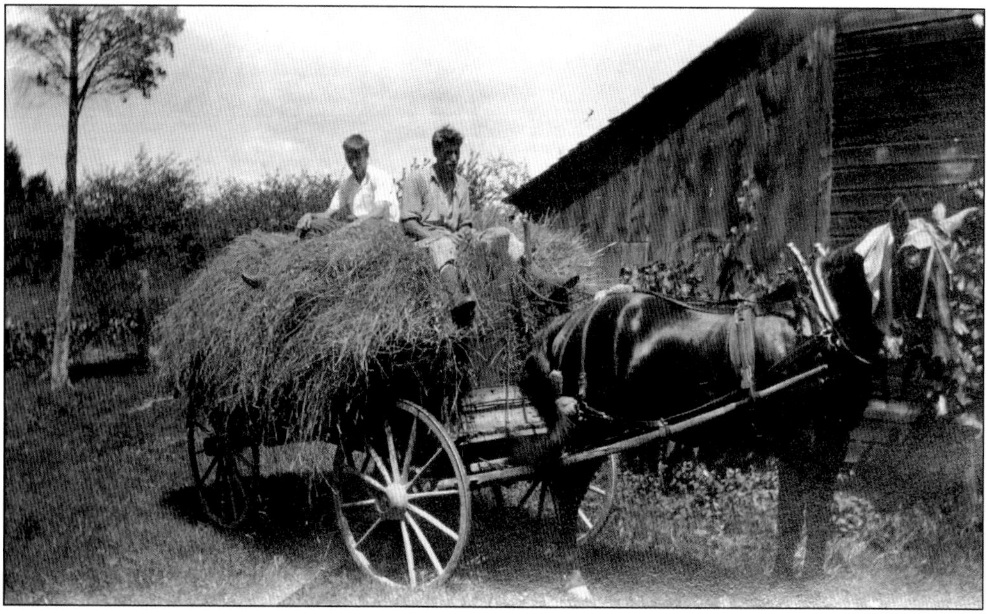

Herbert S. (left) and Harvey J. Terpening are seen here in the summer of 1910. This was the way most farmers gathered hay. Bailers were simply not available. It took a great many wagonloads of hay to feed a family's livestock, so barns tended to be enormous with sizable haylofts. The hay was moved one pitchfork full at a time. (Raymond Krom collection.)

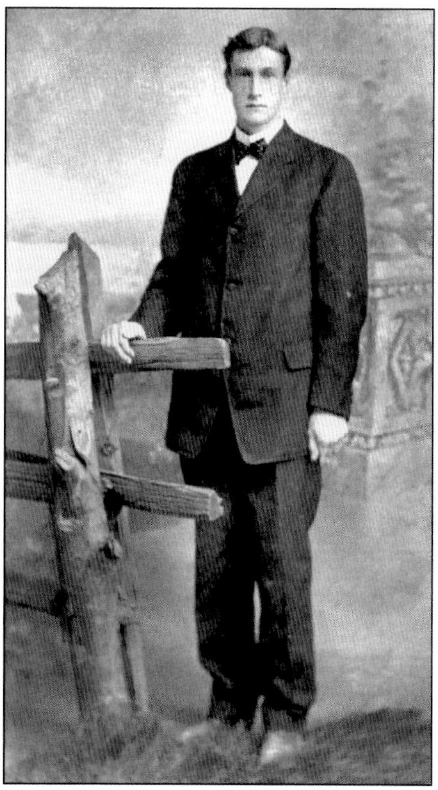

This photograph, taken in 1923, shows Harvey J. Terpening at age 33. He looks good in the suit, but the choice of a split-rail fence for a prop tells the whole story. He was far more comfortable on the farm and wearing attire appropriate for that setting. (Raymond Krom collection.)

Elizabeth Leona Freer married Harvey J. Terpening in January 1917. Elizabeth is the Elsie Freer shown as a girl earlier in the chapter. This signed portrait was a part of her sister Ruth's collection. Terpening was the brother of Herbert Terpening who is shown below. The Freers, Terpenings, and VanAkens were large and prolific families, and we find many local marriages among them.

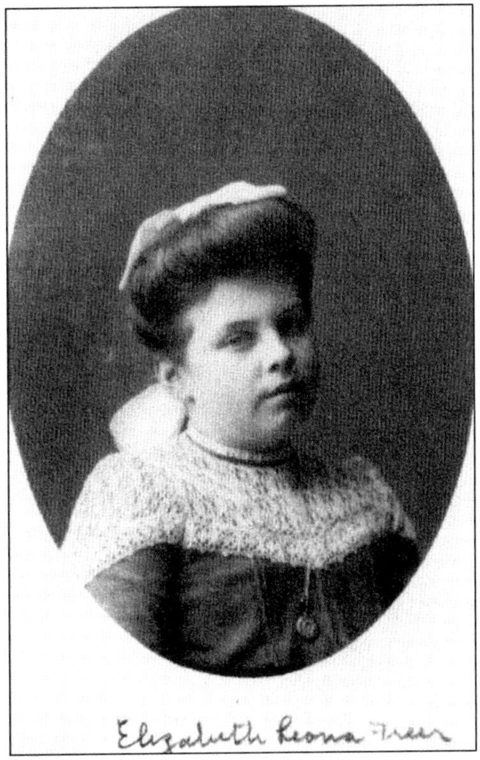

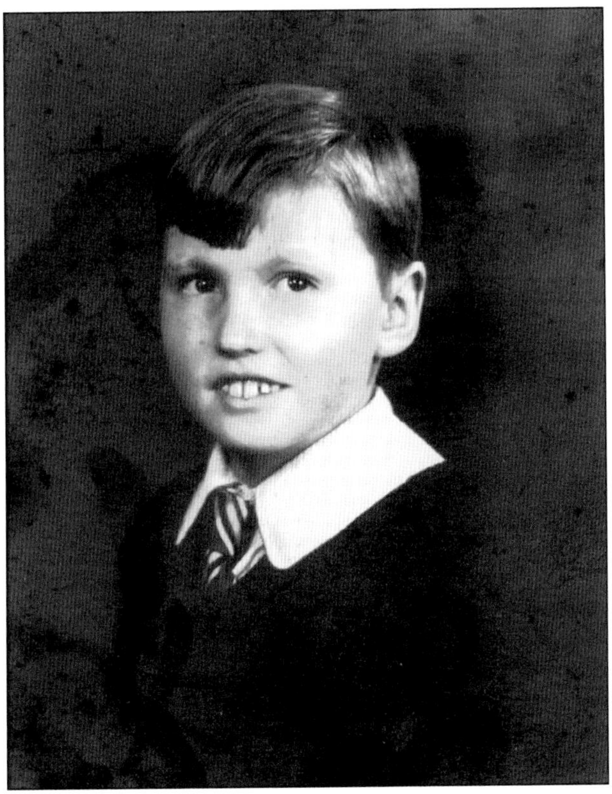

Herbert Terpening was born in 1895 to Lorenzo Terpening Sr. and Symanthy VanAken, who were married in 1873. Strangely, Symanthy has a different name in almost every census. She was Cornelia as a child, later Cynthia, Symanthy, and Lucinda, and her marriage record lists her as Symanthy. Perhaps she disliked the name Cornelia. (Raymond Krom collection.)

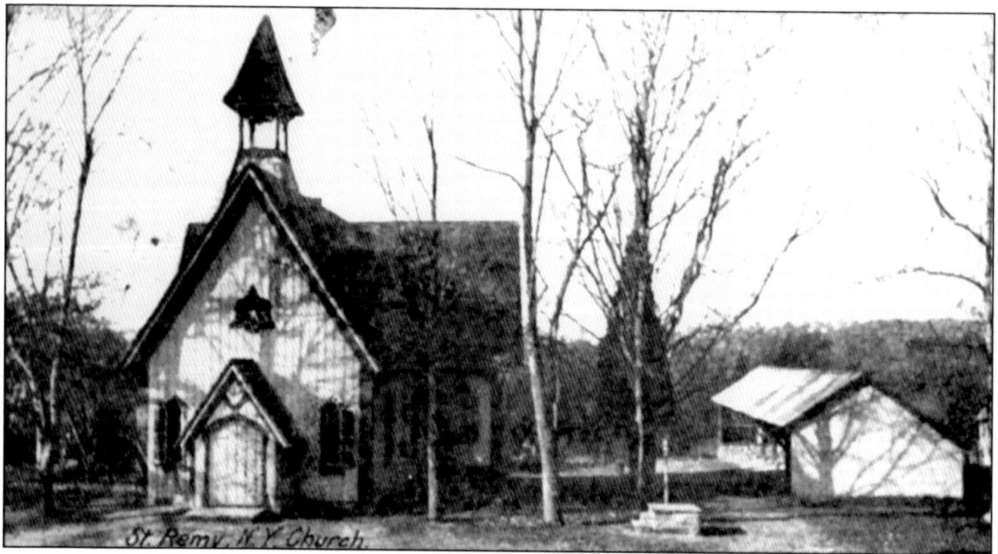

The St. Remy Chapel is one of the finest examples of board-and-batten Gothic architecture in Ulster County. In 1856, the Honorable Abraham Bruyn Hasbrouck donated one-quarter acre of land for its construction. Hasbrouck wished to build a place of worship for the people of the hamlet that he had named. He also donated $100 toward its construction cost of $500. Other subscribers donated from $1 to $20.

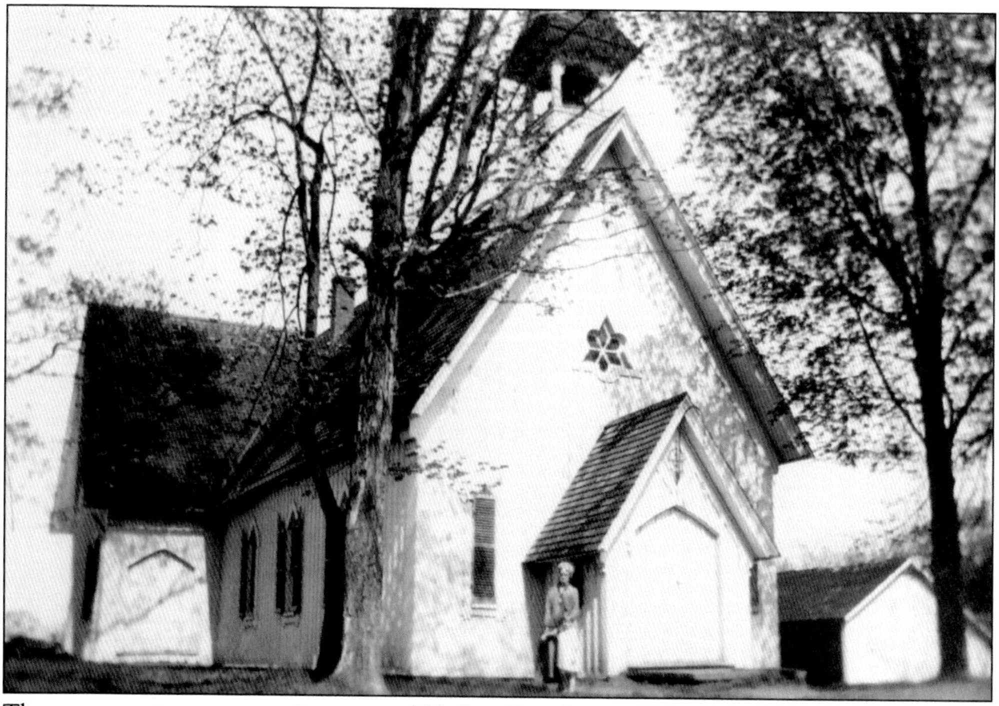

The congregation was an active one and filed its Certificate of Incorporation on May 25, 1878.[41] William Todd was minister. The church building was a favorite of photographers in all seasons. Here we see the edifice in the spring of 1926 or 1927. The woman leaning on a cane is Ophelia Roosa Lawrence. She died in November 1927 and would have been about 71 years of age in this photograph. (Martin Jordan collection.)

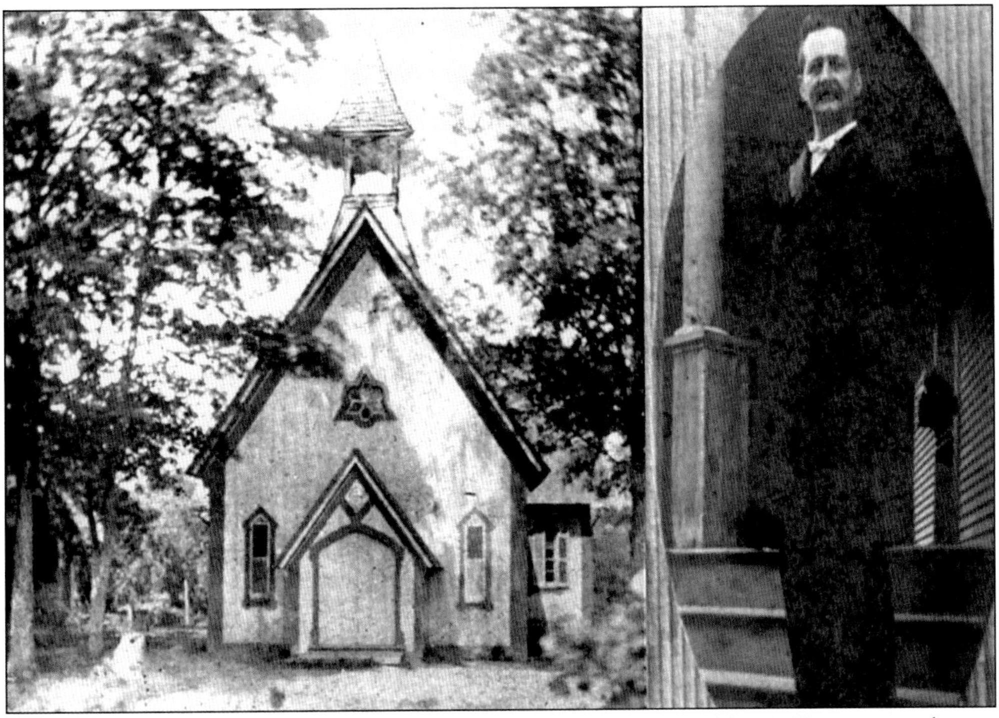

This view of the St. Remy Chapel and portrait of the Reverend Franklin A. Force were taken in 1905 for a postcard. The two images were combined as shown here. The postcard was probably distributed to the parishioners because it commemorated the installation of the Domine on February 1 of that year. Note that the photographer waited for summer weather to take the photographs. (Authors' collection.)

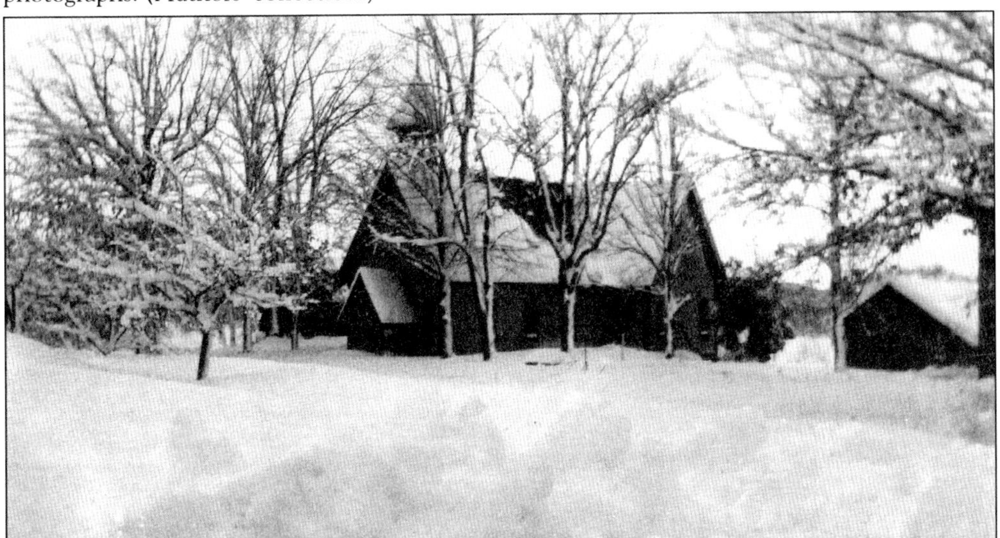

The snowstorms were prodigious in the olden days. This view of the chapel and carriage shed was taken from the Lorenzo Terpening farm during the winter of 1920. These were the days before paved roads and powerful snow-moving machinery. The road was probably cleared by hand, horse, and tractor. (Raymond Krom collection.)

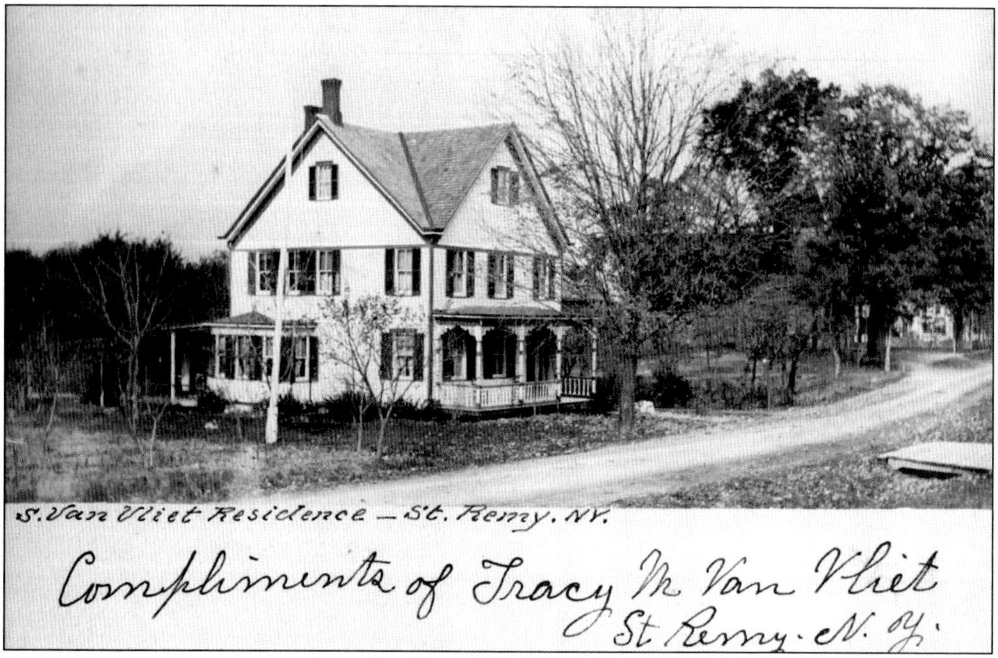

In January 1881, Simon VanVliet married his childhood sweetheart, Amelia Van Wagenen. Simon was the eldest son of Moses VanVliet and built this house for his own growing family. He and his wife raised two sons, Lewis and Tracy, and a daughter, Edna. To feed this family, he created an orchard on the farm. He was active in the business until he and his wife died in 1930. (Authors' collection.)

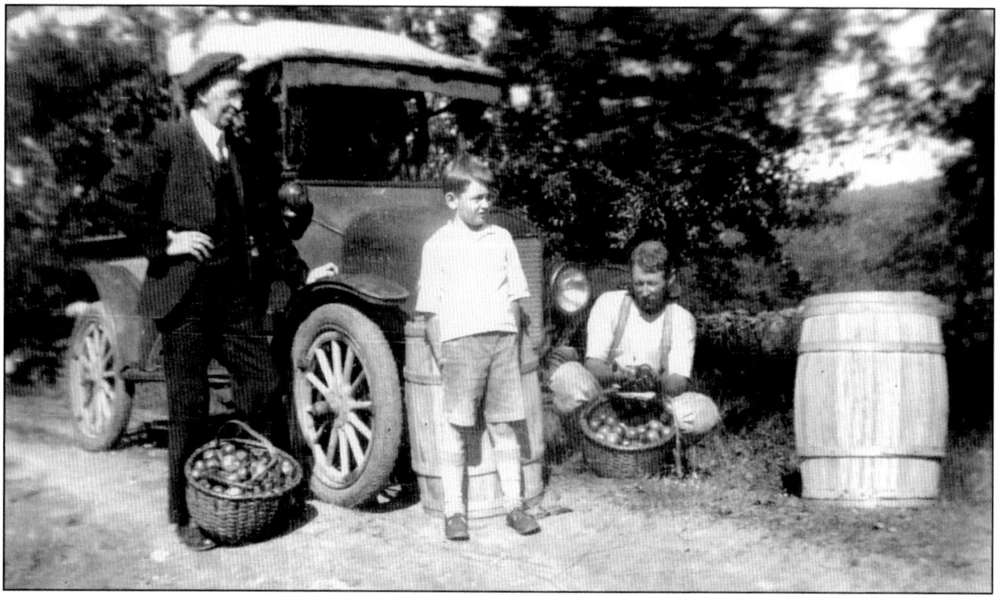

After Simon VanVliet's death, Tracy VanVliet (left) took over the family farm and orchards. Shown with VanVliet are Raymond Krom Sr. (center) and a Terpening, probably Harvey. The vehicle is a Model T delivery truck that VanVliet used to take produce to the docks and for his delivery route to Connelly. The Terpenings raised peaches and often helped out in the VanVliet orchards. (Raymond Krom collection.)

Shown is Harvey Terpening *c.* 1930. The barrels hold apples or perhaps peaches. Barrels were the standard way of shipping produce to market in earlier times. After the young folks had loaded his truck, Tracy VanVliet would drive the barrels to the docks on the Rondout Creek for shipment to New York City. The town of Esopus was well known for the superior quality of its apples (and its applejack). (Raymond Krom collection.)

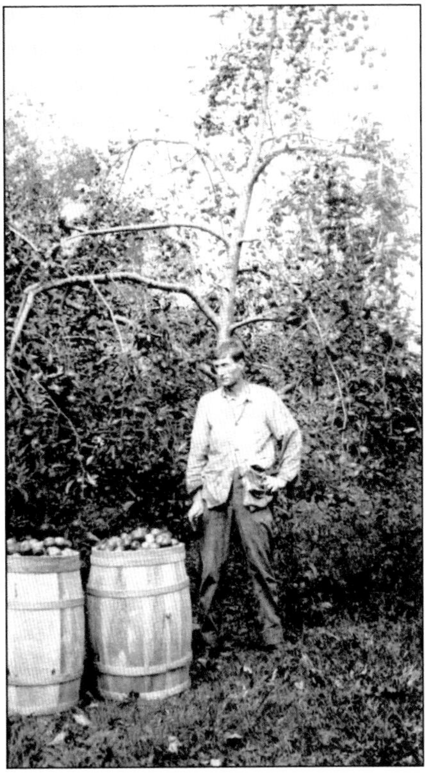

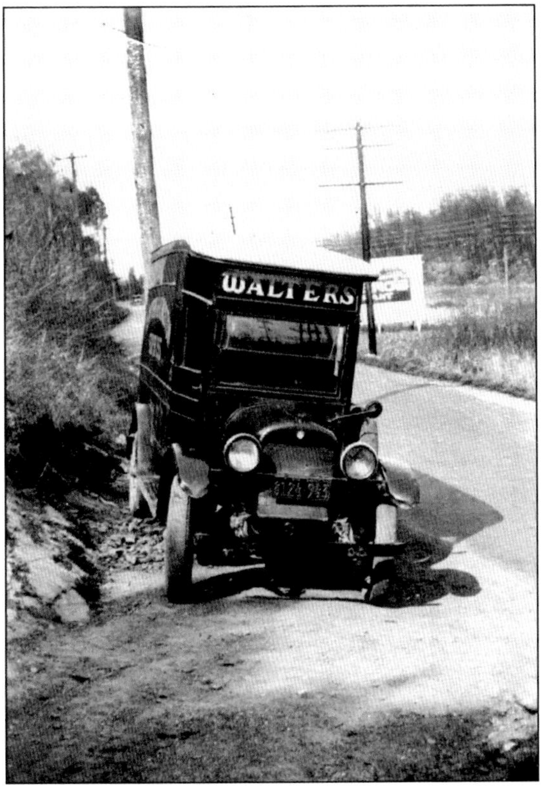

Another local firm was Walters Produce. This is their delivery truck stopped along the road from St. Remy to Rifton in 1933. Note the billboard for Von Berg's Restaurant in the background. This delivery truck was a closed-back version, as opposed to VanVliet's open version. For the curious, the license plate says, "COM 124-943" and "1933" or "1930." (C. Terpening collection.)

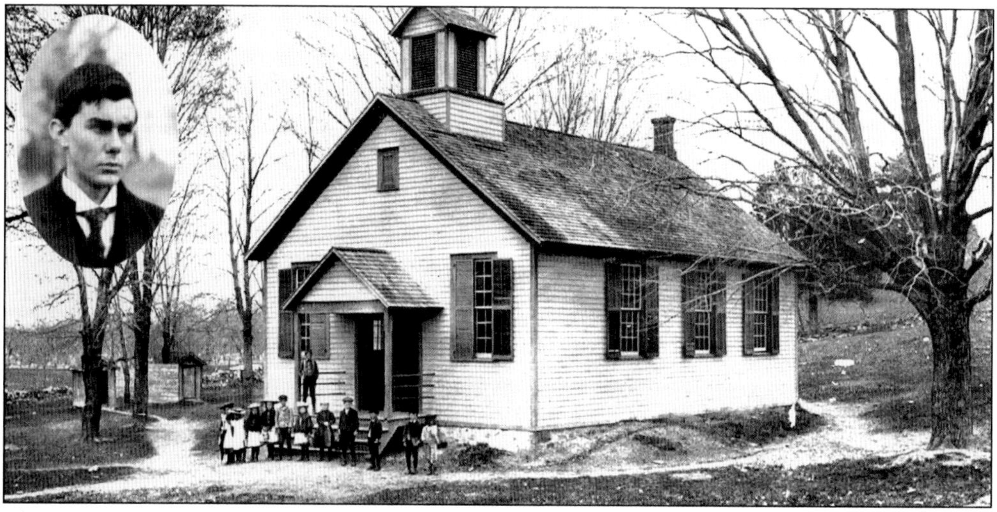

The District No. 5 schoolhouse, on Main Street, is pictured *c.* 1915. In the left rear are boys' and girls' outhouses. The twin doors leading into the school are also labeled according to gender. The inset of the teacher appeared on a postcard version of this photograph. (Gift of Florence Liebhaber.)

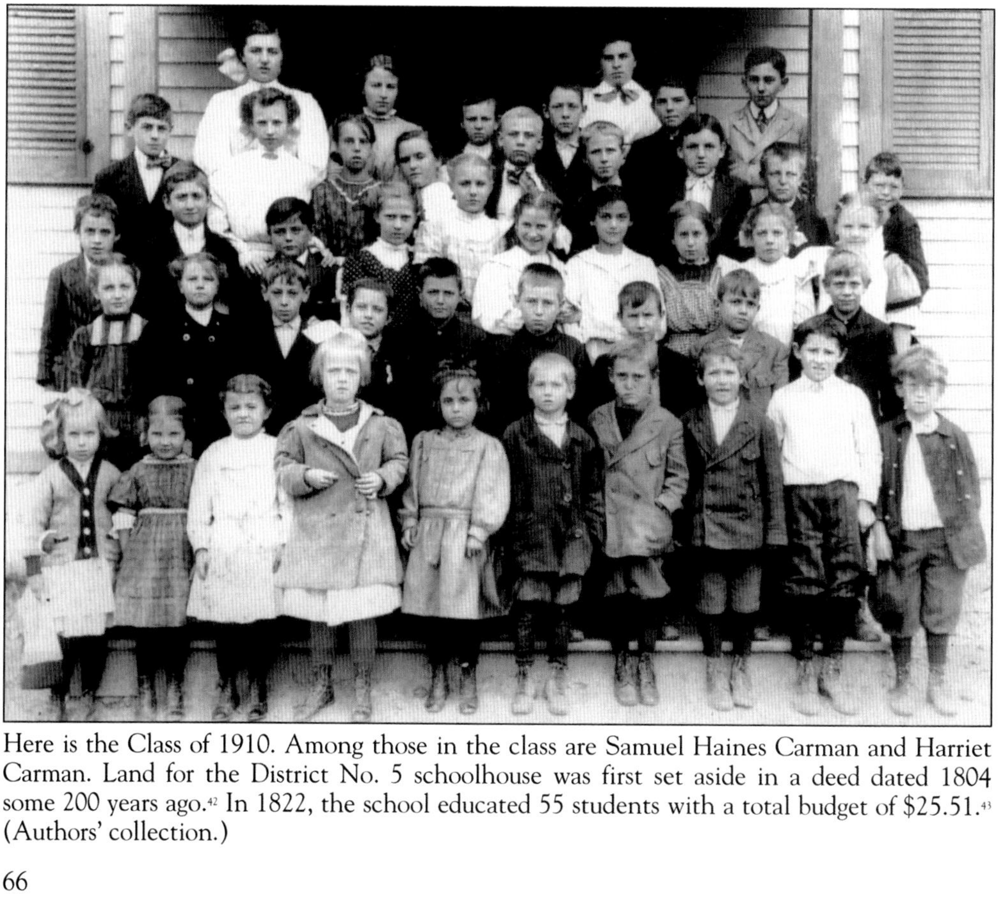

Here is the Class of 1910. Among those in the class are Samuel Haines Carman and Harriet Carman. Land for the District No. 5 schoolhouse was first set aside in a deed dated 1804 some 200 years ago.[42] In 1822, the school educated 55 students with a total budget of $25.51.[43] (Authors' collection.)

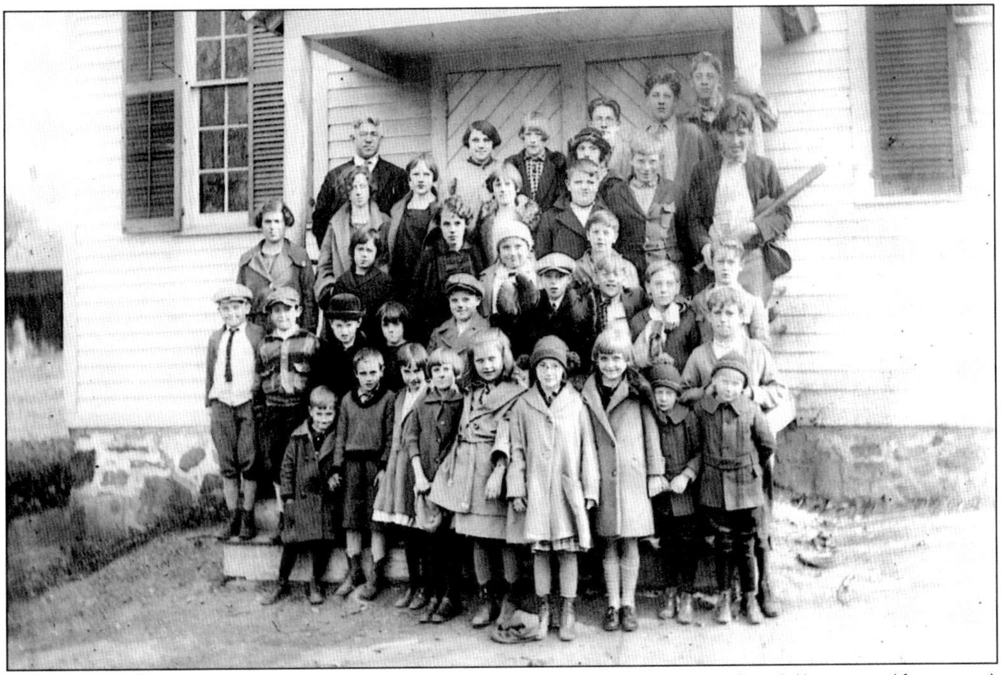

Shown are members of the Class of 1925. From left to right are the following: (first row) ? Emberson, ? Emberson, Isabel Reynolds, two unidentified students, Georgiana White, Dorothy White, unidentified, Peter Helmich, and James Helmich; (second row) Wallace Wood, second from the right; (third row) unidentified, Isabel Krom, Doris Emberson, ? Tyler, and two unidentified students; (fourth row) Clarence Krom, third from the right; (fifth row) Mr. Gulick, two unidentified students, Catherine Helmich, John Helmich, and two unidentified students.

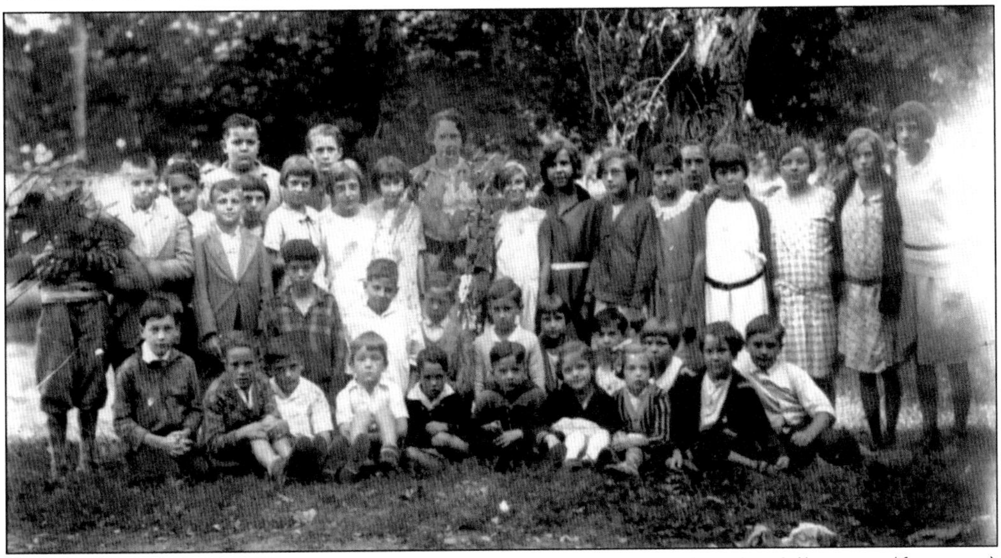

Among the members of the Class of 1928 are, from left to right, the following: (first row) unidentified, ? Emberson, unidentified, Raymond Krom Sr., ? Emberson, and three unidentified students; (third row) seven unidentified students, Isabel Reynolds, two unidentified students, Dorothy White, two unidentified students, Barbara Krom, and three unidentified students; (fourth row) Clarence Krom, unidentified, and the teacher. (Raymond Krom collection.)

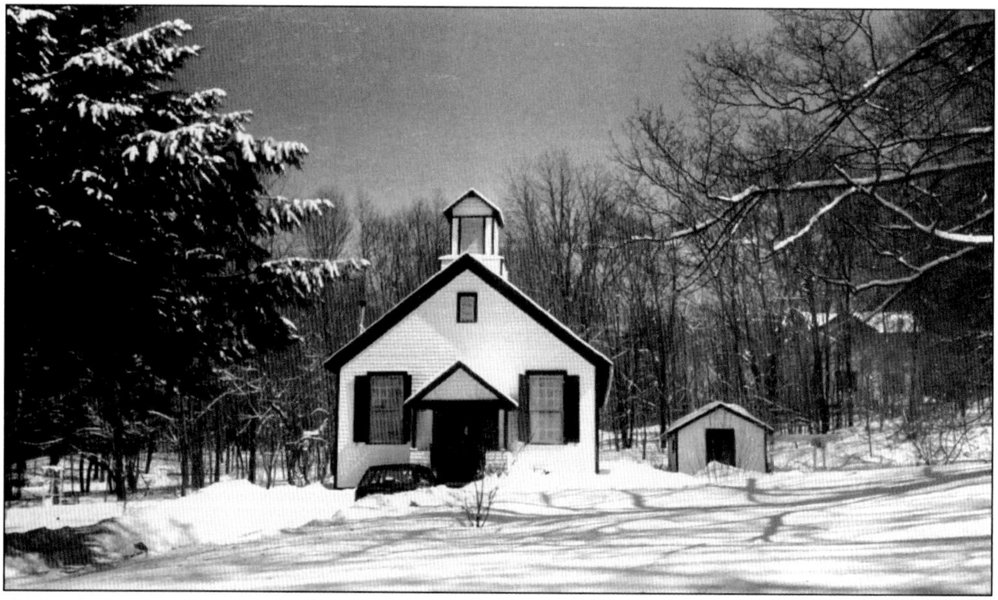

On Friday, October 16, 1959, the St. Remy School closed its doors for the final time. The last nine pupils were transferred to Port Ewen School. Ruth Elliott, the teacher at St. Remy, was transferred to Lake Katrine School, where she filled a vacancy as a second-grade teacher. The schoolhouse was sold as a private dwelling. This is how it looked after the blizzard of March 1993. (Authors' collection.)

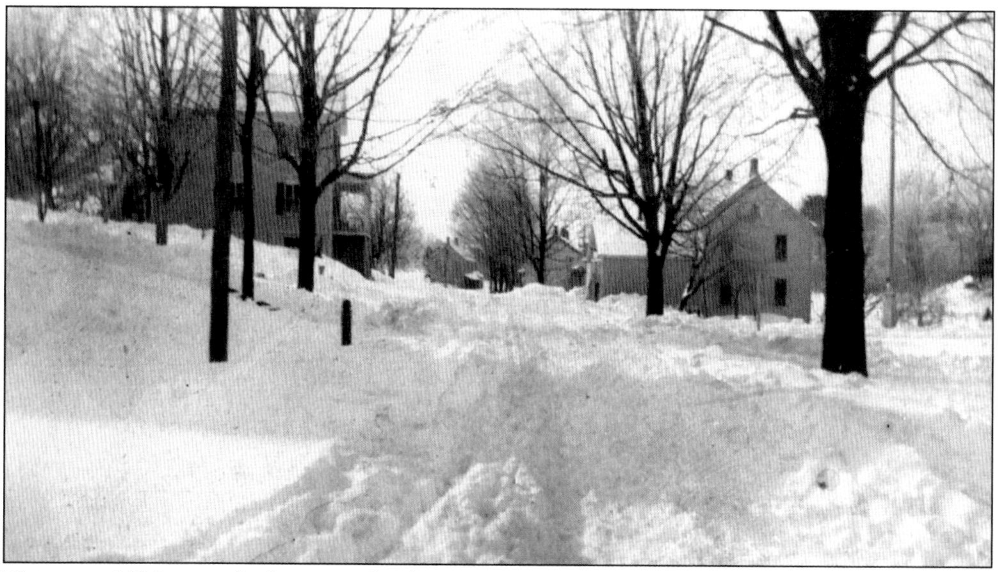

This is a 1920 view looking south along Main Street from Greenkill Road just past the schoolhouse. The roads have not been plowed and probably will not be for some time. Ahead and to the right we see the Ryan House opposite the butcher shop. In the center distance is the bakery. The tiny building at the right is the second U.S. post office in the hamlet.[44] (Raymond Krom collection.)

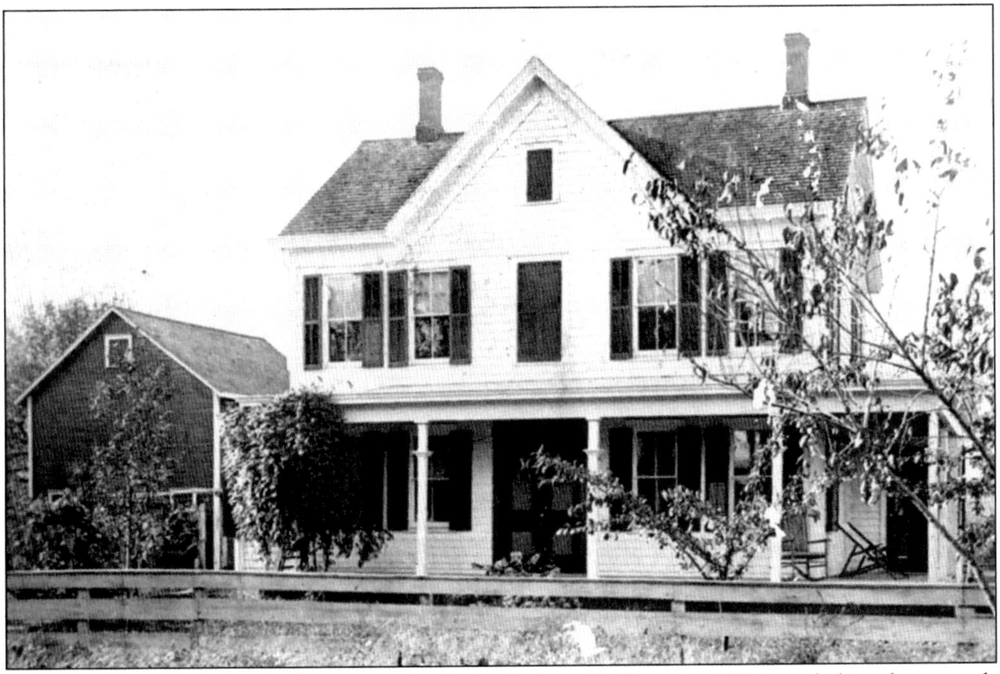

A Carpenter Gothic–style house was built for Joshua V. Freer in 1904, and this photograph was taken in 1906. The house stands behind the Jonas VanAken home of 1843 and in front of the St. Remy Rural Cemetery along the Greenkill Road. Joshua Freer dug the graves. In the mid-20th century, this was the home of the Raymond Krom family. Greenkill Road ran to the ancient house and ferry of Benjamin VanAken. (Authors' collection.)

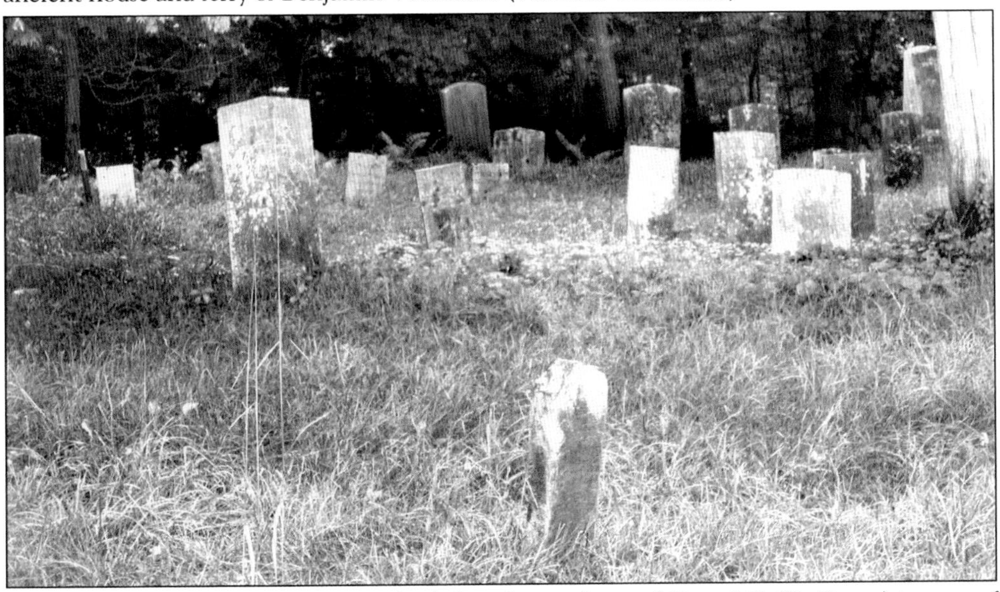

The Greenkill Burying Ground was deeded to the residents of Greenkill (St. Remy) in care of Jan VanAken's eldest son, Pieter, in 1804 "for the benefit and behoof of the Neighbourhood."[45] Many burials date from the mid- to late 1700s. Most of the earliest settlers of St. Remy were laid to rest in this VanAken family burial ground on the family farm. Two ancient cedar trees and stone walls mark this cemetery. (Authors' collection.)

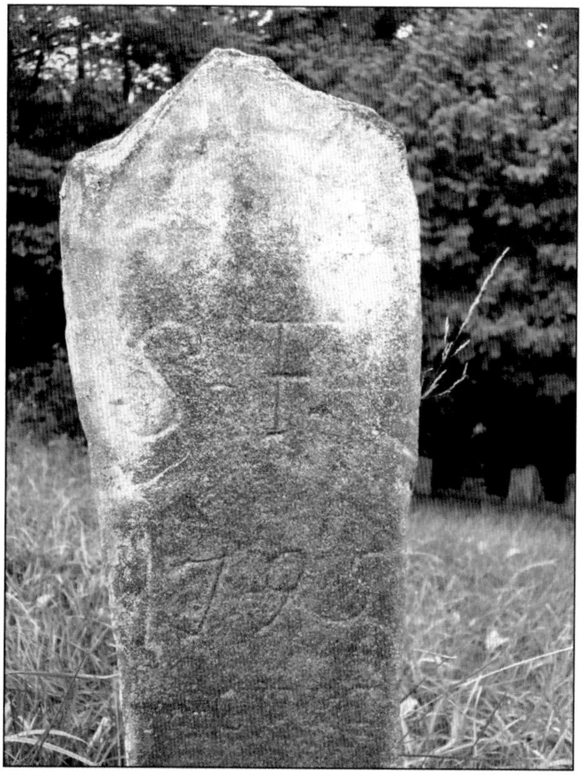

Although many of the stones in the old ground are hard to read and harder to photograph, this stone was very legible after 200-plus years. It reads, "S. Freer 1795." It is believed to be the burial site of Samuel Freer, who was born in 1742. Samuel was the husband of Zara Roosa, who was born in 1744. These old stones are a favorite of schoolchildren, who take rubbings of the inscriptions. (Authors' collection.)

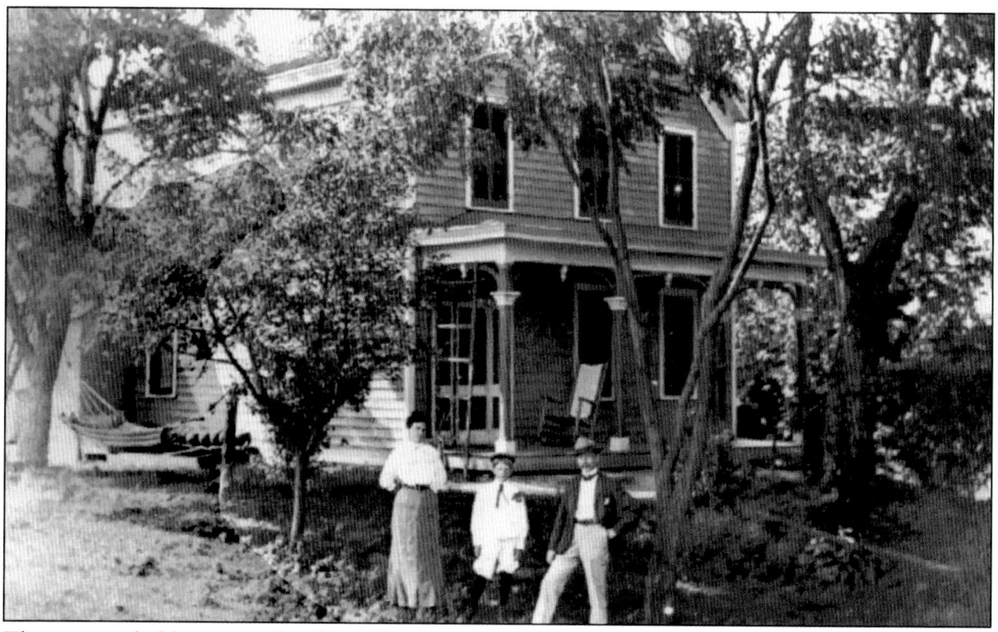

This was probably originally a Freer house. It was constructed between 1875 and 1891 and has been home to the Reynolds family for the past 50 years. It stands across from the St. Remy Fire Station, and its owner is a culinary expert of world renown. This photograph dates from the 1920s, when Lou and Virginia (Elizabeth) VanVliet owned the house. The youngster is Harold. (Beatrice Jordan collection.)

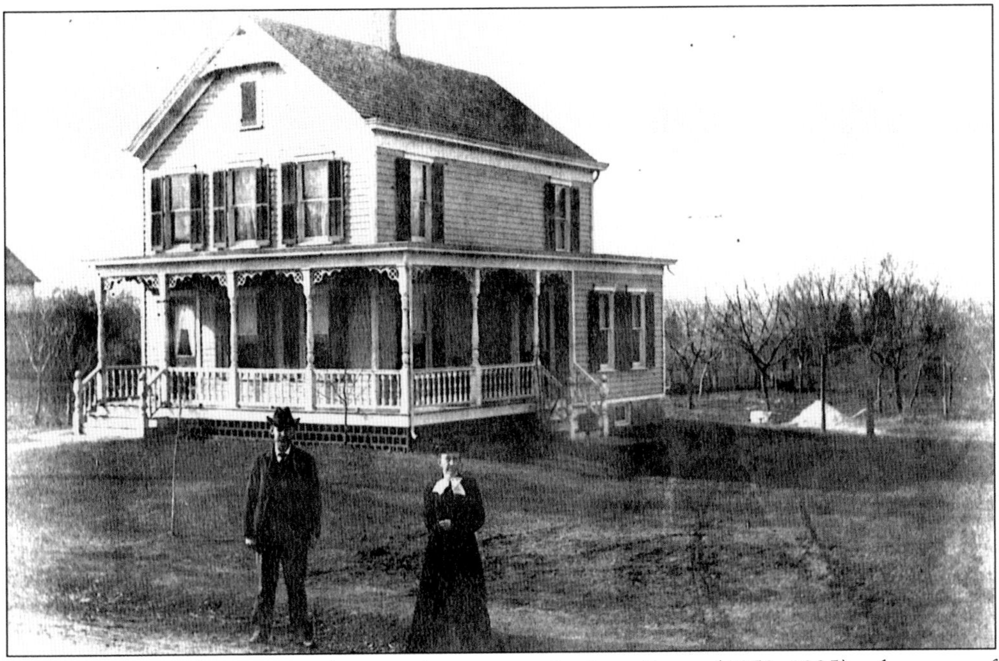

In this early-20th-century photograph, we see Luther Freer (1859–1925), the son of William H. Freer and Maria Houghtaling, and his wife, Cornelia D. Roosa (1849–1915), the daughter of Levi C. and Maria Roosa. In the background are the VanVliet orchards, and at the left rear is the St. Remy Chapel. Levi Roosa is mentioned in the Beers *Commemorative Biographical Record*. The house later became a Krom homestead. (Authors' collection.)

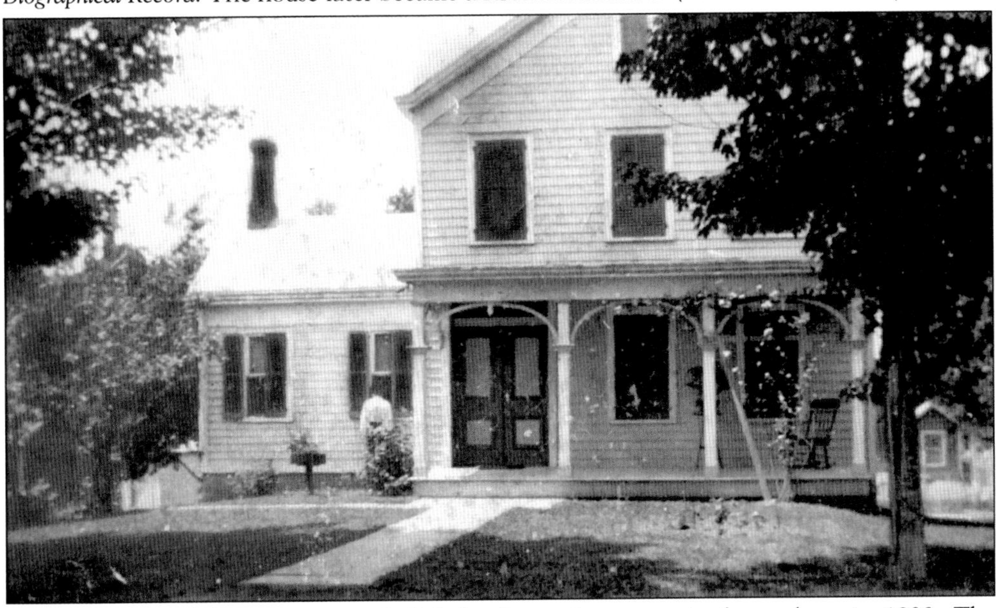

The home of Ralph Lawrence and Ophelia Roosa Lawrence is shown here in 1922. The house was probably built in 1863.[46] It is not known who is gazing into the kitchen window—perhaps Ophelia Lawrence, lost in happy reminiscence. She died at the age of 70, four years after this photograph was taken. The house was subsequently purchased by the Freer family. (Beatrice Jordan collection.)

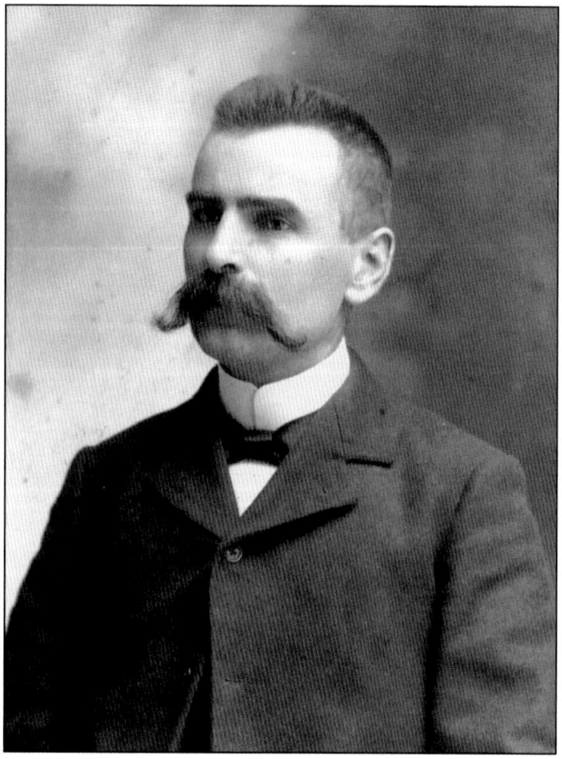

Ralph Lawrence (1856–1916) and his wife, Ophelia, were the owners of the Lawrence house shown in the lower photograph on page 71. Lawrence, like many other early residents, was a farmer. The barn on his property is still standing and was rebuilt in the 1990s. He and his wife were married *c.* 1881 and came to St. Remy in 1883. (Martin Jordan collection.)

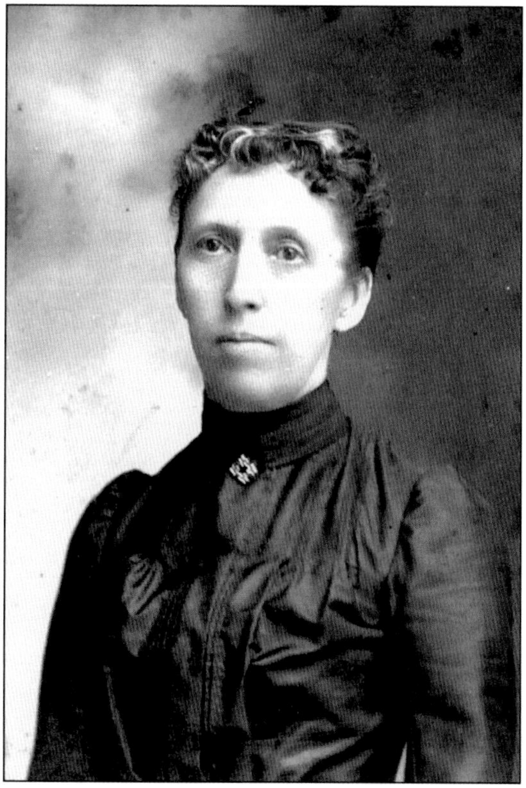

This is an 1880s portrait of Ophelia Roosa Lawrence (1856–1926). She is the woman who created the hair sample book shown earlier in this chapter. She earned a teacher's certificate in 1873. She and her husband, Ralph Lawrence, had one child, Katherine. Katherine Lawrence married Harry Ellsworth on October 16, 1907.[47] (Martin Jordan collection.)

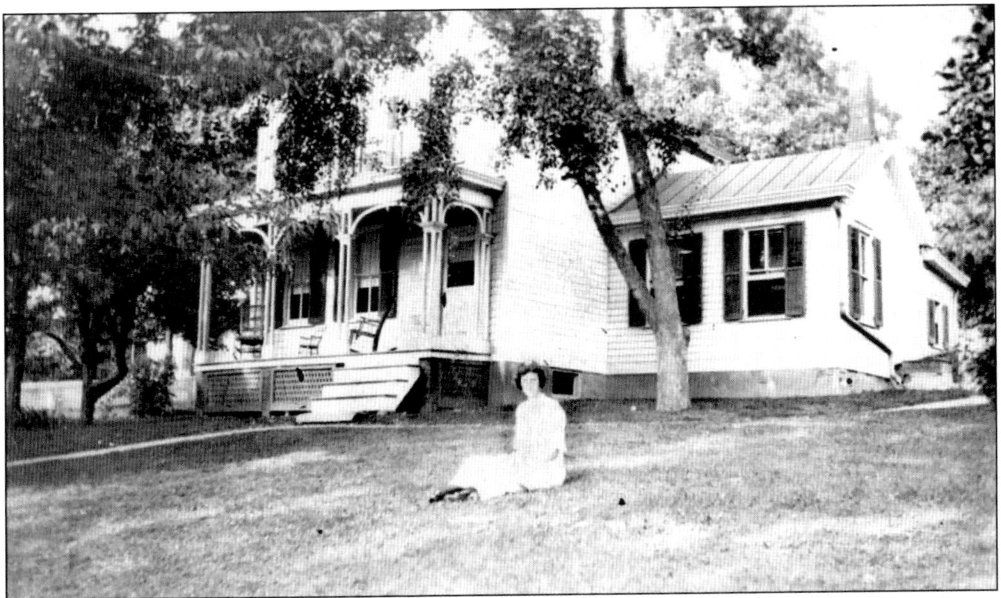

This photograph is labeled, "William Freer 1900." The house may be that of William Garret and Anna M. Freer. It is located near the junction of Union Center Road and Main Street. Anna Freer was born in 1870, which would make her 30 years of age in 1900. It is known that Josh and Louise Freer owned the house from 1938 until the 1960s.

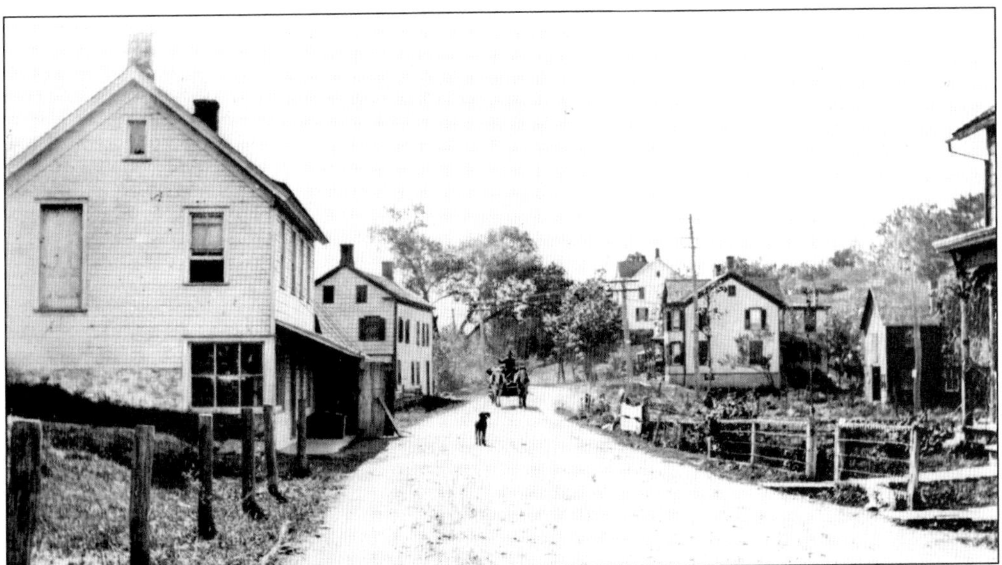

This is a 1900 view of St. Remy's Main Street in the business district of town. In the left foreground is the bakery, which was built by Anna and Samuel Deyo in 1841.[48] In the left background is the *c.* 1839 building containing the post office, barbershop, and one of the general stores. That building burned down *c.* 1916. The post office dates from January 1888. In the right foreground is the dance hall, now an apartment house. The blacksmith shop is to the right of center. Note the two telegraph lines. (Authors' collection.)

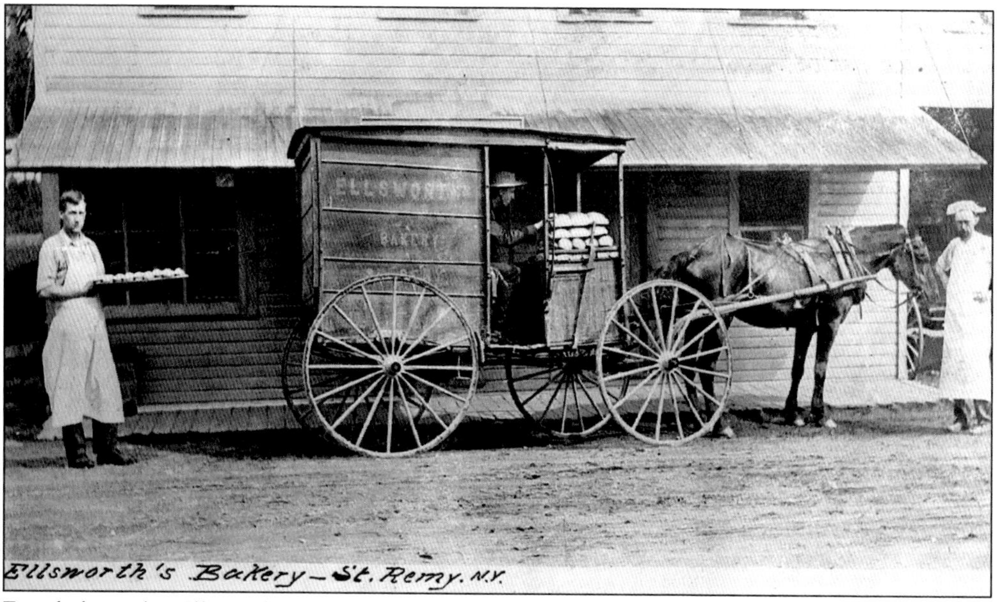

Entitled simply "Ellsworth's Bakery—St. Remy, N.Y.," this *c.* 1900 photograph shows a proud baker and his assistant preparing to deliver their tasty wares to the residents of St. Remy and Rifton. It must have been difficult to drive the wagon with those breads stacked up front. The bakery had large windows, and people passing by could see the goods and oven. It was an active business well into the 20th century. (Authors' collection.)

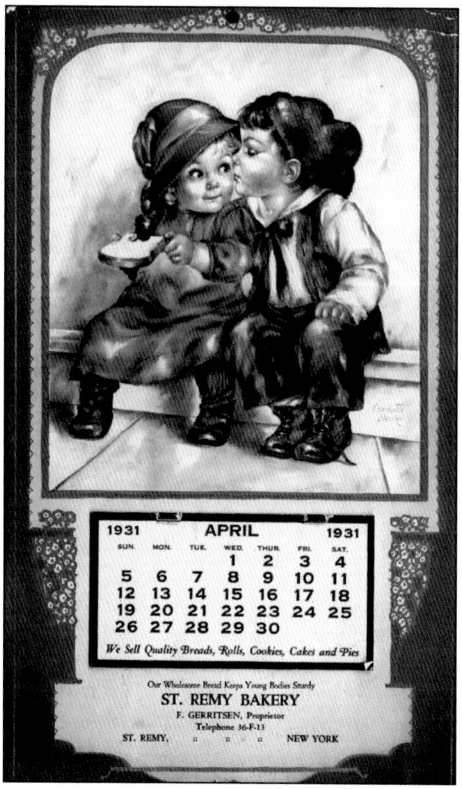

Black and white hardly does this beautiful calendar justice. The original is in full color, more than 15 inches tall, and bordered in dark green and gold. The year is 1931, and the calendar text reads, "We Sell Quality Breads, Rolls, Cookies, Cakes and Pies." The bottom portion reads, "Our Wholesome Bread Keeps Young Bodies Sturdy . . . St. Remy Bakery . . . F. Gerritsen, Proprietor . . . Telephone 36-F-13." The artwork is by Charlotte Becker. (Authors' collection.)

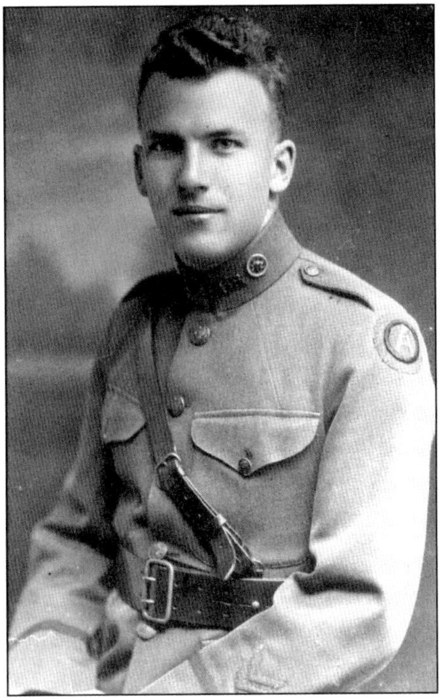

Lt. Eugene Lichtenberg of St. Remy is pictured in 1919 wearing his World War I uniform. He was stationed in France until August of that year. Born in 1895, he was adopted by the Lichtenbergs as an infant. Eugene Lichtenberg Sr. was an engineer and owned Hilltop House from 1903 to the 1920s. (Authors' collection.)

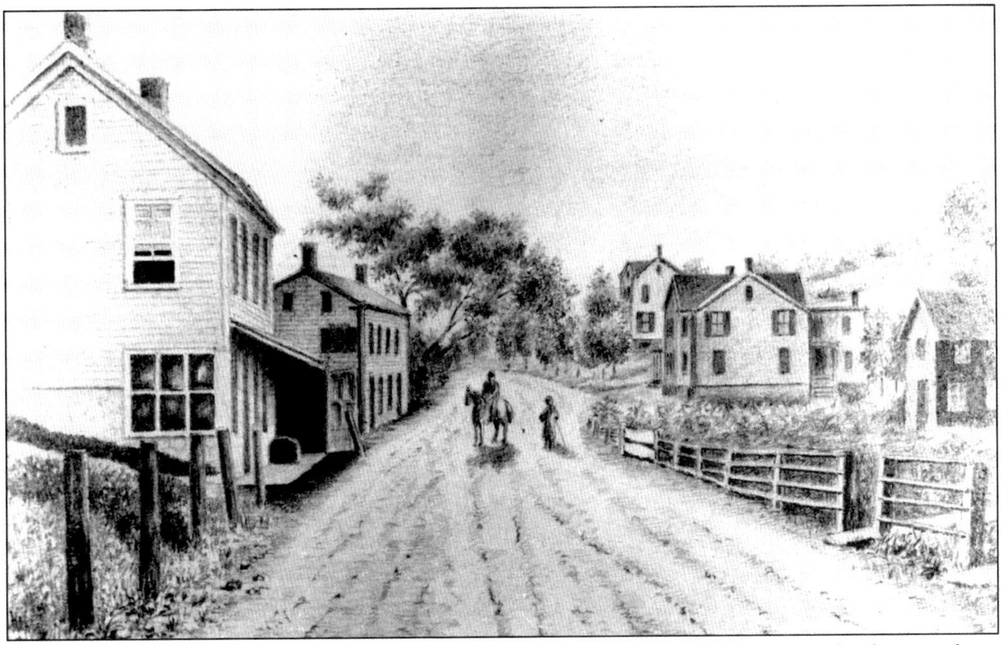

Eugene Lichtenberg Jr. made this sketch of St. Remy in 1905. He apparently drew it from the Main Street postcard (the lower picture on page 73), making a substitution at the center. He and his family lived in Hilltop House, in the right background. At the right and in front of his home are the Samuel Haines house and the St. Remy Blacksmith Shop. (Original in Willis DeHart collection.)

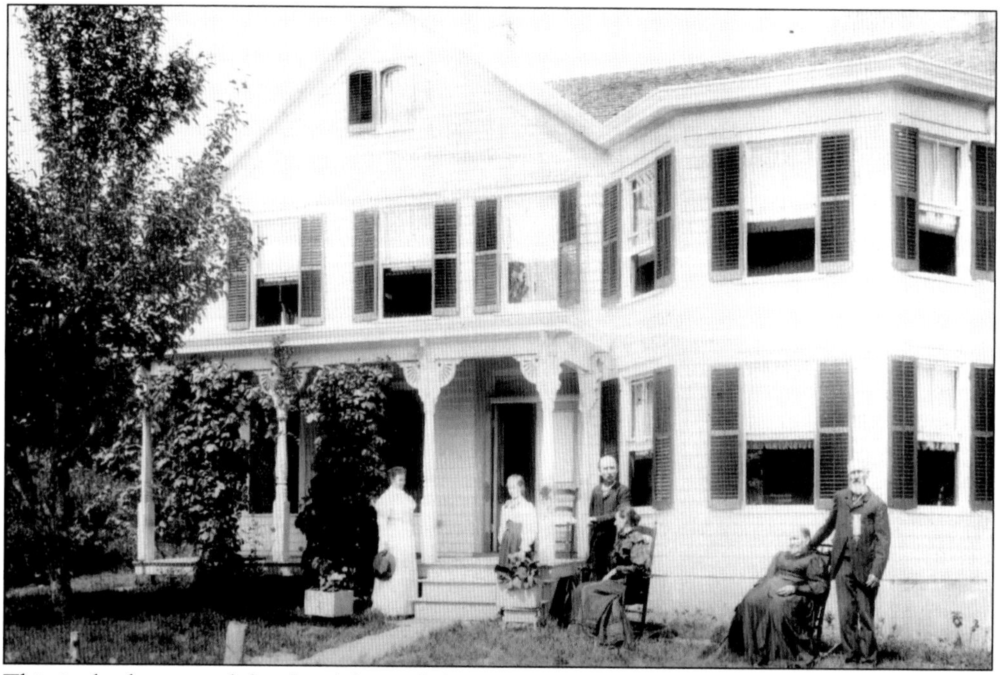

This is the home and family of Samuel G. Haines in 1895. Pictured are, from left to right, neighbor Martha Connelly, Martha Watson Haines, Samuel G. Haines, Mary Frances Decker Haines, Mary E. Lawson Decker, and Peter M. Decker (wearing his Mexican War medal). The rear part of the house was constructed in the 1840s, the main part (left) in 1872, and the north wing in 1895 as a living space for the Deckers.

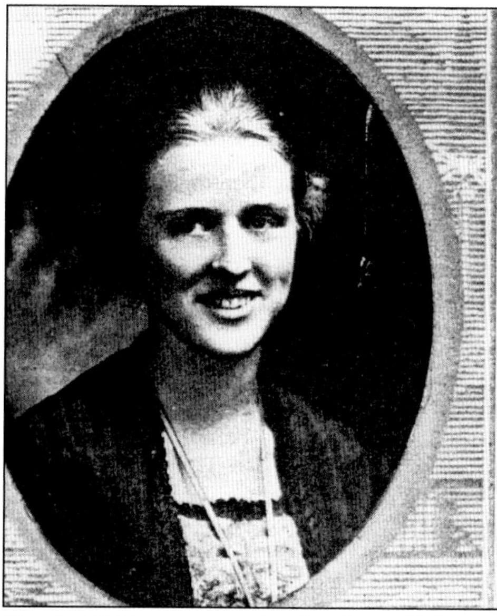

Harriet H. Carmen
St. Remy, N. Y.

RECORD: Glee Club, 3, 4; Prisma, 3, 4: Musical Association, 4; Senior B. B., 4

If you heard someone say, "Harry is such a nice girl!" just what would you have thought? Well, we won't let you think. This is Harry. All reliable beauty ads. please note: She is your ideal silver blond. Parle-t-elle francaise? Oiu! Oui! She enjoys the distinction of belonging to that select and refined third year French class. Ask Miss Cordes.

Harriet H. Carman was the daughter of Martha Watson Haines and Harrie Addison Carman. This is her yearbook picture. She died at the age of 29. Her only sibling was Samuel Haines Carman, to whom this book is dedicated and who provided much of the information contained herein. (Authors' collection.)

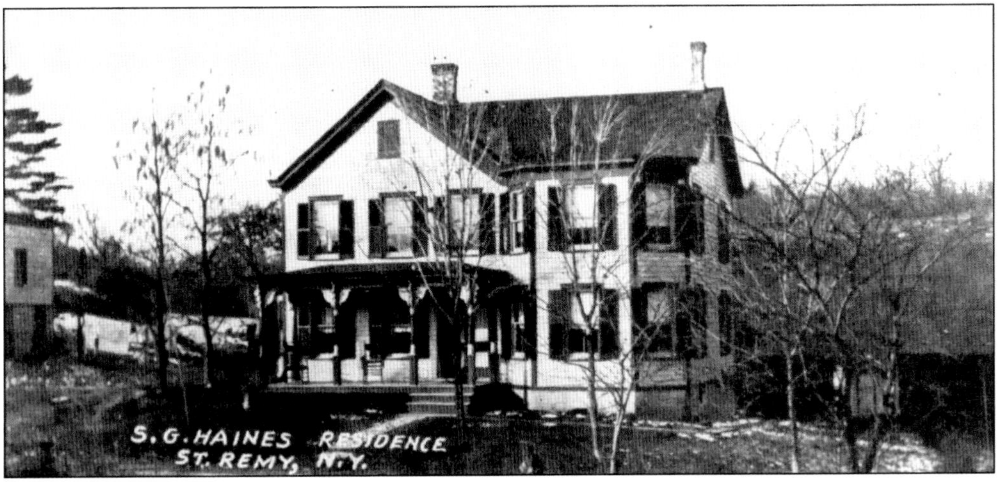

This postcard of the Haines-Decker house was made about five years after the photograph on the facing page was taken. Samuel Haines was the town blacksmith and purchased the VanAken blacksmith shop in 1893, after working in Elmore's Corners and Amesville. Mary Francis Haines was an herbal medicine woman who sometimes augmented her cures with commercial preparations. She lived to be 98 years of age. (Authors' collection.)

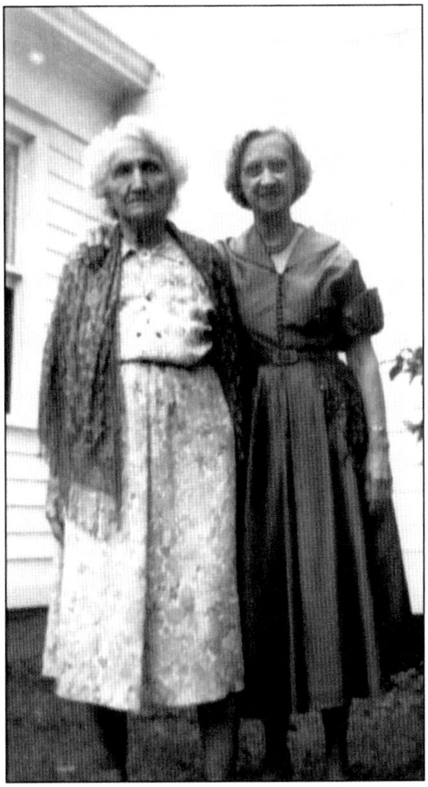

Mary Francis Haines (left) poses with her friend and neighbor Margaret Ryan in the late 1940s. Haines is already more than 80 years old. The photograph was taken next to the Ryan homestead adjoining the present-day Fire Station No. 1. The Ryan family had six sons who fought in World War I. (Authors' collection.)

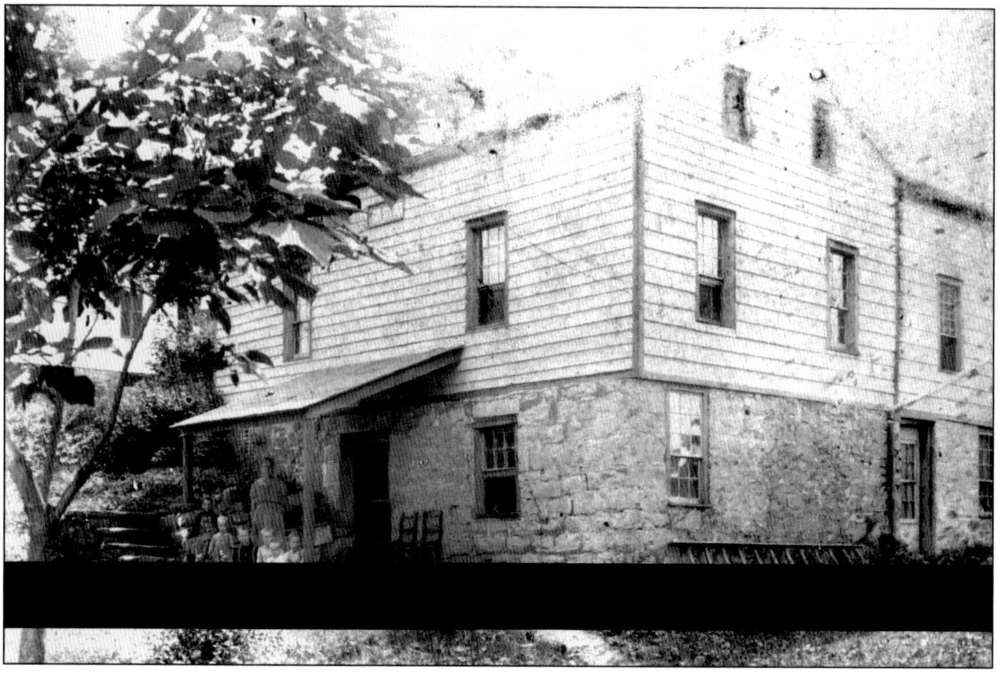

This is one of the oldest houses in St. Remy. It is an original VanAken house, constructed of timber frame over stone around the time of the Revolutionary War. The rear wing was added in 1817. This photograph dates from c. 1870 and shows Martha Connelly and her children. George Connelly was a butcher until 1875 and then became a boatbuilder. The older children are, from left to right, Mary, Walter, Arthur, and Henrietta. (Authors' collection.)

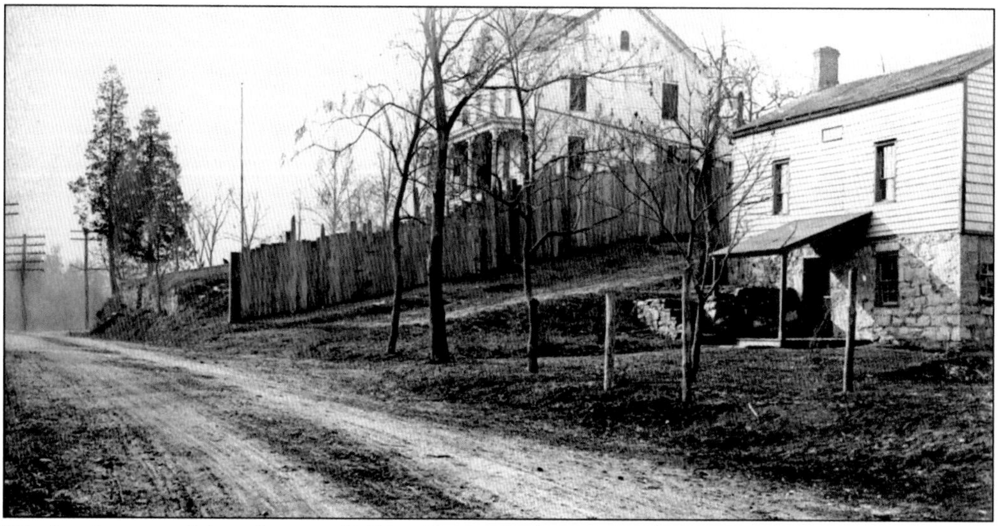

The last house on Main Street is Hilltop House, built in 1870[49] by George and Martha Connelly and given to their son Arthur in 1880. Arthur Connelly began his trade as a boatman on the Erie Canal[50] and then became a boatbuilder with his father on the Rondout Creek. The old telegraph lines[51] of the Independent Telephone Company and the American Telephone and Telegraph Company are clearly visible along the road. (Authors' collection.)

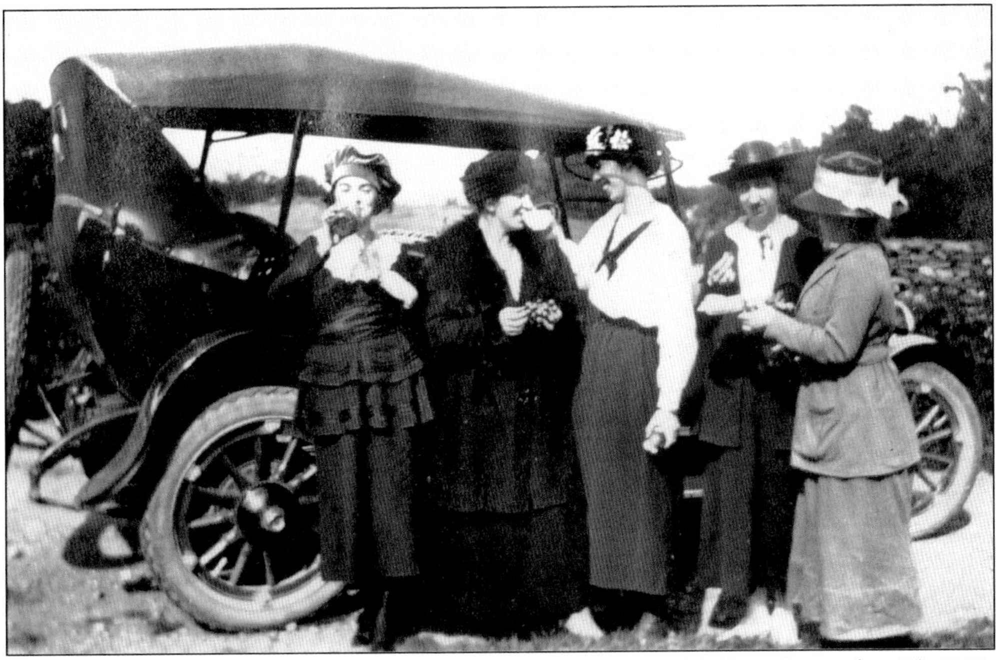

These young women from St. Remy are off for an outing in Fishkill on September 15, 1919. From left to right are Leona Terpening, Della Grady, Girtraude Douglas, Elizabeth Ryan, and Elizabeth Hunter. They liked to show off their collection of hats. (Authors' collection.)

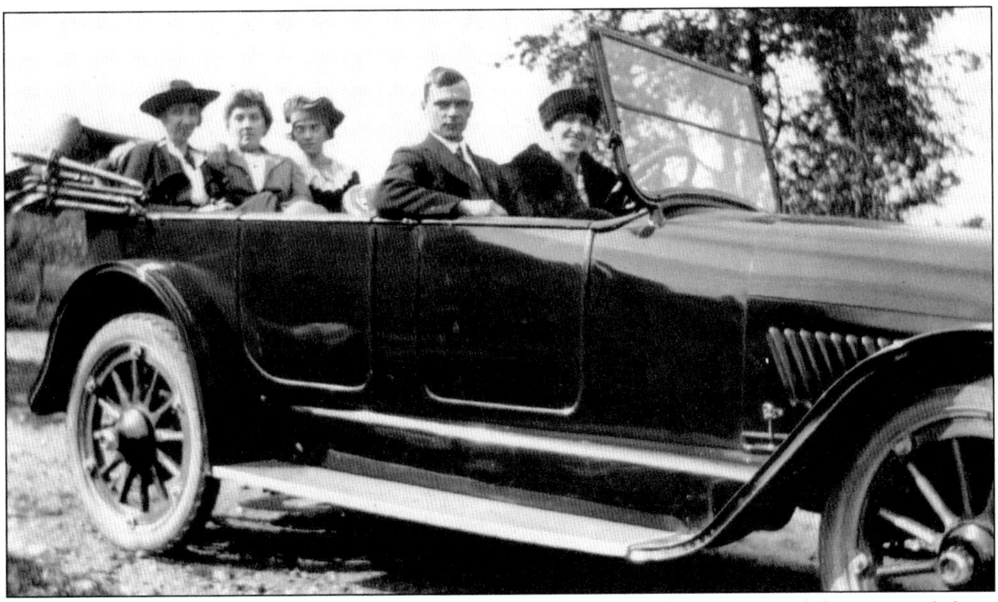

Another photograph from the outing of September 15, 1919, shows more of the automobile—the make of which has not yet been determined. Any guesses? The weather must have been nice in the afternoon, for the roof has been lowered. From left to right are Elizabeth Ryan, Elizabeth Hunter, Leona Terpening, an unidentified man (possibly Eugene Ryan), and Della Grady. Girtraude Douglas was the photographer. (Authors' collection.)

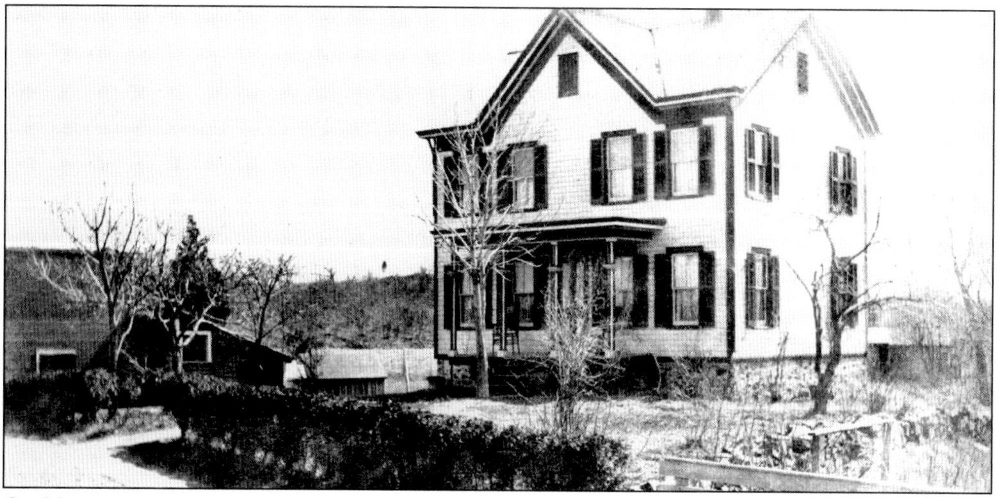

On Union Center Road stands another of the four Carpenter Gothic–style homes in St. Remy. This was a VanAken home said to have been built in 1865.[52] Old maps show the owner as Mrs. VanAken in 1875 and A.W. Frost in 1891. The 1900 and 1905 censuses list Jacob Cline and Wiletta Frost and their daughter Jennie. The house is still a residence. (Authors' collection.)

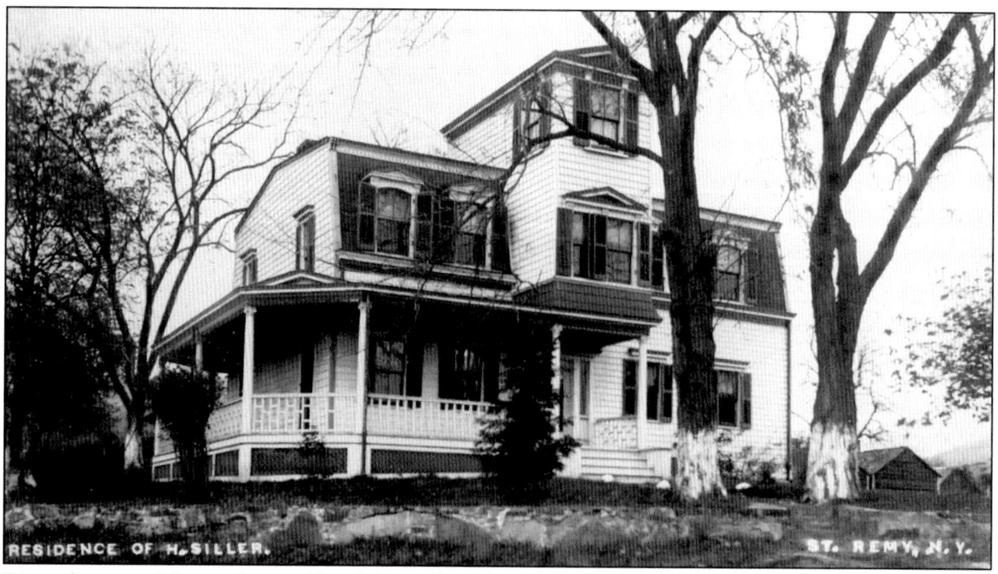

Directly across Union Center Road from the Clyne-Frost residence stands this interesting early-20th-century house. The 1905 census lists the occupants as Hugo and Julia Siller and their four adult children. The Sillers do not appear in the 1900 census, and the house is not shown on the 1891 map, so Hugo and Julia may be the original owners. This homestead was to become the Holland Poultry Farm after World War II. (Authors' collection.)

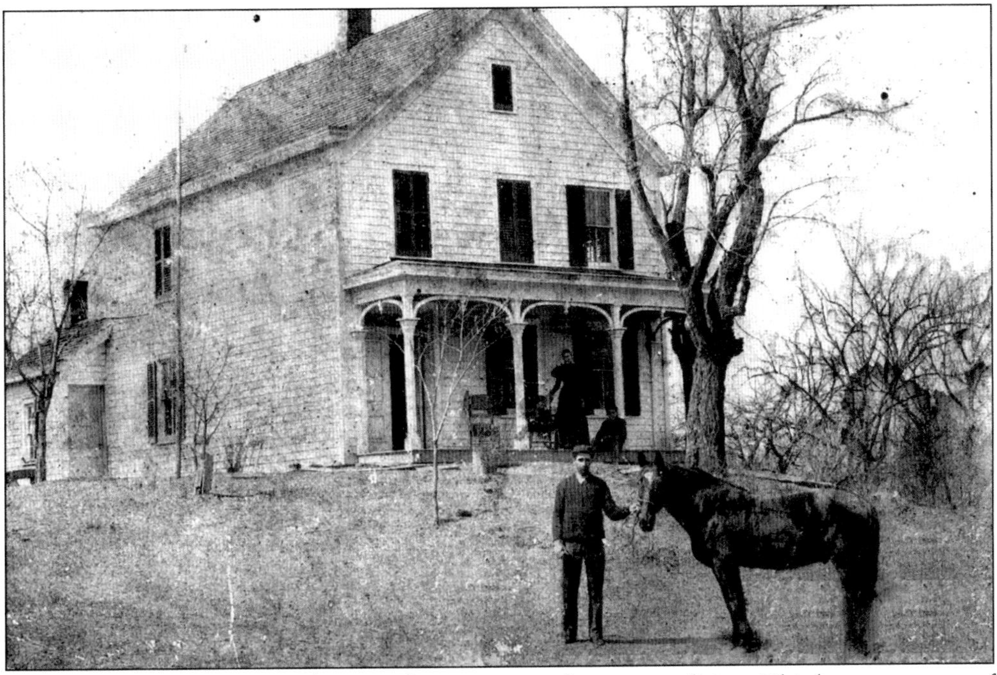

The original of this c. 1887 photograph is in extremely poor condition. This house was part of the 30-acre farm of Abram W. and Elizabeth VanAken and probably dates from 1860–1870. Jonathan and Mary VanAken (both shown) owned the house and farm from 1883 until 1902.[53] (Raymond Krom collection.)

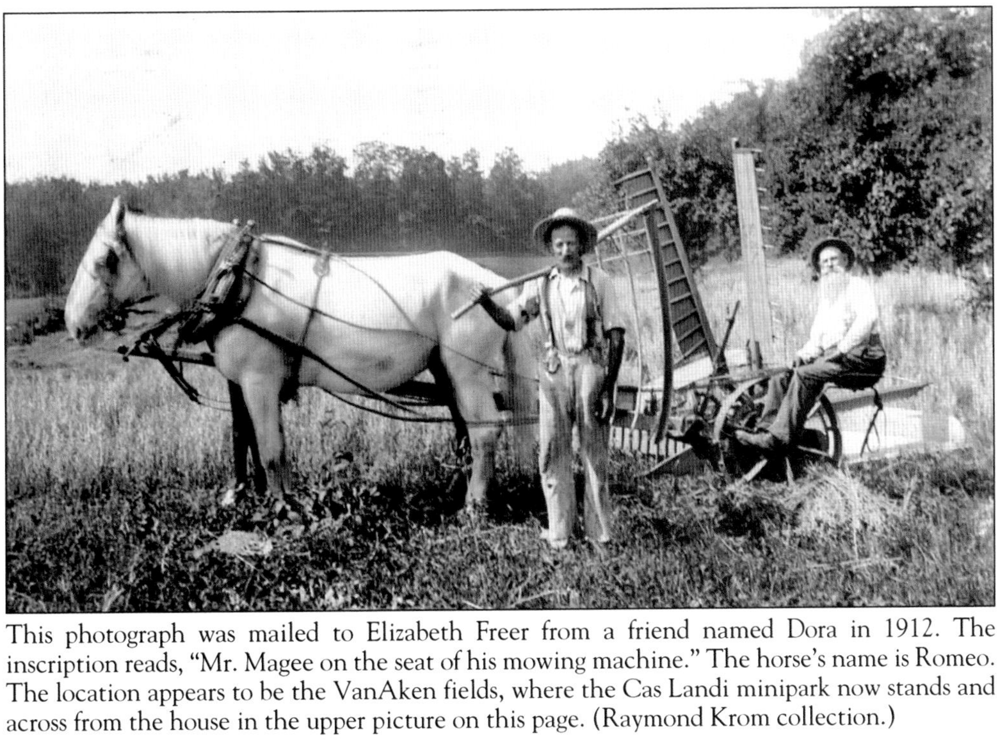

This photograph was mailed to Elizabeth Freer from a friend named Dora in 1912. The inscription reads, "Mr. Magee on the seat of his mowing machine." The horse's name is Romeo. The location appears to be the VanAken fields, where the Cas Landi minipark now stands and across from the house in the upper picture on this page. (Raymond Krom collection.)

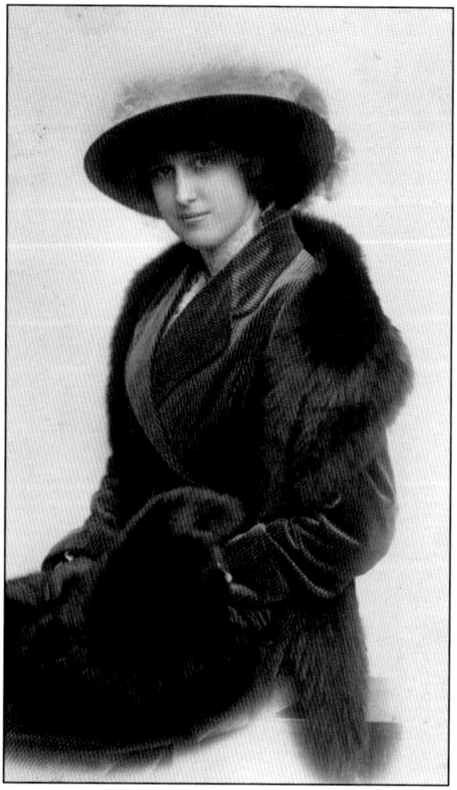

Irene Porter, born c. 1880, was the "belle of the ball" in the St. Remy–Ulster Park area. As can be plainly seen from the photograph, she was a sophisticate through and through. The fur is genuine. She traveled extensively but maintained contacts in St. Remy. The local children liked to watch her periodically drift into town.[54] She may have been the daughter of Charles A. Porter and Elmira Freer of New Salem. (Authors' collection.)

This is one of a number of postcards sent back and forth between Irene Porter and her friends. The postmark is St. Remy, 1910, and the address is simply "Siegfried Pa." The receiving post office no doubt knew her well. (Authors' collection.)

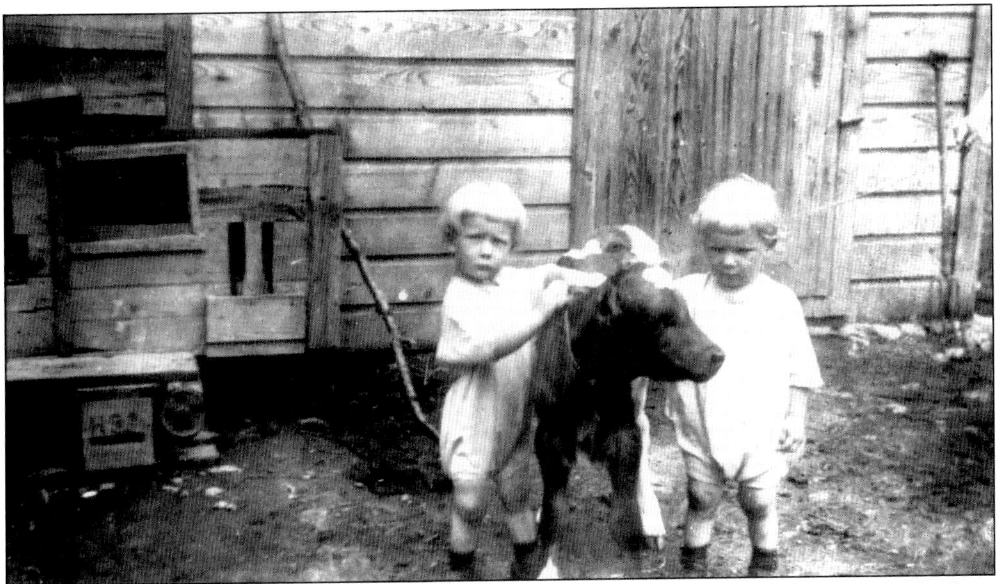

These are the Helmich twins, Peter and James, around age two. No, that is not a strange-looking dog. The boys are playing with their calf. Their mother's hand is just off to the right, holding a leash. The boys were born in 1920, and their house was two doors south of the fire station. Peter Helmich, a lifelong member of the fire department, died in May 2003. (C. Terpening collection.)

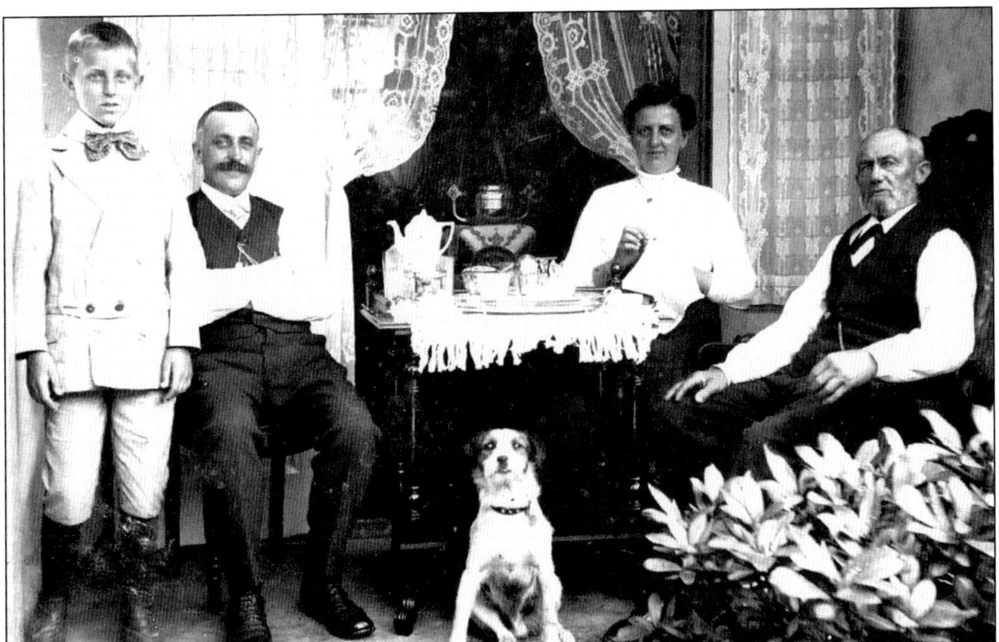

This c. 1920 Helmich family portrait includes the dog. From left to right are John (the eldest child), Cornelius, Hilda, and grandfather J. (perhaps Johannis) Helmich. Cornelius Helmich emigrated from Holland in 1907 and Hilda from England in 1895.[55] (C. Terpening collection.)

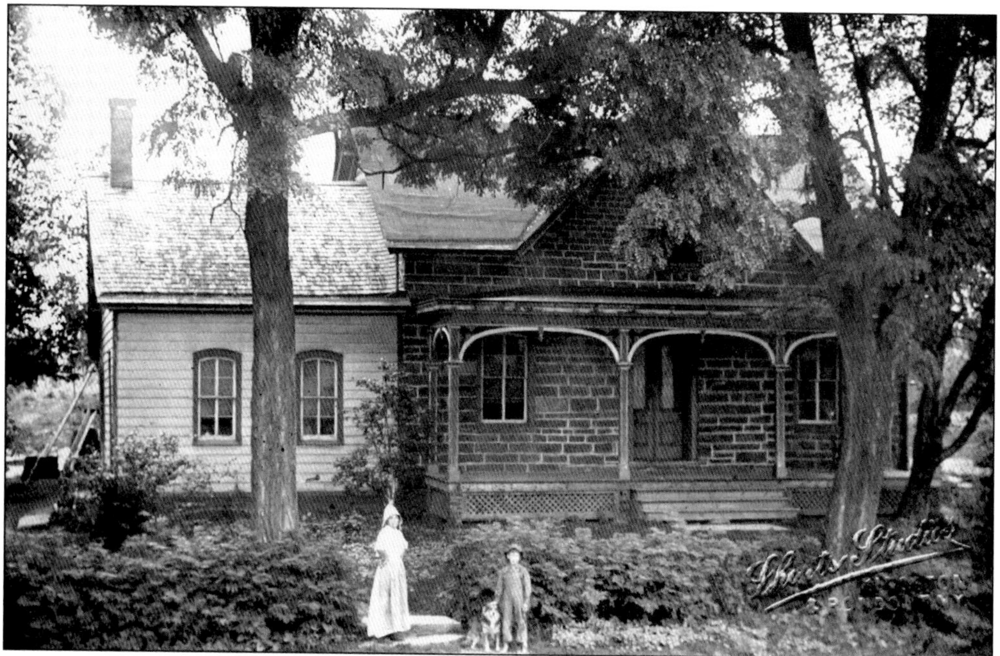

The Twin Brook Farm house is unusual. It is an older stone house with a wood-framed addition, but the reader should notice the style of stone. The front of the house is built of cut stone, not fieldstone. This is uncommon on early houses. Our earliest proven reference is the 1850 census, which shows Oliver and Harriet Terpening as owners and lists the home as a stone house. The house probably dates from several decades earlier. (Raymond Krom collection.)

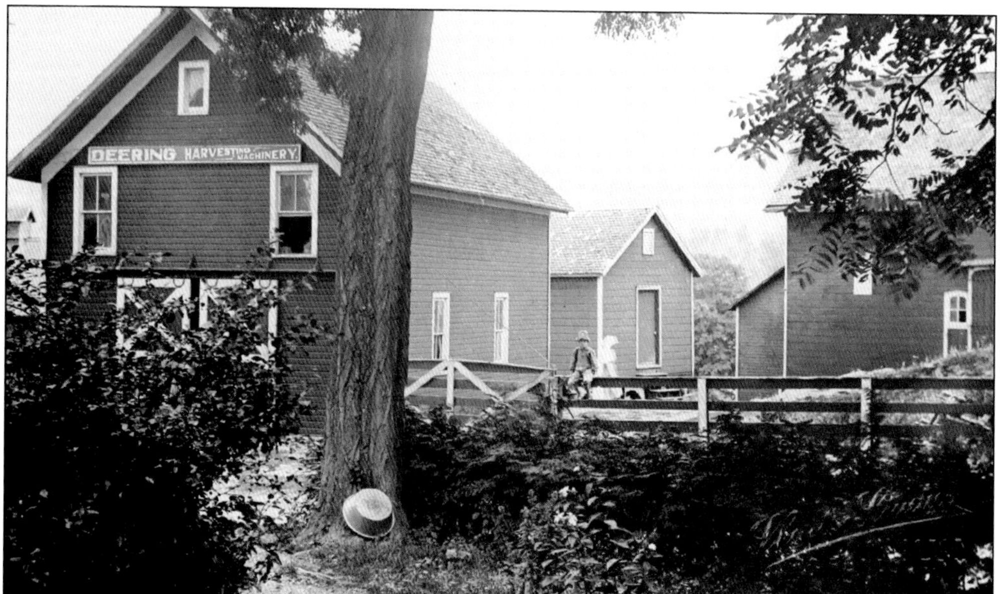

These are the Twin Brook Farm barns. Oliver Terpening was the father of Lorenzo Sr. He sold the farm to Ira Lambert before 1891. Clarence and Clara Freer bought the farm next. Their son Elmer was born in 1903, and these photographs were taken *c.* 1910. The photographs on this page show Elmer Freer and his mother, Clara Deyo Freer. (Raymond Krom collection.)

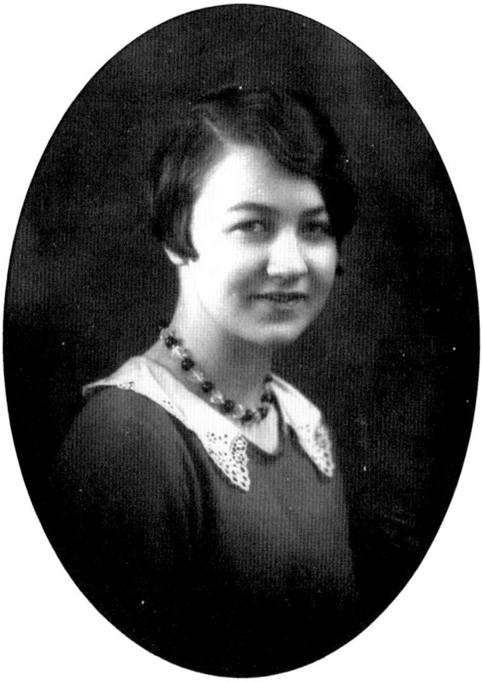

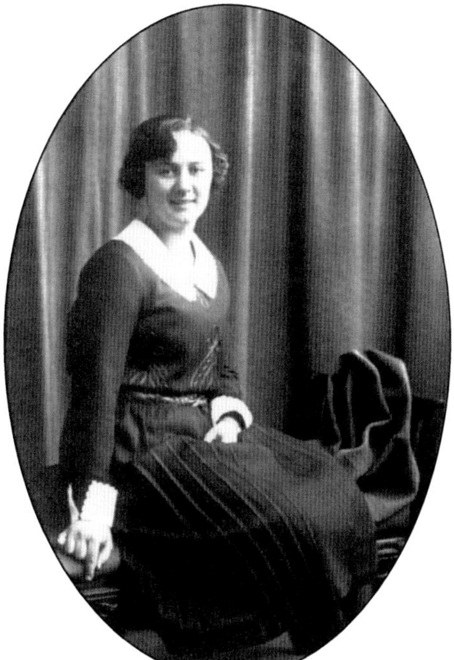

Pictured are May York (left), born in 1911, and Bernice York at age 15 in May 1921. They were the older sisters of Myron York, who kept the family farm with his wife, Betty Walker, until his death in 1996.

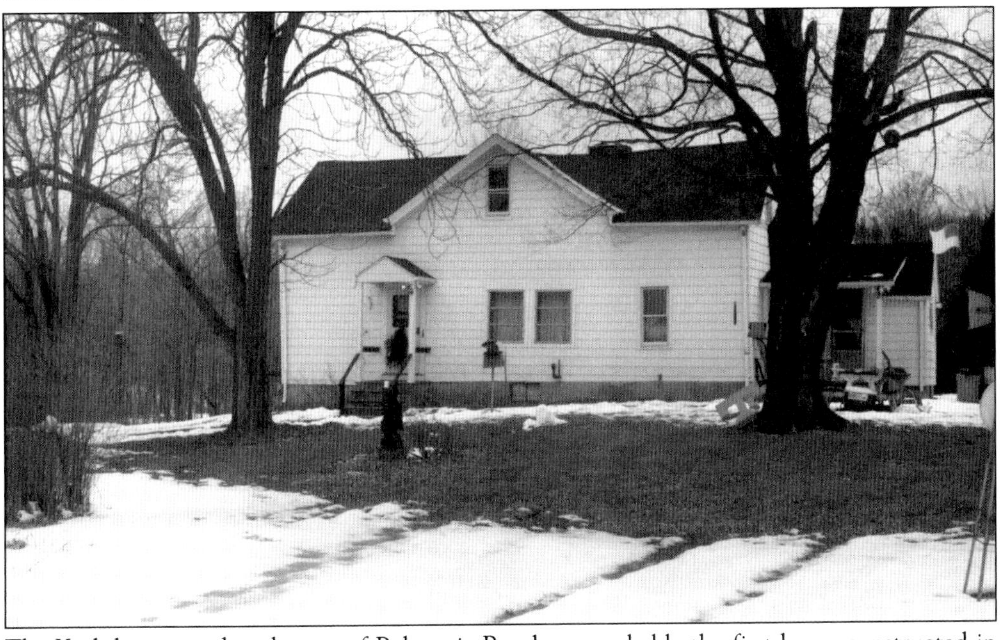

The York homestead at the top of Pokonoie Road was probably the first home constructed in St. Remy in the 19th century. Myron York found a French newspaper dated February 1802 inside the walls when making a repair in the 1960s. The center room, loft, and cellar were built in 1802, probably by Gerrit I. Freer. The left and right sections were complete by 1840. Lewis York purchased the farm in 1860 from William G. Freer.[56] (Authors' collection.)

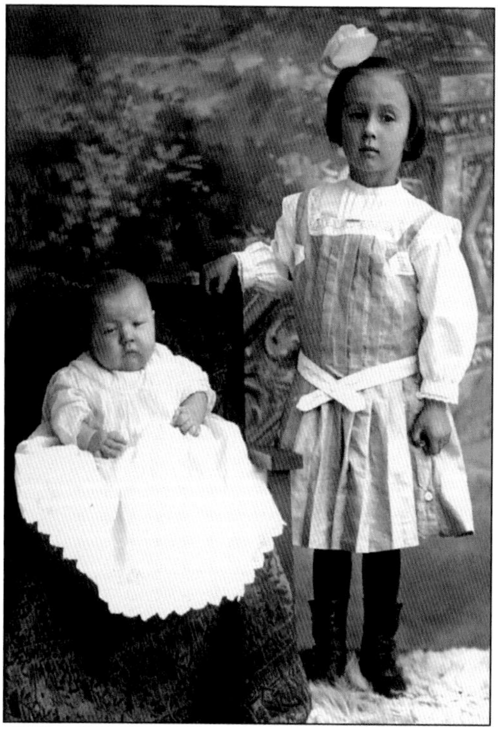

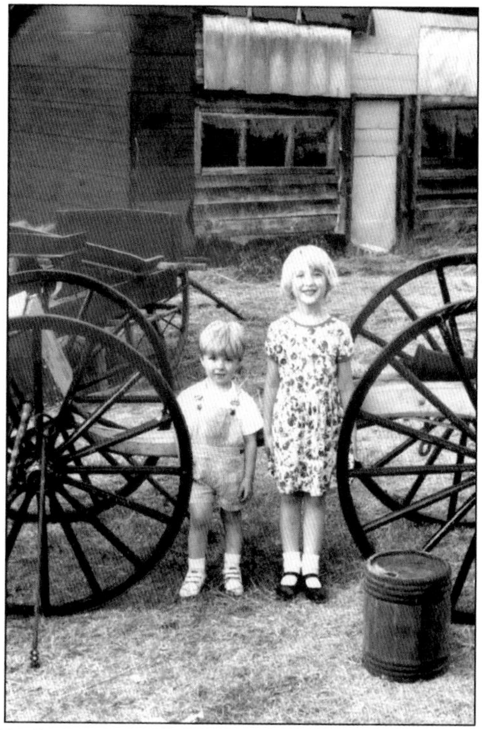

On the left are May (left) and Bernice Roosa York in 1911. May married Otto Havlin in St. Remy in 1932 and then moved to Kingston. She is buried in the St. Remy Cemetery. On the right are Matthew and Rebecca York, the grandnephew and grandniece of May and Bernice and the last generation of Yorks to live on the farm. Notice the family resemblance between Bernice and Rebecca. (Authors' collection.)

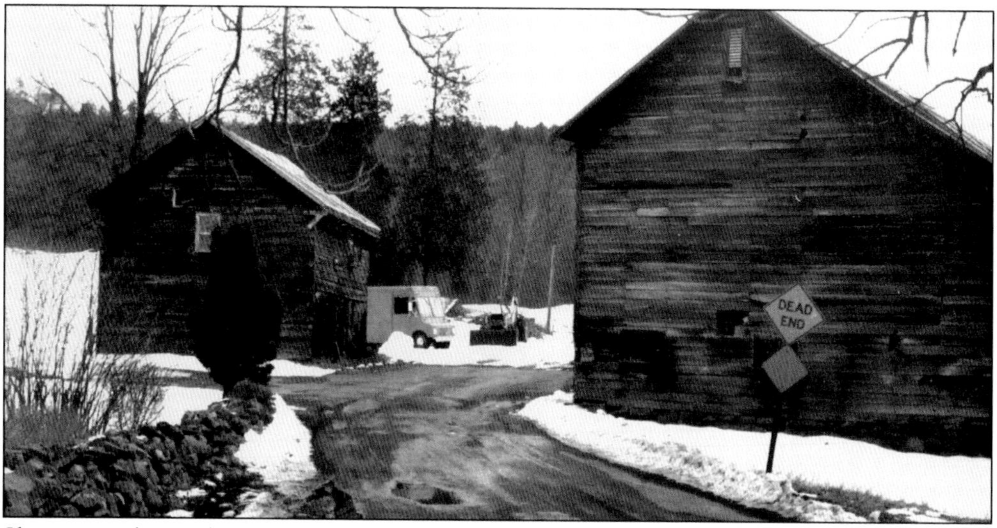

Shown are the York Farm granary (left) and the large barn. The barn is somewhat unusual because its interior contains a combination of Dutch and English features. The original small farm contained only 12 acres, but it grew gradually until it spread over 101 acres of rolling field and hilly woodland. At one corner of the property is an original Kingston Commons land marker. (Authors' collection.)

This aerial view from c. 1939 was not taken from an airplane. Neither was it taken from a balloon. The view is Main Street just south of St. Remy, and the photograph was taken from the very top of the St. Remy fire siren tower. This tower was used as a World War II airplane-spotting post. Carefully selected or conscripted residents would spend several hours a day scanning the sky for hostile aircraft.[57] Fortunately, none ever appeared. (C. Terpening collection.)

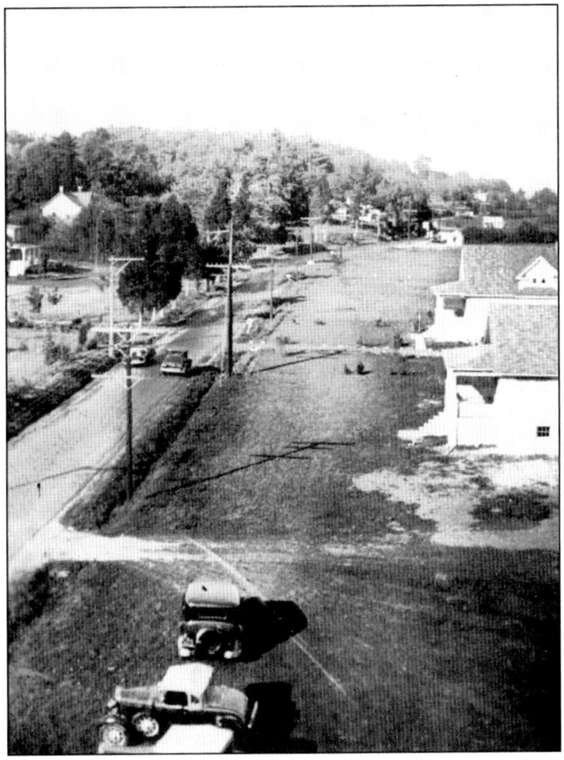

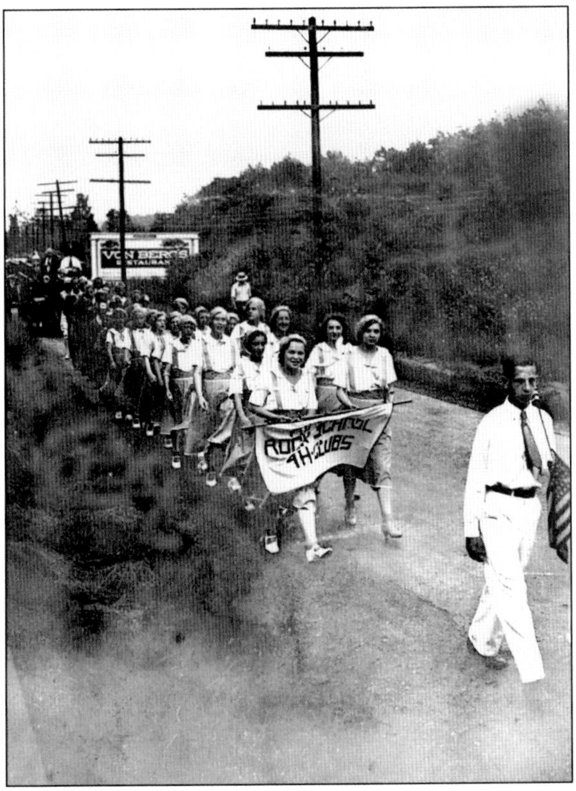

The Rock School 4H club takes part in this c. 1930 parade. They are proudly bringing up the rear of the line of marchers. The road appears to be Main Street between St. Remy and Rifton, and the billboard advertises Von Berg's Restaurant in Kingston. In the early days, every hamlet had a band and civic groups, and to this day, everyone still loves a parade. (C. Terpening collection.)

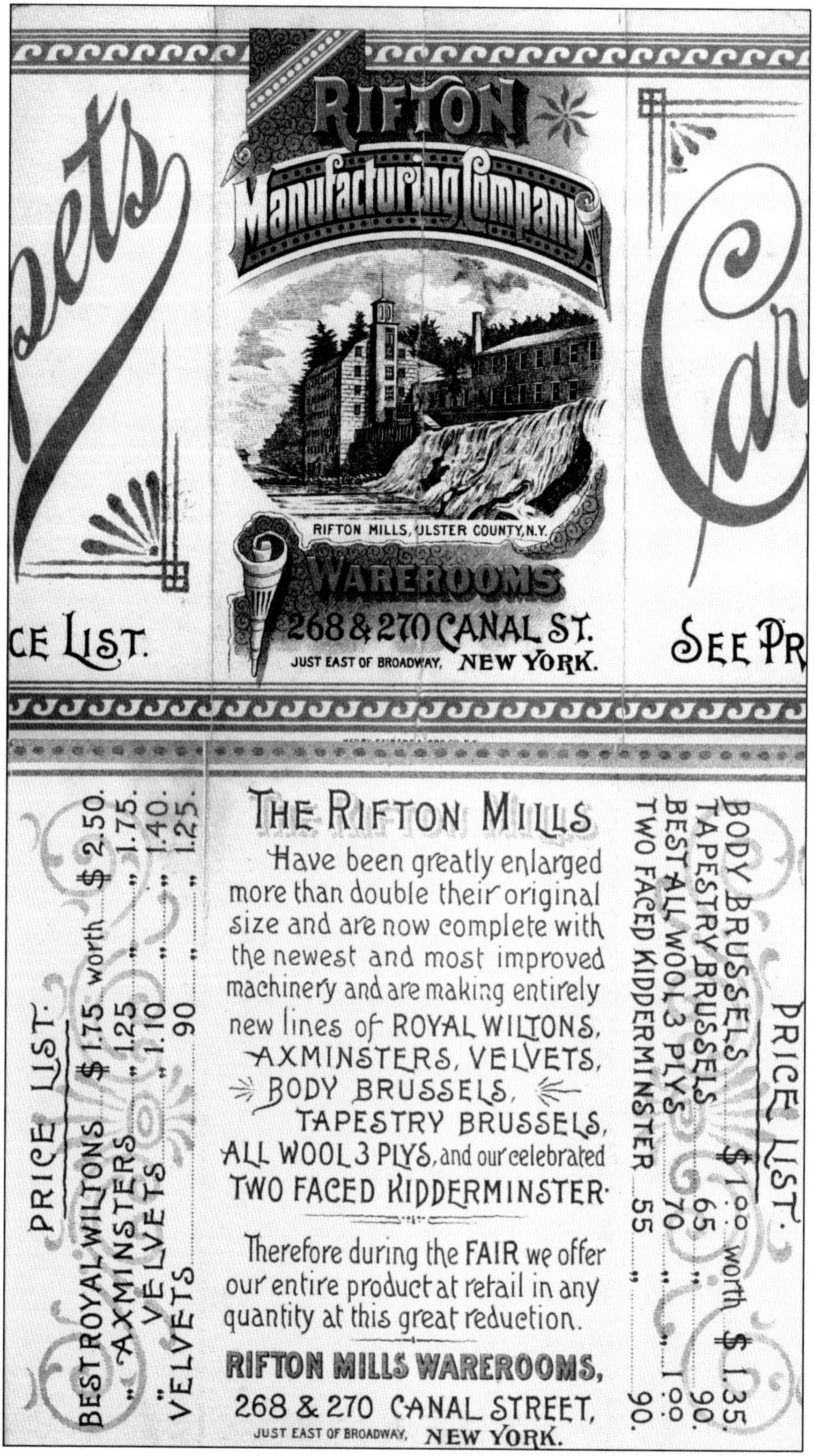

RIFTON
Manufacturing Company
RIFTON MILLS, ULSTER COUNTY, N.Y.
WAREROOMS
268 & 270 CANAL ST.
JUST EAST OF BROADWAY, NEW YORK.
...pets
...CE LIST.
Car...
SEE PR...
PRICE LIST.
BEST ROYAL WILTONS $1.75 worth $2.50.
" AXMINSTERS 1.25 " 1.75.
" VELVETS 1.10 " 1.40.
VELVETS 90 " 1.25.
THE RIFTON MILLS
Have been greatly enlarged more than double their original size and are now complete with the newest and most improved machinery and are making entirely new lines of ROYAL WILTONS, AXMINSTERS, VELVETS, BODY BRUSSELS, TAPESTRY BRUSSELS, ALL WOOL 3 PLYS, and our celebrated TWO FACED KIDDERMINSTER.
Therefore during the FAIR we offer our entire product at retail in any quantity at this great reduction.
RIFTON MILLS WAREROOMS,
268 & 270 CANAL STREET,
JUST EAST OF BROADWAY, NEW YORK.
PRICE LIST.
BODY BRUSSELS $1.00 worth $1.35.
TAPESTRY BRUSSELS 65 " 90.
BEST ALL WOOL 3 PLYS 70 " 1.00
TWO FACED KIDDERMINSTER 55 " 90.

Four

RIFTON

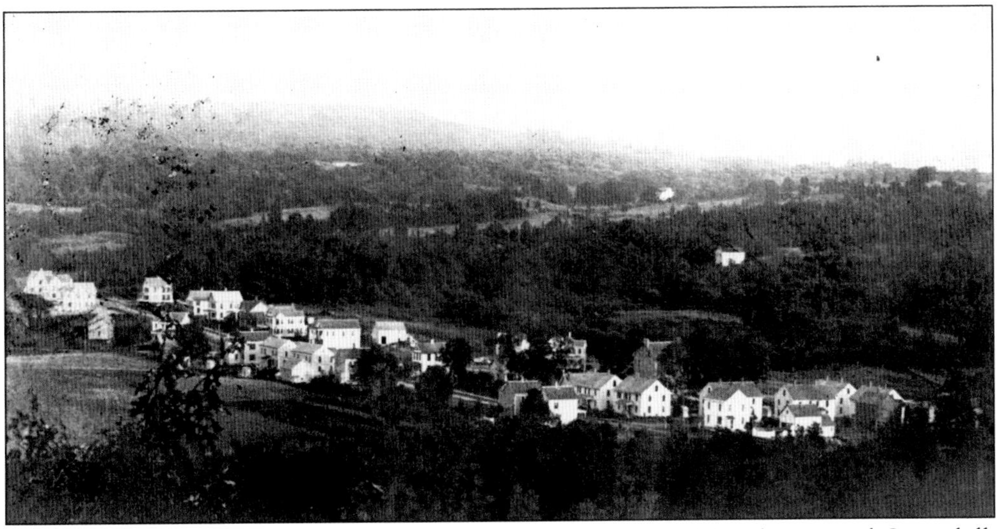

The Rifton that we know today was once three closely related hamlets named Swartekill, Rifton Glen, and Dashville. The communities of Saltpeterville, Arnoldton, and Perrine's Bridge have also been absorbed into the mix. Rifton was the latecomer to the group. In 1861, Jeremiah W. Dimick[58] purchased the mill at Arnoldton and changed the name of the surrounding community to Rifton Glen. Rifton (sans Glen) officially became a village on May 20, 1901, with several pages of ordinances to back things up. For example, scorching[59] was prohibited and punishable by a $2 fine. Above, we see a photograph entitled "New Rifton 1905." On the facing page is a foldout pricelist of the Rifton Mills. The mills are what made the village possible, and after their closure, the village of Rifton was officially dissolved in 1919 by the state legislature. The Rifton area has received a thorough treatment in other works,[60] but new information and new photographs sometimes come to light. This chapter will concentrate on them and, in a few instances, better-quality versions of previously published photographs. We refer the reader to the older works for a more complete reference.

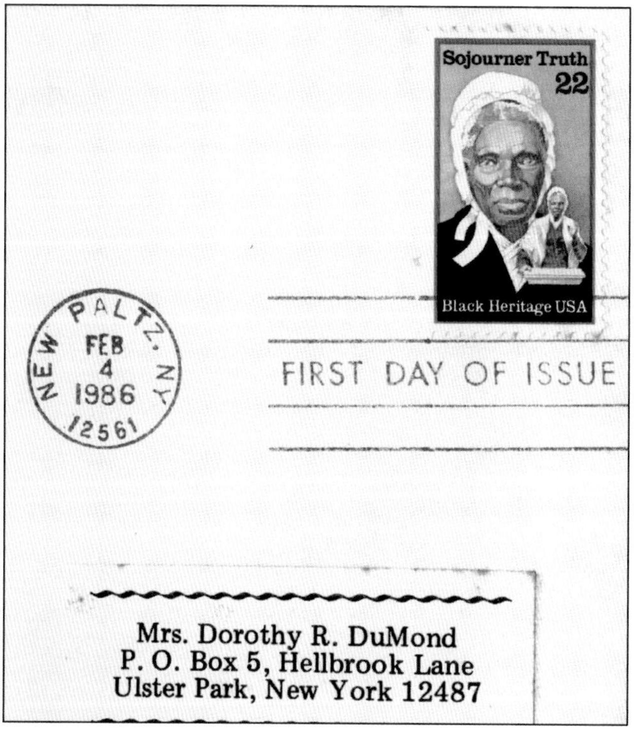

Swartekill was the northernmost of the hamlets, located where the Swartekill (creek) falls into the Wallkill. The Hardenburg farm near the falls was the birthplace of the famous suffragette and orator Sojourner Truth. The original Hurley Patent once crossed the Rondout and Wallkill for a short distance, meeting the Kingston Patent in Swartekill. This was the cause of confusion about Sojourner's birthplace until town historian Dot Dumond put all of the evidence together and revealed the true story.

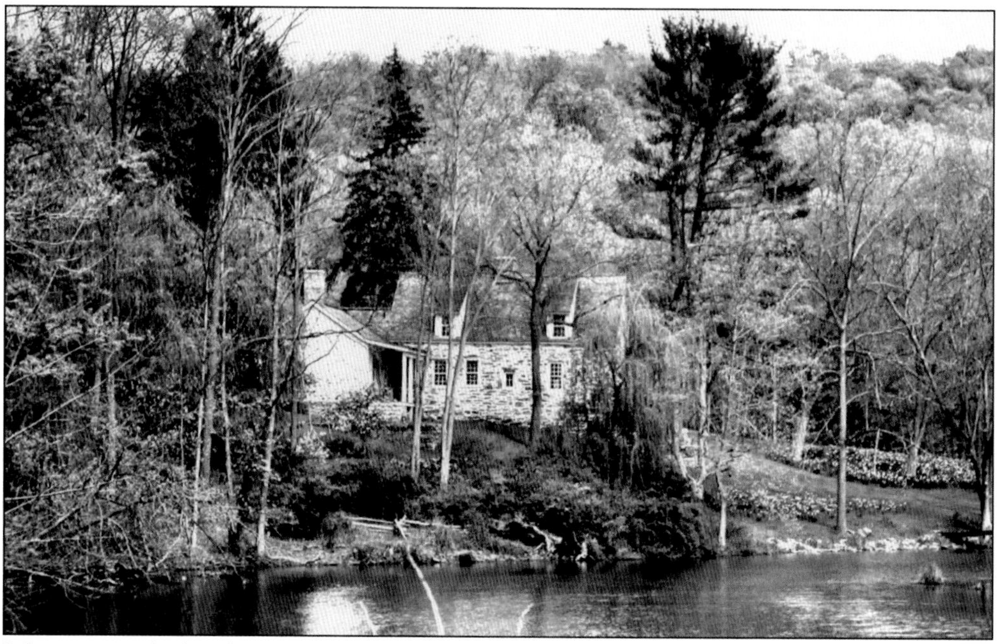

Johannes Hardenburgh owned this house and farm on the Swartekill (creek) in Swartekill. This is where Isabella Baumfree (better known as Sojourner Truth) was born *c.* 1797. Hardenburgh was apparently quite wealthy, for he had seven slaves in 1790.[61] Baumfree was listed among the possessions in his estate papers. She was subsequently auctioned off (with a lot of sheep) to John Neeley in 1806 for the tidy sum of $100. (Authors' collection.)

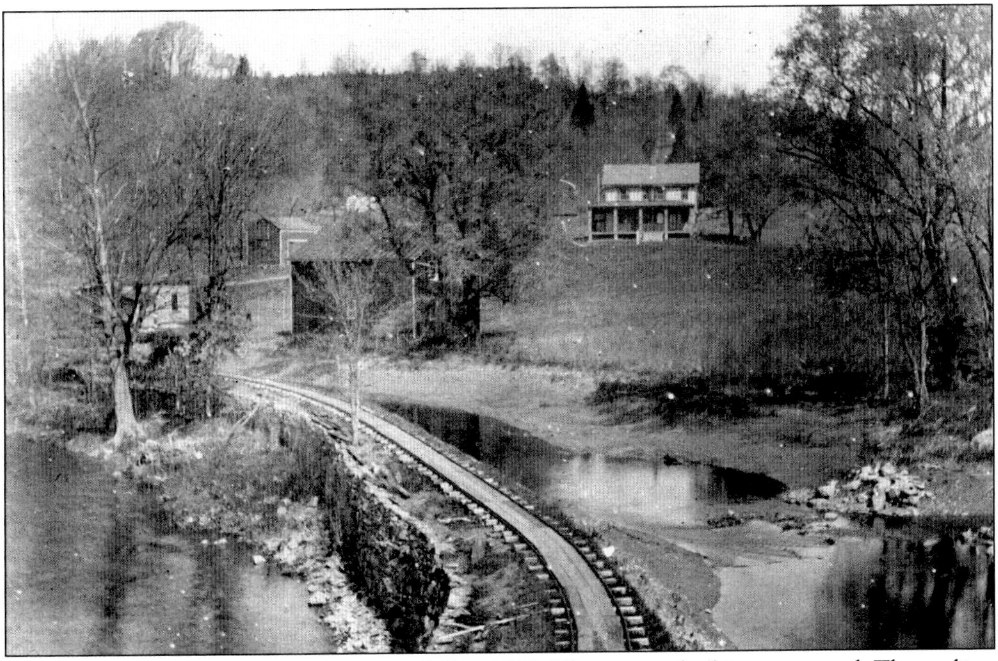

This is part of the powder mill in Swartekill c. 1900. The view is looking westward. The earliest record of the mill dates from 1865. A narrow-gauge rail bed runs through the picture. The ties are covered with wooden planking. The train cars were not pulled by engines but rather by mules (Beatrice Jordan collection.)

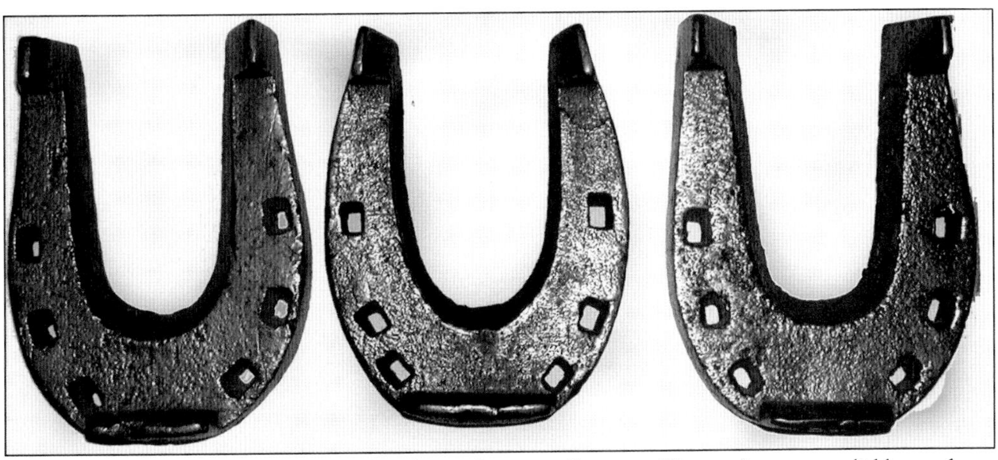

The planks between the rails were for the mules to walk upon. The mules wore solid brass shoes about four inches long, probably with brass nails. These were used to prevent sparking if a shoe touched the iron rail. These three shoes are made of shiny yellow brass, as beautiful as the day they were amassed. We wonder where the fourth one went. (Photograph by the author; shoes in a private collection.)

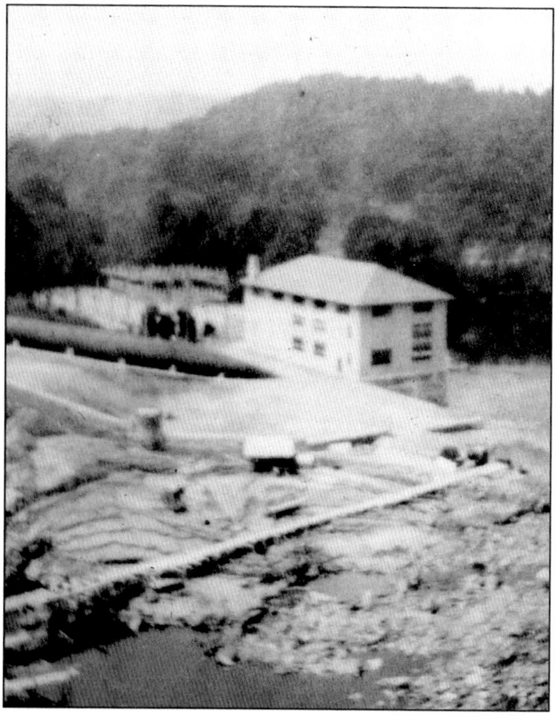

There were several types of mills—pressing, corning, drying (house), and glazing—all separated from each other and from the storage buildings by some distance. Water was supplied by a canal running along the Swartekill.[62] The first record of powder production dates from 1865, when the Smith and Rand Powder Company filed a map of their holdings with the county clerk. In 1869, the firm merged with the Lafflin Powder Company to become the Lafflin and Rand Powder Company. (Beatrice Jordan collection.)

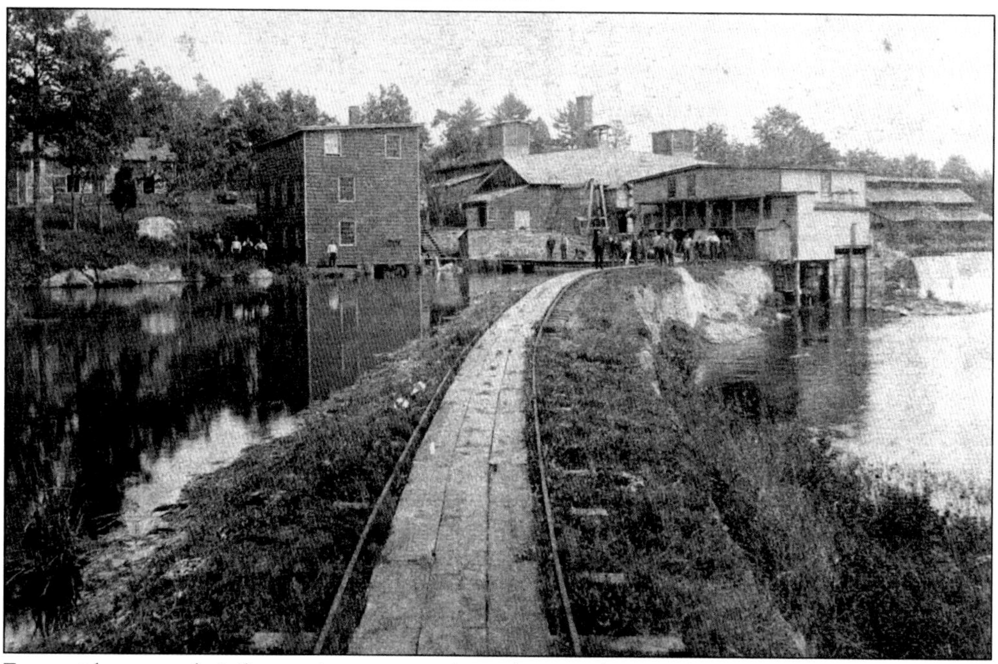

Even with care and vigilance, there were at least three mishaps at the mills. On January 6, 1894, the drying and corning mills blew up, killing three. A fourth person was killed when the boiler house "shook down." At 11:10 a.m. on March 18, 1896, the glassing (*sic*) and drying mills blew up. Five men were killed in the mishap. One of them was not found until May 3. Finally, on April 2, 1902, the rolling mill and charcoal storehouse burned down. Thankfully, no one was injured in that incident. (Beatrice Jordan collection.)

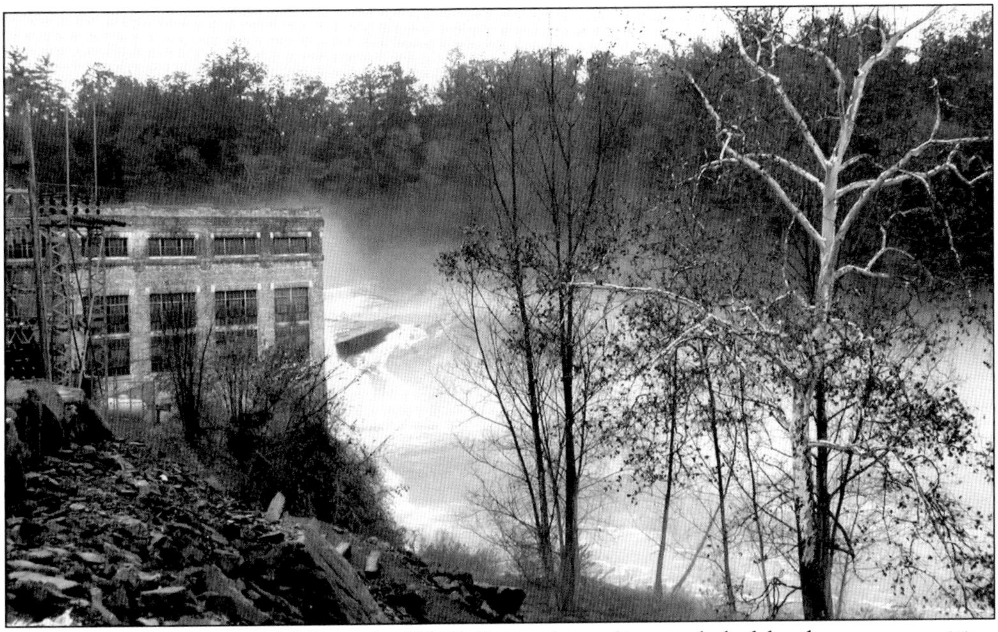

Dashville, with its powerful falls on the Wallkill, was the earliest settled of the three communities, and there was a succession of mills at the falls where the kill makes a right angle turn through the rock, sometimes more than one at a time. Ezekiel Eltinge built a gristmill, a sawmill, and a fulling and carding mill by 1824. Shown here is the last water-powered "mill" at Dashville—the United Hudson Electric Corporation[63] generating station. (Authors' collection.)

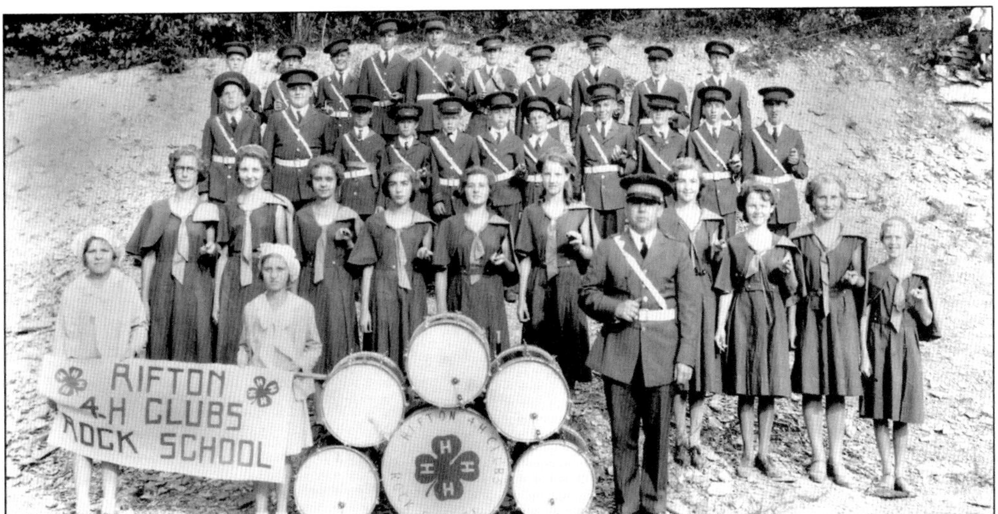

Pictured at a Highland parade in 1930 or 1931 are, from left to right, the following: (first row) Juanita Remus, Audrey Kidd, and Paul Wiren; (second row) Sophie Orleich, Olga and Emily Buzdygan, Ethel Eckert, Beatrice Bailey, Doris Wiren, Sophia Palkowics, Betty Kent, Karen Tervo, and Margaret Prehn; (third row) Gene Wiren, Arnold Terpening, Watson Bailey, Gene Philips, Edwin Suominen, Walt Bailey, Howard Eckert, Lerot Davis, Walt and Charlie Prehn, and Hayward Mitchell; (fourth row) Arne Tervo, Harry Mitchell, Nat Philips, Ed Balfe, Ernie Terpening, Pete Albers, Donnie Kidd, Rosener Wheeler, Julius Eckert, and Bob Arnstron.

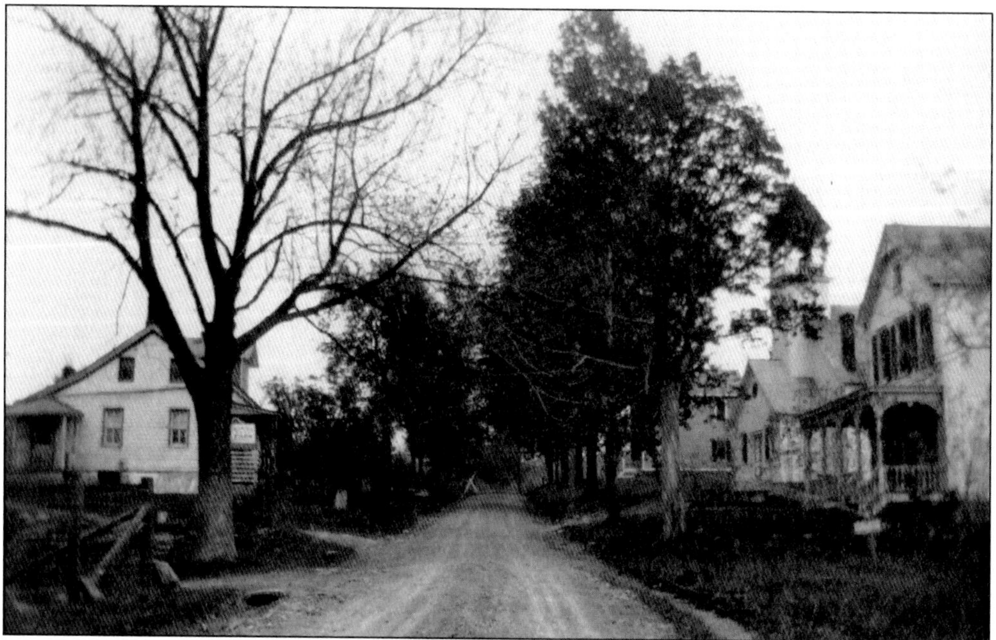

This is a rare view looking up Church Hill Road *c.* 1920. The inscription on the rear of the photograph reads, "On the left, the old farm house where I [William Smith] was born, Feb. 1, 1884. This was grandfather Smith's home, later my father's place, after grandfather passed away in 1908. On the right is the M.E. church. View is east." The Methodist church is at the center right. (Beatrice Jordan collection.)

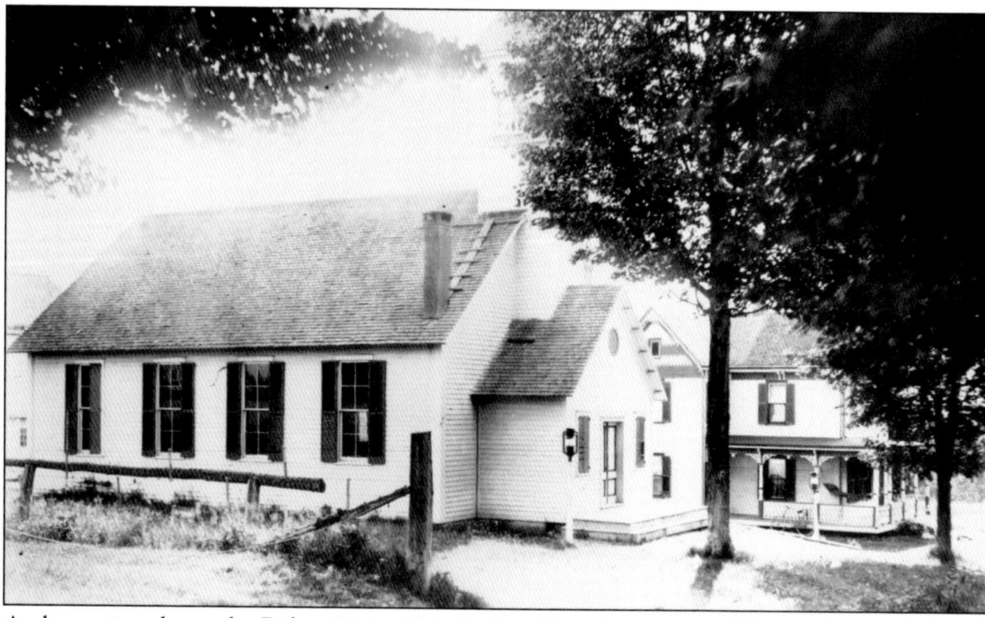

A closer view shows the Rifton United Methodist Church *c.* 1898. This print comes from the original glass-plate negative, courtesy of Florence Prehn. The photograph was taken looking approximately west. The original church was built in 1892 at a cost of $2,200. One source states that the *Dashville* church burned down *c.* 1917. Other sources say that it was torn down and rebuilt as an icehouse by C. Tegar in 1927.

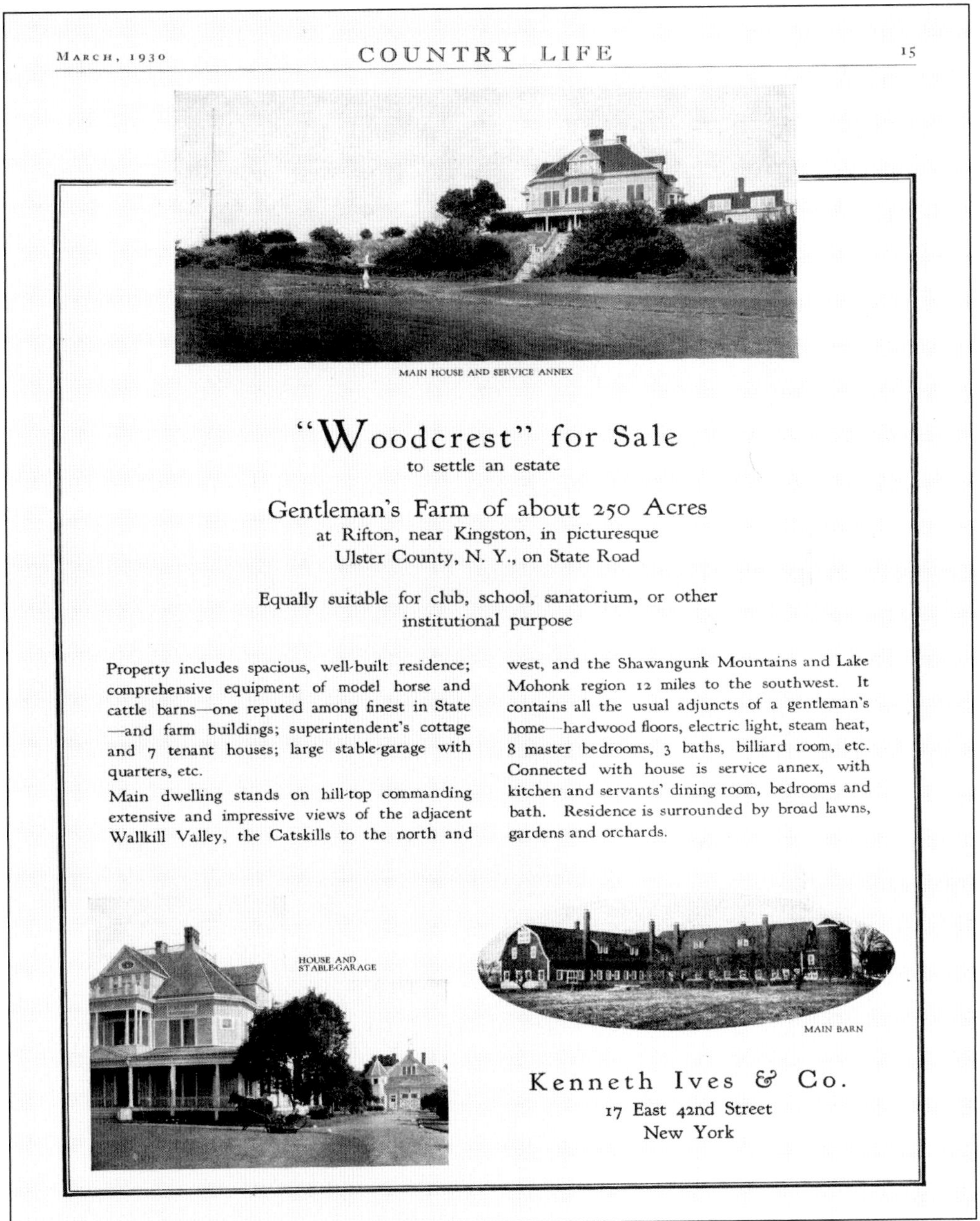

MAIN HOUSE AND SERVICE ANNEX

"Woodcrest" for Sale

to settle an estate

Gentleman's Farm of about 250 Acres

at Rifton, near Kingston, in picturesque
Ulster County, N. Y., on State Road

Equally suitable for club, school, sanatorium, or other institutional purpose

Property includes spacious, well-built residence; comprehensive equipment of model horse and cattle barns—one reputed among finest in State—and farm buildings; superintendent's cottage and 7 tenant houses; large stable-garage with quarters, etc.

Main dwelling stands on hill-top commanding extensive and impressive views of the adjacent Wallkill Valley, the Catskills to the north and west, and the Shawangunk Mountains and Lake Mohonk region 12 miles to the southwest. It contains all the usual adjuncts of a gentleman's home—hardwood floors, electric light, steam heat, 8 master bedrooms, 3 baths, billiard room, etc. Connected with house is service annex, with kitchen and servants' dining room, bedrooms and bath. Residence is surrounded by broad lawns, gardens and orchards.

HOUSE AND STABLE-GARAGE

MAIN BARN

Kenneth Ives & Co.
17 East 42nd Street
New York

Woodcrest was the estate of Jeremiah W. Dimick, who owned the carpet mills along the Wallkill. Although Dimick died c. 1915, the estate was still not settled in 1935. The 20th accounting, taken in January 1936, shows a total estate value of $1,433,028.65! This included 30 buildings in New York City and large tracts of land in Rifton. The mills and water rights had already been sold c. 1920. Dimick's widow, Altha Covey Dimick, was considerably younger than Jeremiah and remarried to a Mr. Beaufort. She received a life estate payment of $43,000 that year.[64] Woodcrest is now owned by the Hutterian Society of Brothers. Woodcrest Bruderhof is the first of two fine communities in the town of Esopus; the second, similar in scope but without major historic structures, is Maple Ridge Bruderhof in Ulster Park. (Authors' collection.)

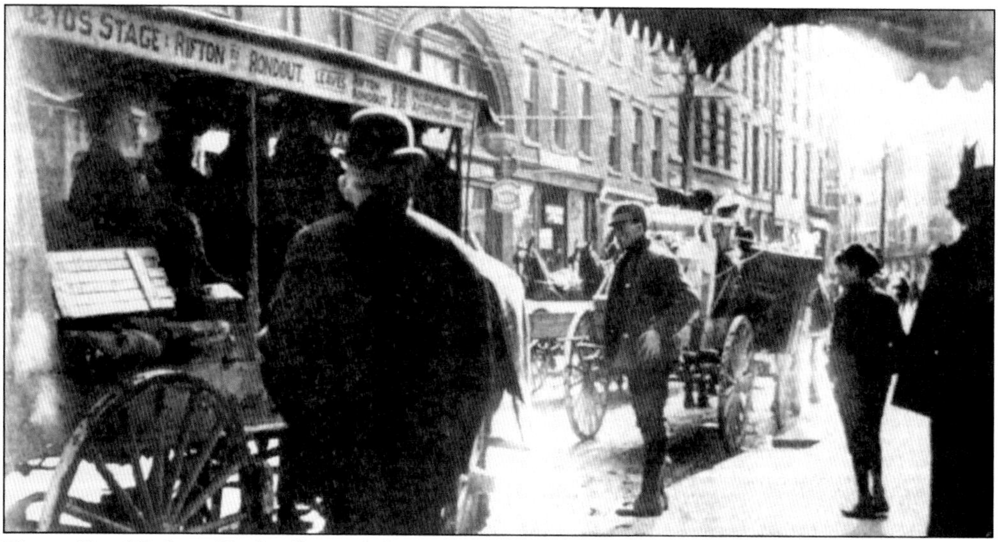

The mills of Rifton, Dashville, and the growing village of Rondout required transportation for their workers and families. From the 1880s until *c.* 1920,[65] a stagecoach bus ran from Rifton to Rondout, passing through St. Remy, Freerville, and Eddyville on the way. It was run by the William Deyo Company and originally left Rifton at 8:30 a.m. and Rondout at 2:30 p.m. William owned three stages altogether.[66]

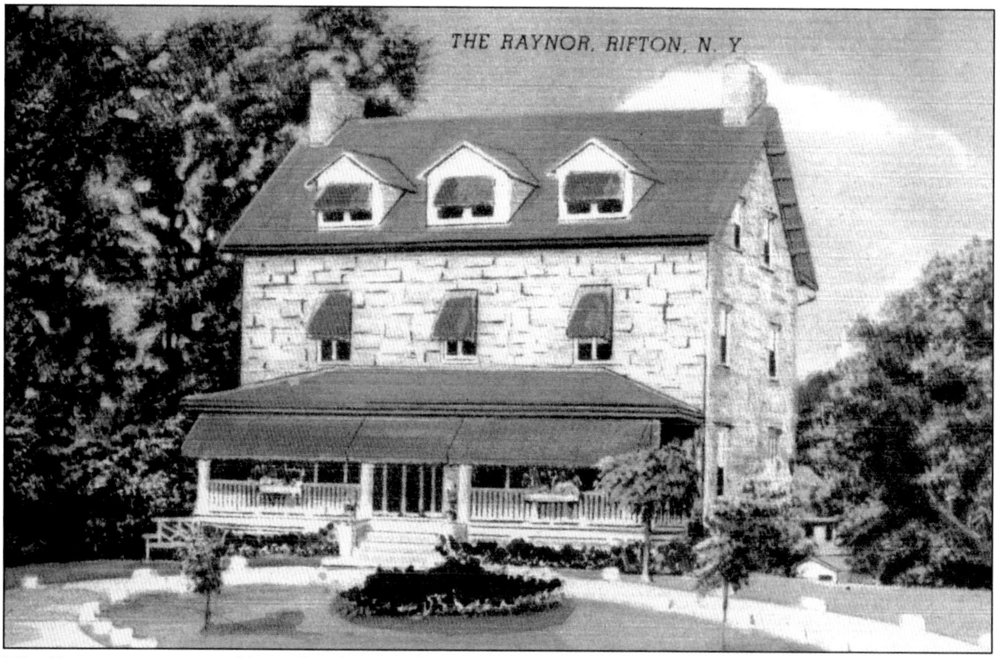

The Raynor tourist and boardinghouse also appears in the New Rifton photograph earlier in the chapter. Although built of stone, it is not an ancient house. It was constructed *c.* 1890. It stands along Route 213 between Maple and Pine Streets and is now a private home. In this postcard drawing, it sports medium-green roofs, orange shutters, and bright-red flowers in all of the beds and boxes. (Authors' collection.)

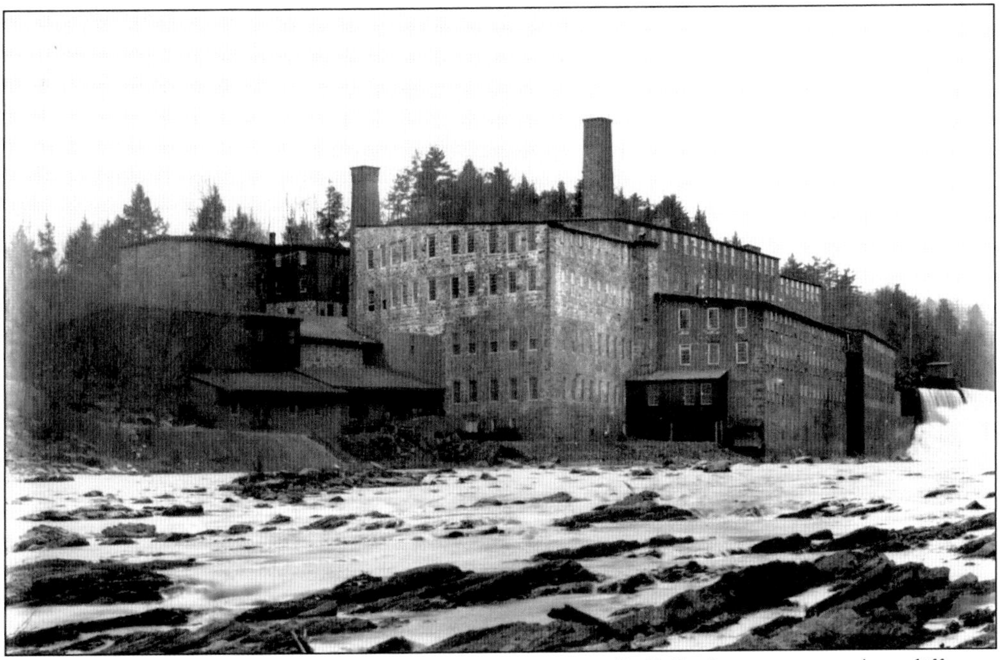

We present here the imposing "new mill" at Buttermilk Falls from a somewhat different perspective than that commonly seen on postcards. Both images on this page are from original glass-plate negatives. The new mill made fine carpets and rugs from 1889 until 1915. In its later years, it also generated electricity for parts of Rifton and itself. (Florence Prehn collection.)

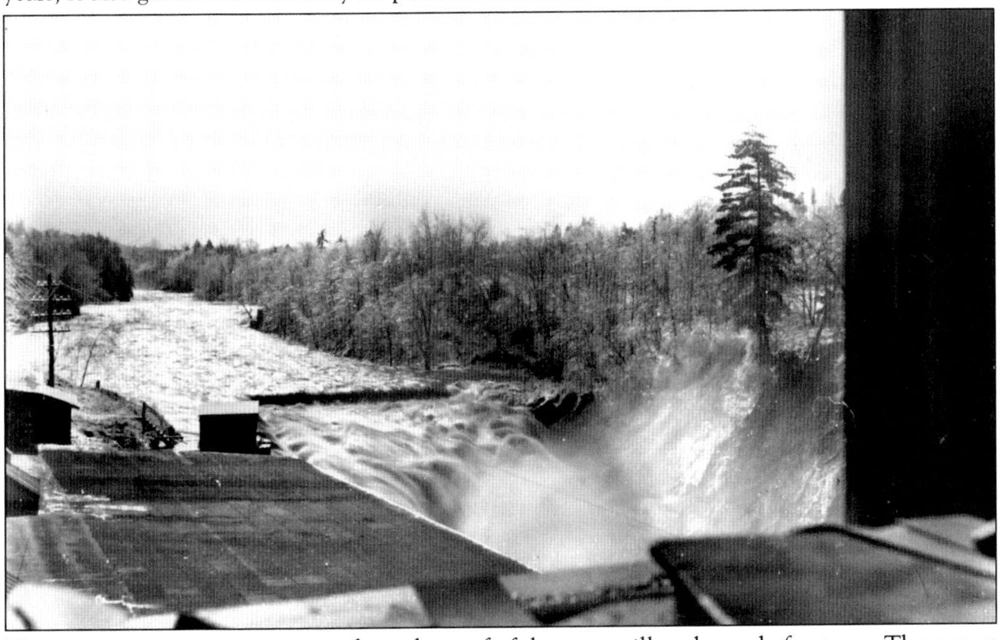

This is a very rare view upstream from the roof of the new mill at the end of a storm. The carpet machinery and generators must have been running at full force on this day. To the left is one of the poles supplying electrical power to the village. Contrary to some stories, the mills were not closed by Dimick because of a strike. The mills ran until Dimick's death and for a time thereafter before being sold in 1920.[67] (Florence Prehn collection.)

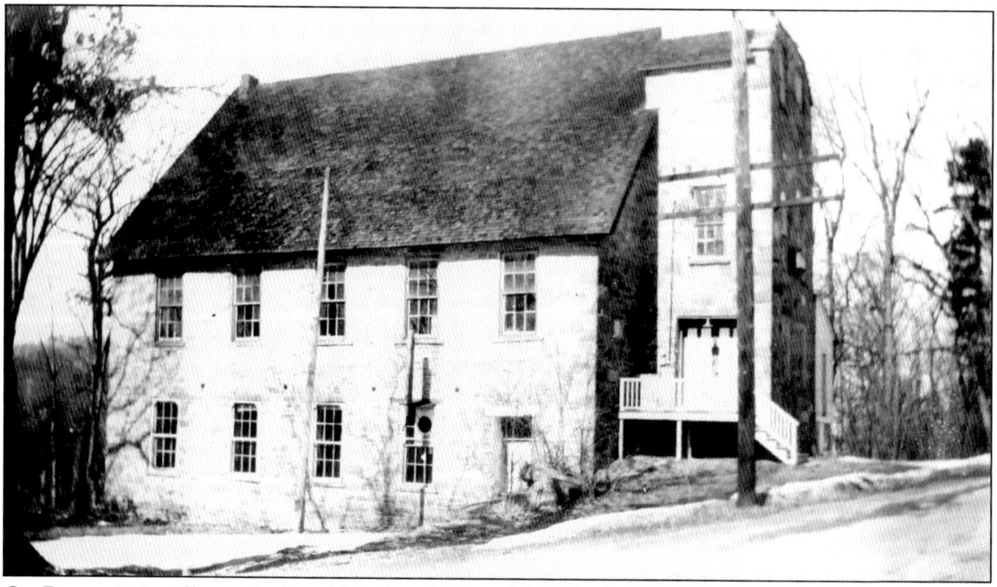

On Route 213 still stands the old Rifton Village Hall, built by Dimick for the new village. It is now a private home. The first floor held a school. Local children had a choice of attending the Rock School or this one. The second floor held the village municipal offices. The inscription on the reverse of this *c.* 1930 photograph reads, "Town Hall (Top Floor), School (Bottom Floor)." (Beatrice Jordan collection.)

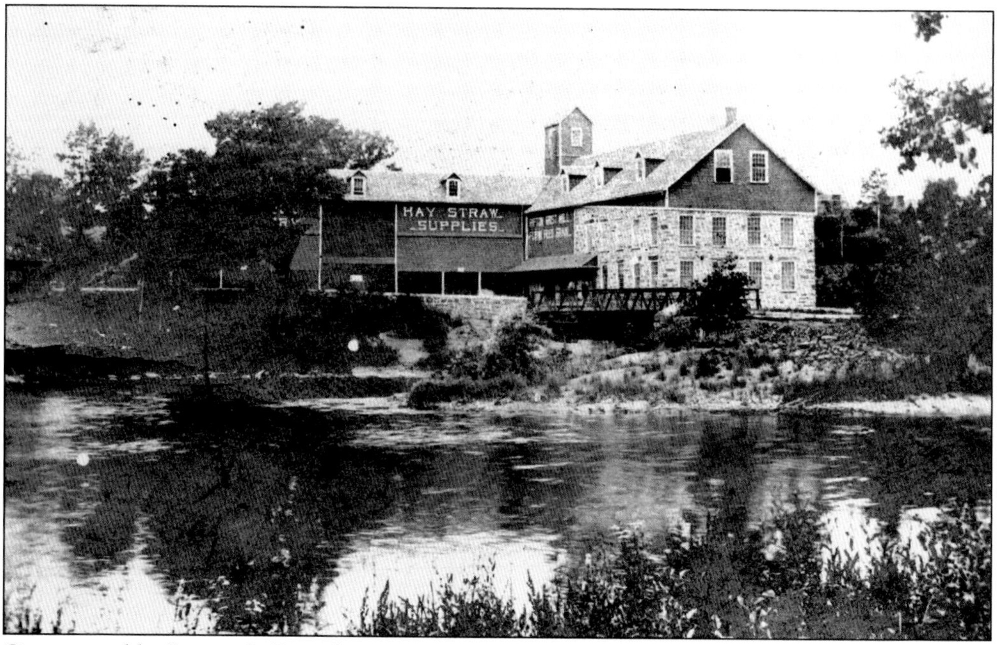

Constructed by Jeremiah Dimick in 1892 and enlarged in 1895 to incorporate a general store, the mill at Rifton Falls is shown here. The falls were less than 20 feet high[68] but broad enough to supply plenty of power to the turbines. The lettering on the right (near the stone portion) reads, "Rifton Grist Mill Flour Feed Grain." On the left-hand face it reads, "Hay Straw Supplies." (Beatrice Jordan collection.)

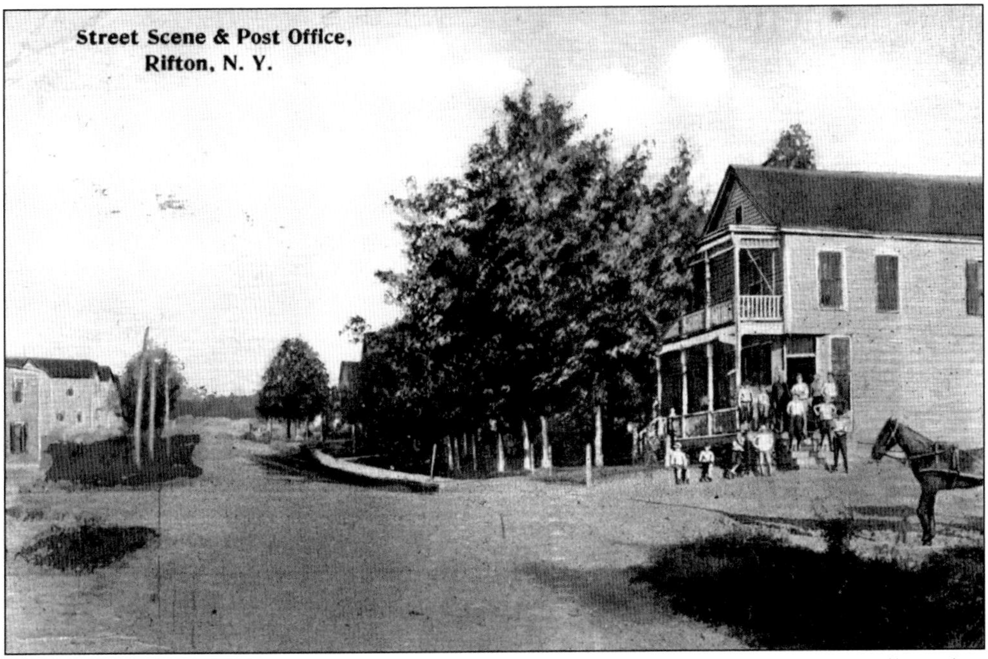

The quiet Rifton of the post-Dimick era was a far cry from the bustling industrial village that existed only two decades before. As in so many mill towns, many residents moved on in search of work when the mills closed down. Some stayed and found work at the electrical plant or in Kingston or Rosendale. Others farmed or kept stores, but the humming of the mills had fallen forever silent. (Authors' collection.)

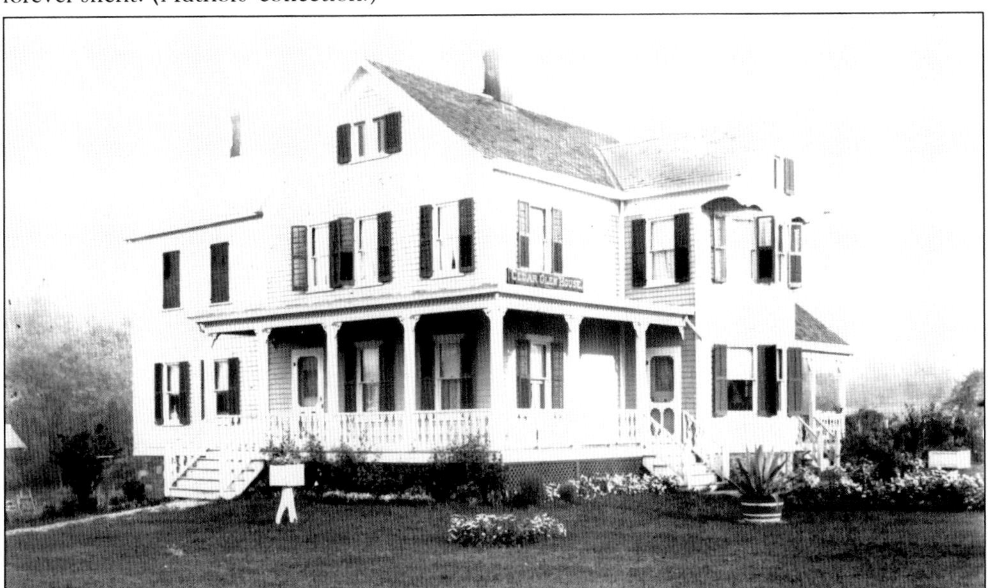

Here the authors ask the help of the reader. The house is called "Cedar Glen House," as can be seen on the sign attached to the porch roof. The authors have been unable to place this boardinghouse. The photograph comes from a glass-plate negative of the 1890s. It is known that there was a Cedar Glen poultry farm on Old Post Road near Maple Street. The authors would be appreciative of any further information. (Florence Prehn collection.)

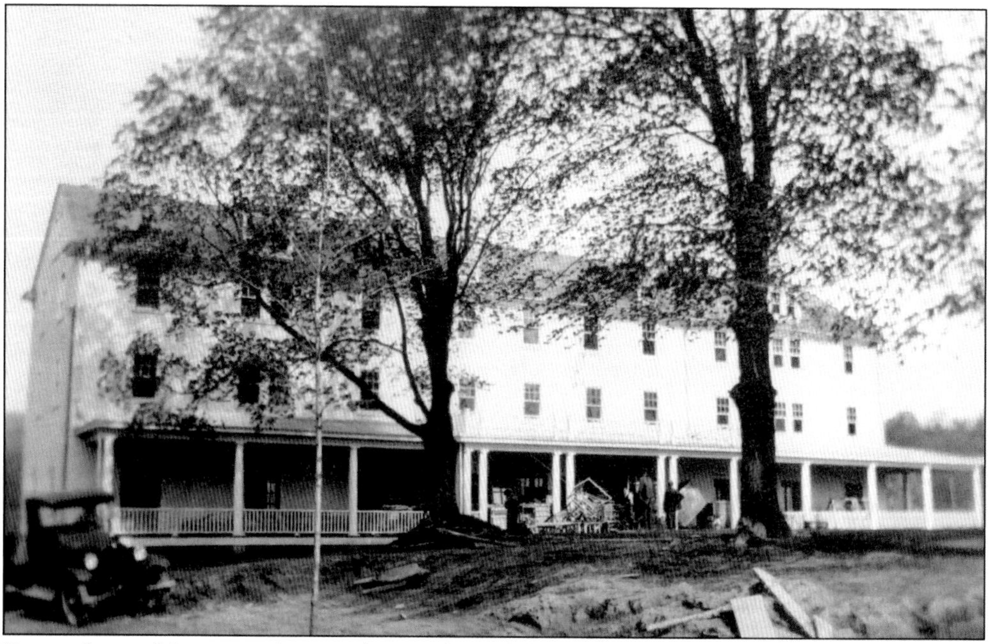

Descendants of the original owners have informed the authors that this is not the *Freeman* Hotel, as listed in some references, but rather the *Friedman* Hotel. This photograph shows the hotel under construction in the early 1920s. The Friedman Hotel, or Rifton Hotel, was one of several large boardinghouses that used to grace Rifton. A few stood into the 1960s, but eventually, they all burned or were torn down. (Beatrice Jordan collection.)

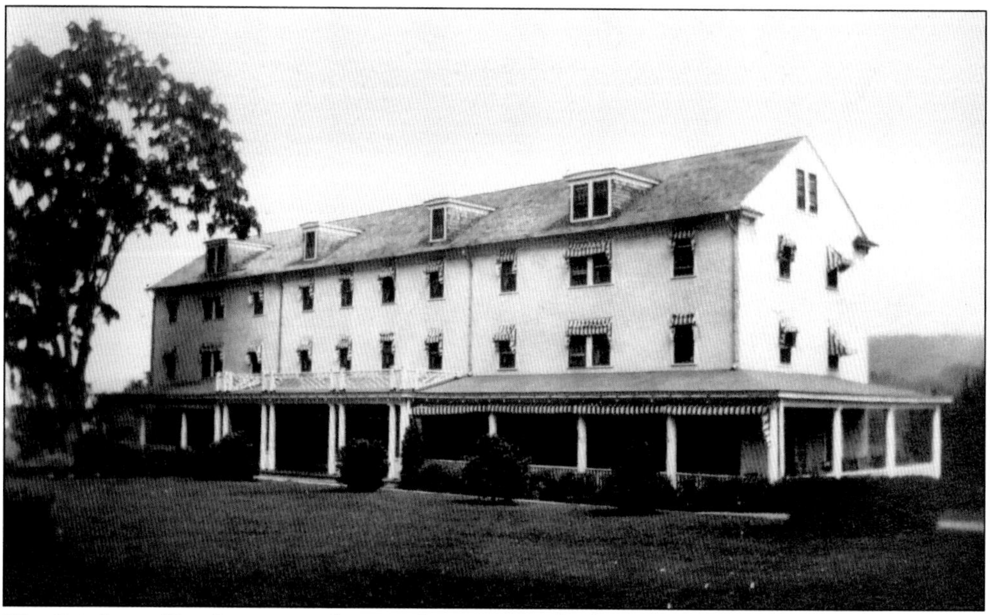

The Friedman Hotel is pictured soon after opening for business. The Rifton Hotel was more of an upscale place, but some of its neighbors had interesting reputations. During and after Prohibition, Rifton was widely known for having the best applejack in the country.[69] Leggs Diamond himself was said to have had a hand in its distribution to New York City. As late as the mid-1950s, arrests for bootlegging were made in the hills behind the old Black Swan.[70]

A proud Martin "Duke" Jordan Sr. stands by his Pierce Arrow bus in 1923. Duksey Jordan had the bus route from Kingston to New Paltz via Eddyville, New Salem, and St. Remy. He eventually lost the route because he was too good hearted and let many people ride for free.[71] During the days when the Rifton and Dashville power stations were being constructed, the bus had a full complement of paying riders, with more on the running boards.[72]

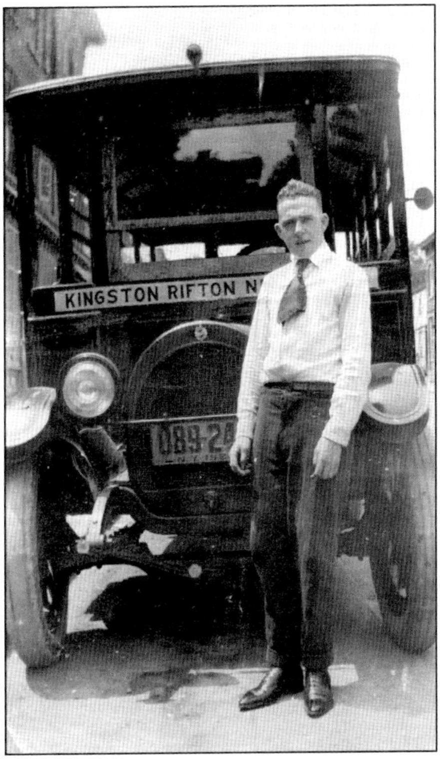

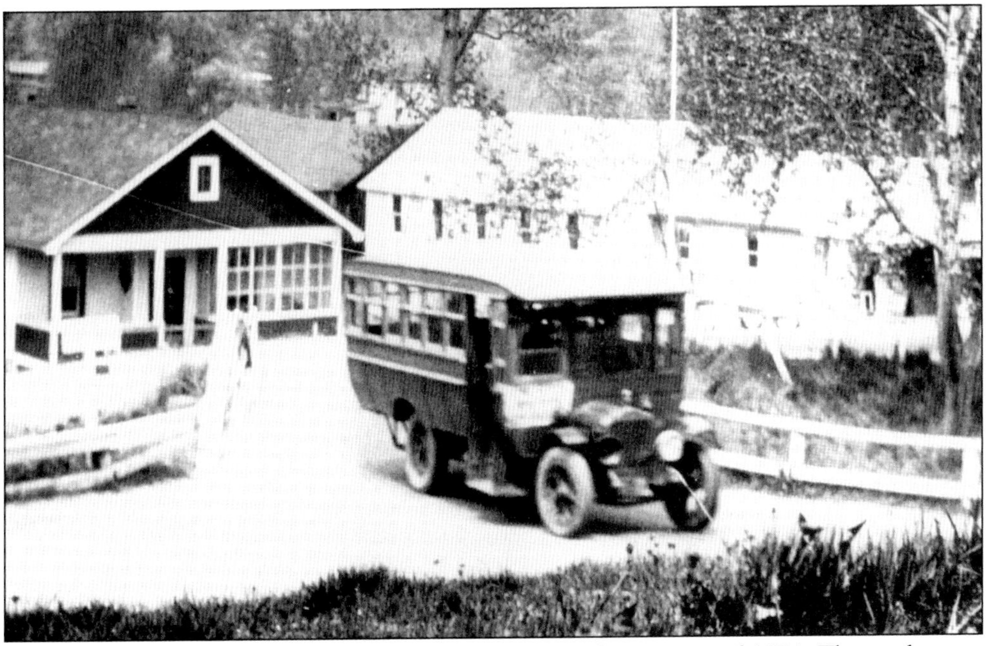

This is Duksey Jordan's bus at the Eddyville station in the summer of 1924. The reader may wonder why the right headlight is missing. Martin Jordan explained that one morning Duke was proceeding up Thompson's Hill toward Rifton along his usual route. After cresting the hill, he found a cow standing in the middle of the road. "There was nowhere to go. The bus got banged up, the cow died, and Mr. Thompson wanted payment for the cow." (Martin Jordan collection.)

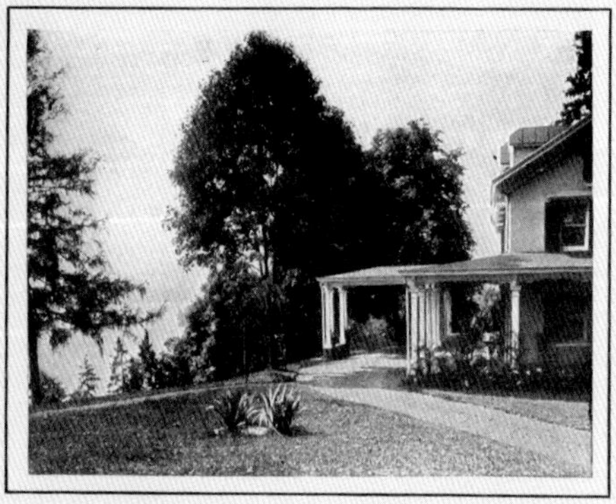

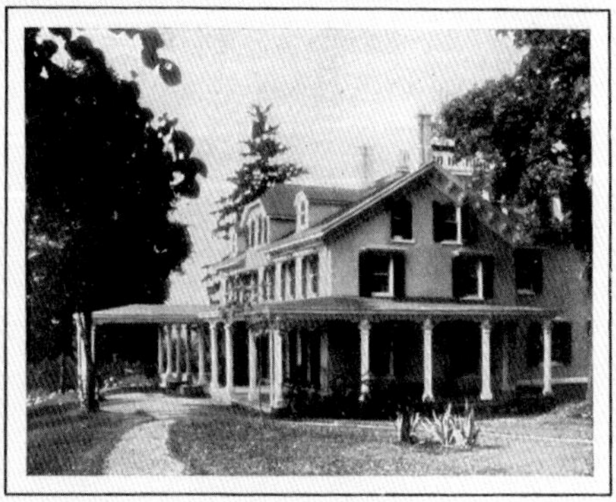

"Rosemount"

Long famous as the

Hudson River Estate

of the late

Judge Alton B. Parker

at Esopus, N. Y.

on west bank, 8 miles below Kingston

is now for the first time offered

For Sale

About 168 acres, mostly uplands, with approximately half mile river frontage. Highly developed; largely devoted to apple orchards; nearly 3000 trees in prime condition; productive of income sufficient for upkeep of estate.

Pleasant, old-fashioned residence of heavy stone and concrete construction in setting of fine trees on ridge well above river. Superb view of Hudson for many miles, unmarred by proximity of any railroad. To the rear rises a still higher ridge with picturesque fringe of woodland, all within the property.

Main floor contains large, hospitable living room opening into an enclosed section of broad verandah, library, foyer hall, dining room, pantry, etc.; kitchen and laundry are on lower level. On 2nd floor—6 family bedrooms, 2 glassed-in sleeping porches, 3 baths; above, extra guest room and bath, 4–5 servants' rooms with bath, storage space. Excellent heating plant, water supply, 9 open fireplaces..

Deep-water dock admitting large boats; fine bathing; also dock house with living apartment. Other accessories include gate lodge, 4 other cottages, 2-car garage, stable, barns, greenhouse with living quarters, cold storage building holding 200 tons of ice, chicken houses, etc.; also facilities for handling apple crop. In addition, peaches, cherries, grapes and raspberries in abundance, charming perennial flower garden, and vegetable garden. Driveways give access to all points, including dock.

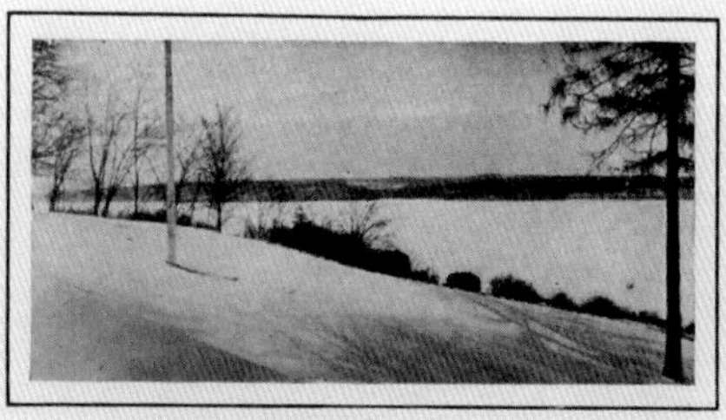

Kenneth Ives & Co.

17 East 42nd Street New York City

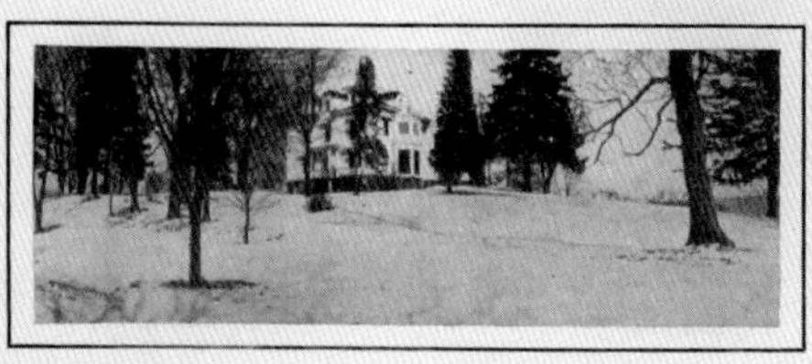

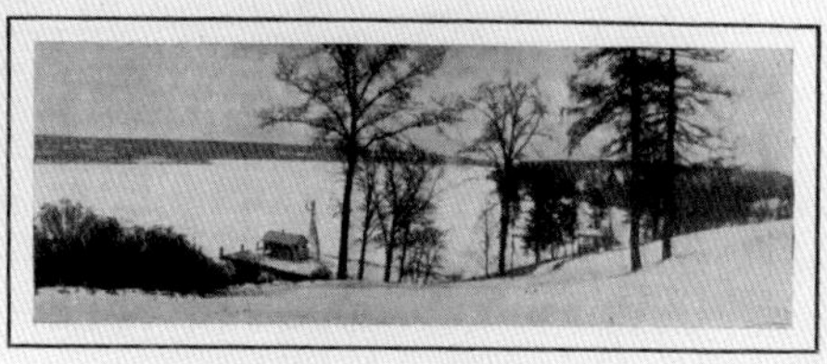

Five

EAST OF HUSSEY'S HILL

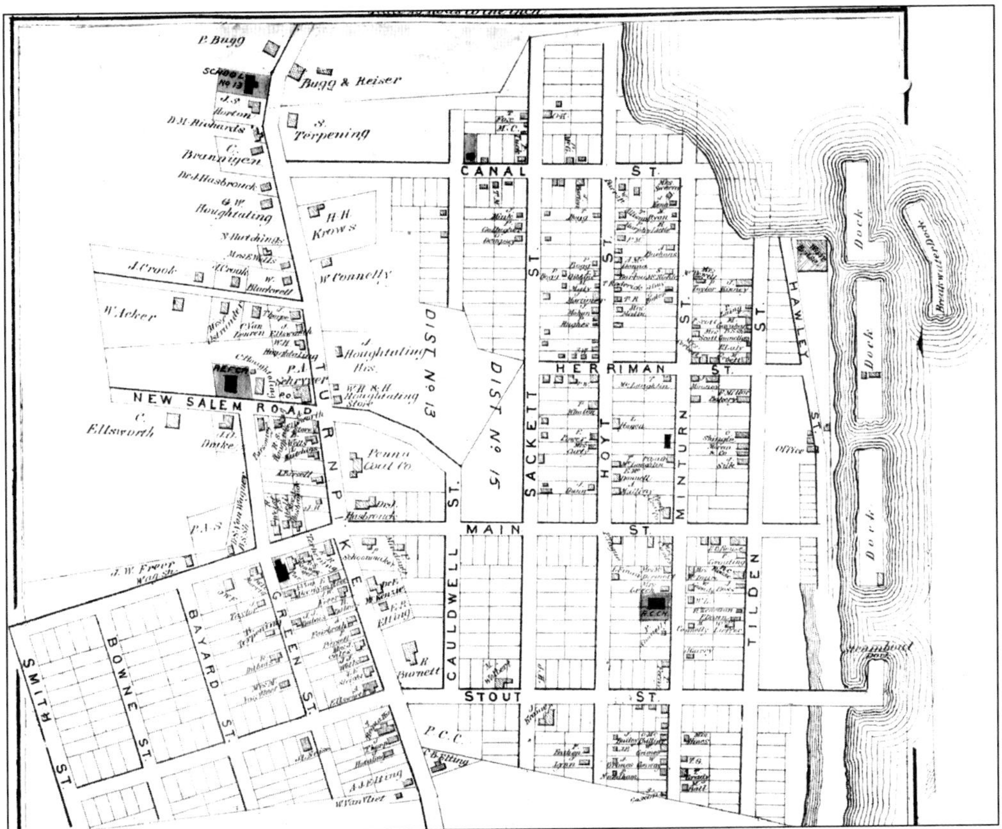

This detailed street map of Port Ewen was published in *Atlas of Ulster County* in 1875. In the first half of the 19th century, Port Ewen was just a farming and ice-cutting hamlet. All of the industrial growth had been along the waterfront in Connelly and Sleightsburg. It was not until the coming of the Pennsylvania Coal Company that Port Ewen became the center of town. Opposite is a real estate advertisement for Rosemount, the estate of Judge Alton B. Parker. Parker was the Democratic presidential candidate in 1904, and the Rosemount Mansion had at its core a 1745 stone house where British officers partied the night before the burning of Kingston. Their crews and 30-ship fleet lay anchored off Esopus Island. The estate was on a huge patent owned by loyalist Thomas Jones. Jones was stripped of his land by a legislative act in 1783.

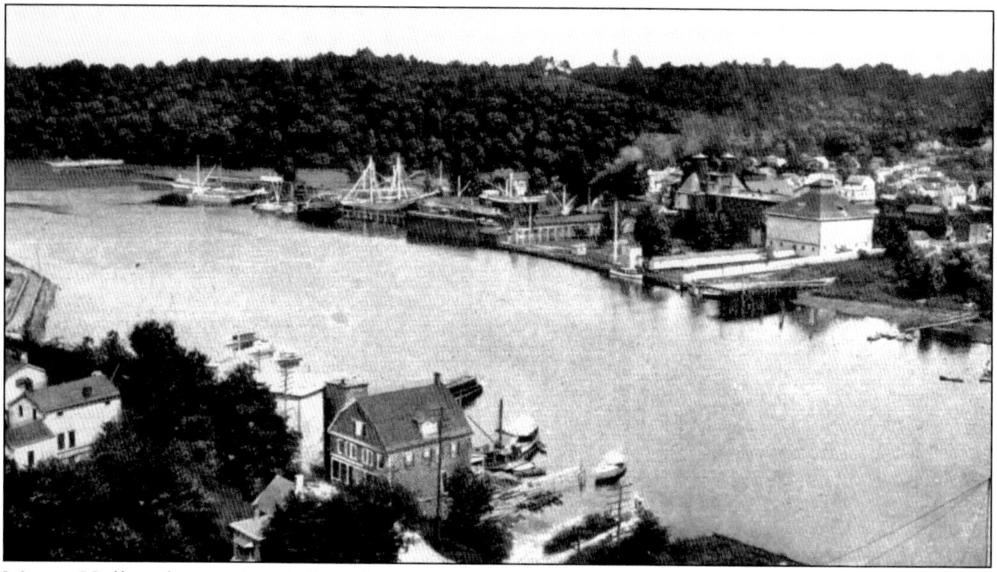

Mingo Hollow lies in South Rondout (now Connelly). Mingo, or Minqua, is a Lenape word that implies a temporary shelter or stopover place and is likely a holdover from the days of Kit Davits's trading post. As late as 1840, Amerindians sheltered here. According to former resident Bob Scherer, "During the time of the big depression tramps occupied a colony known as 'Hobo Jungle' adjacent to the railroad tracks . . . and bootleg whiskey was stored here in caskets during prohibition."[73]

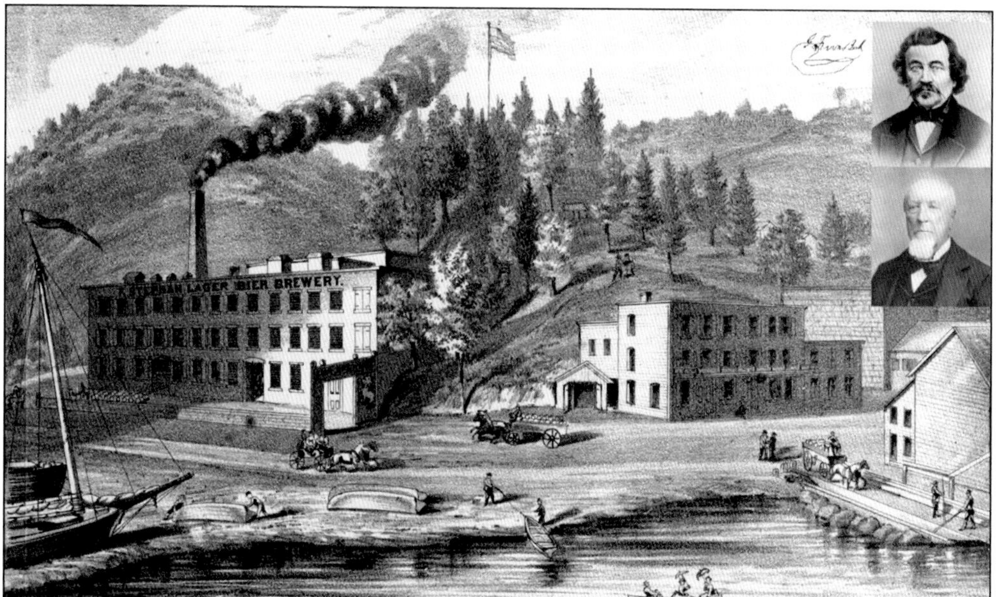

German immigrants brought to South Rondout a love of lager and the recipes and skills to produce it. Pictured above are George VonBeck (top), who established the brewery *c.* 1854, and his son-in-law Frederick Stephan Sr., who ran it from 1867 to 1877. Distribution to thirsty patrons occurred at VonBeck's famous Mansion House saloon across the Rondout via VonBeck's ferry. Penniless on arrival, VonBeck lived the American dream. When he died in 1870, his estate was valued at $500,000.[74]

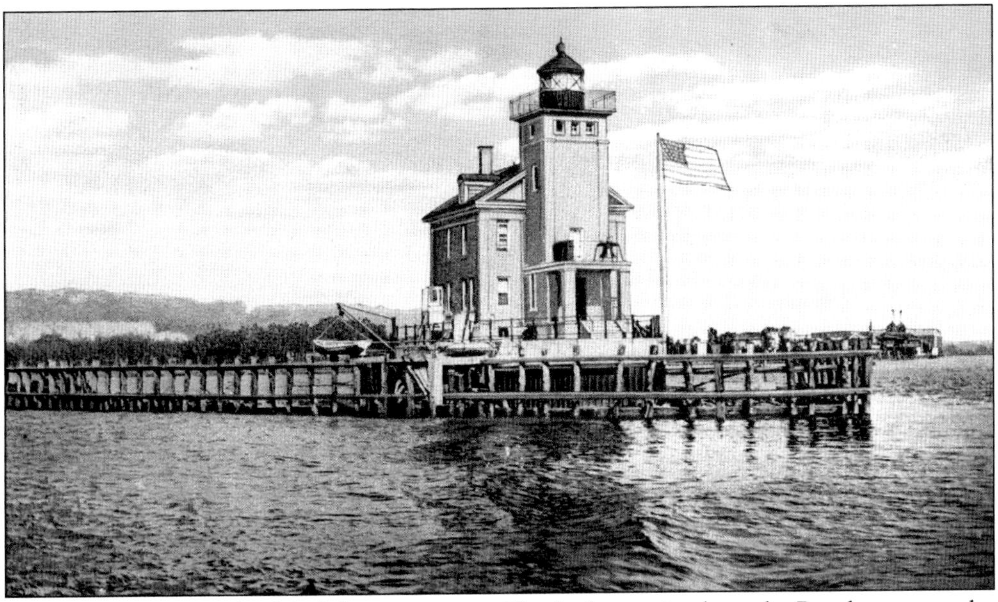

This is the "new," or third, lighthouse opposite Sleightsburg spit where the Rondout meets the Hudson. Construction began in 1913 and was completed in 1915, when this postcard photograph was taken. This was the largest and final family home lighthouse built on the Hudson River. In 1946, it was electrified and automated by the Coast Guard. Since 1988, the Hudson River Maritime Museum has been carefully maintaining and preserving the building. Their haunted lighthouse tours are great fun. (Authors' collection.)

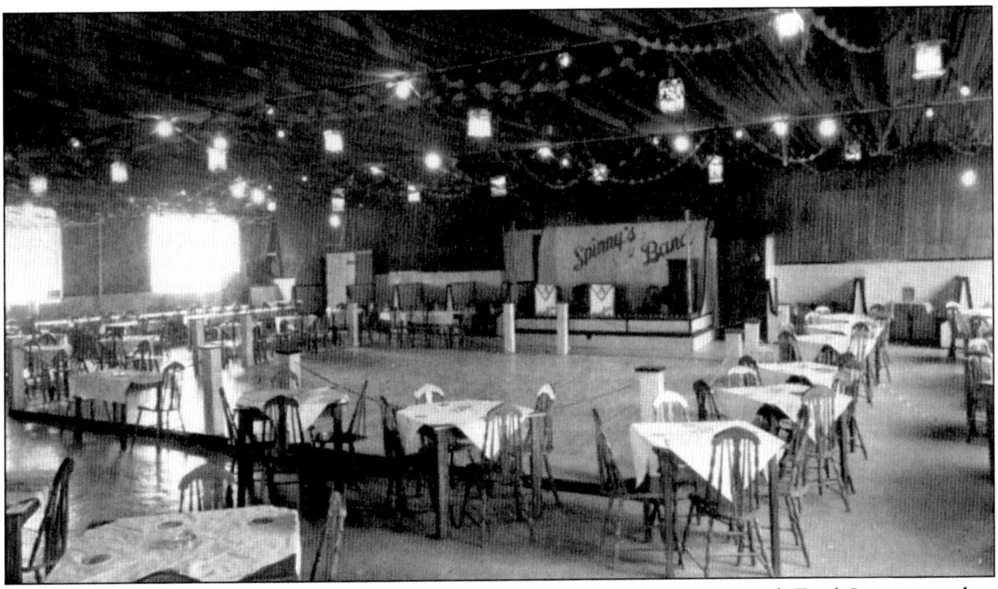

Shown is Spinny's nightclub as it appeared on a 1937 advertising postcard. Fred Spinnenweber rebuilt his bus and taxi garage into this club in 1933,[75] after the repeal of Prohibition. The Fourth of July party that year cost just $2 a person and was complete with hats, noisemakers, and a turkey dinner. There was also beer and soda with an "all night license." The building was originally William Stephenson's store and now houses the Esopus Town Hall. (Beatrice Jordan collection.)

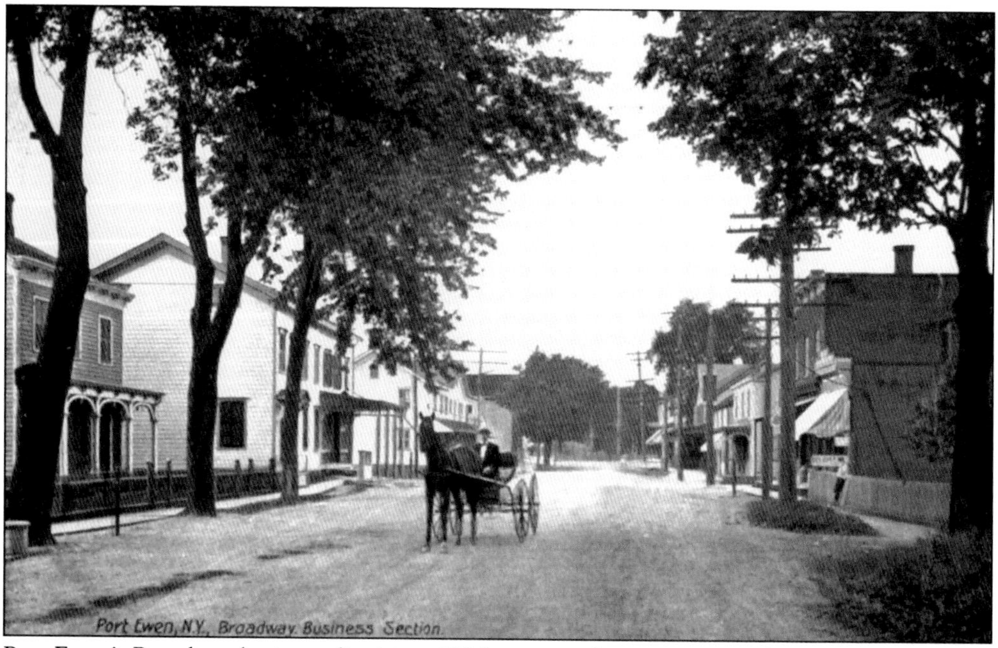

Port Ewen's Broadway business district *c.* 1905 is certainly reminiscent of "Main Street USA." Beginning as an Indian footpath along "Hudson's River" in the 1600s, it soon became part of the main thoroughfare, a "king's post road" between Fort Orange (Albany) and New Amsterdam (New York City). Stages and coaches carrying the mail and wealthy passengers stopped here to change horses or for a meal and libations of a local sort. (Authors' collection.)

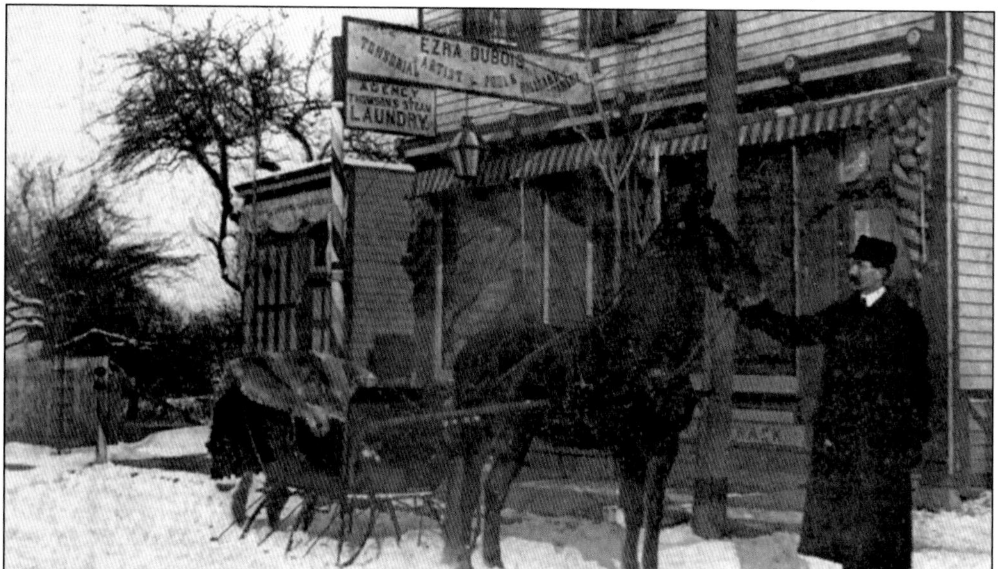

This is the Broadway Barber Shop of Port Ewen in 1905. The gentleman is believed to be Ezra DuBois. Ezra was no mere barber. His sign carries the verbiage "Ezra DuBois Tonsorial Artist—Pool and Billiard Parlor." At the left is an agency of Thomsen's Steam Laundry. Port Ewen has remained the commercial hub of the township to this day. (Raymond Krom collection.)

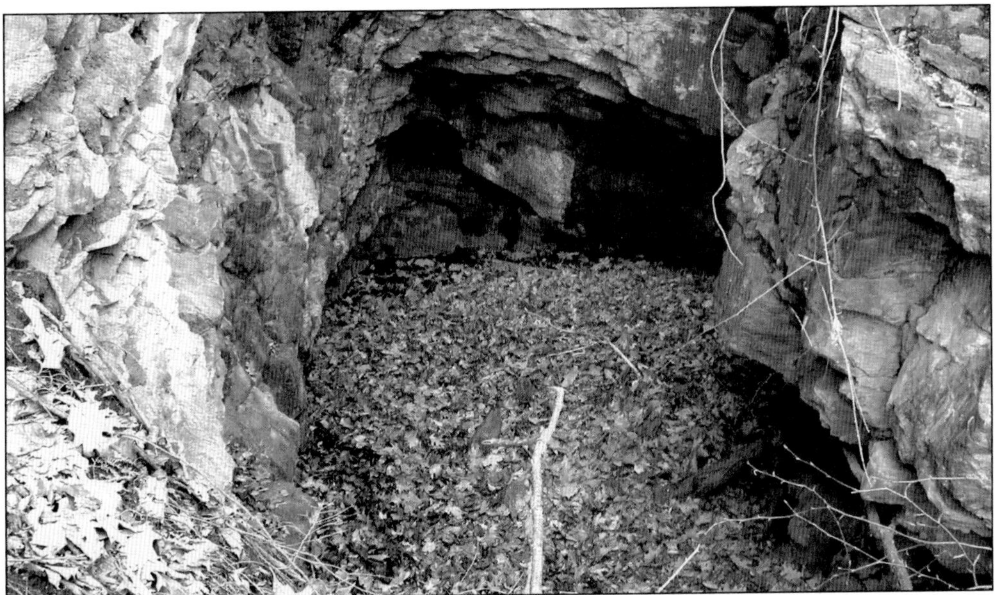

As gold fever swept our nation, mining companies sprang forth. On the local scene, legends of Amerindian and pirate treasures lent credence to the furor. The Hussey Hill Gold Mine (entrance above) was established on November 12, 1877, through real estate and mineral rights purchased by the Hudson River Gold & Silver Mining Company. Eighteen months later, the assets of the company, including steam engine, shafting, and on-site machinery, were bought at foreclosure by Plaintiff Simon S. Westbrook. (Authors' collection.)

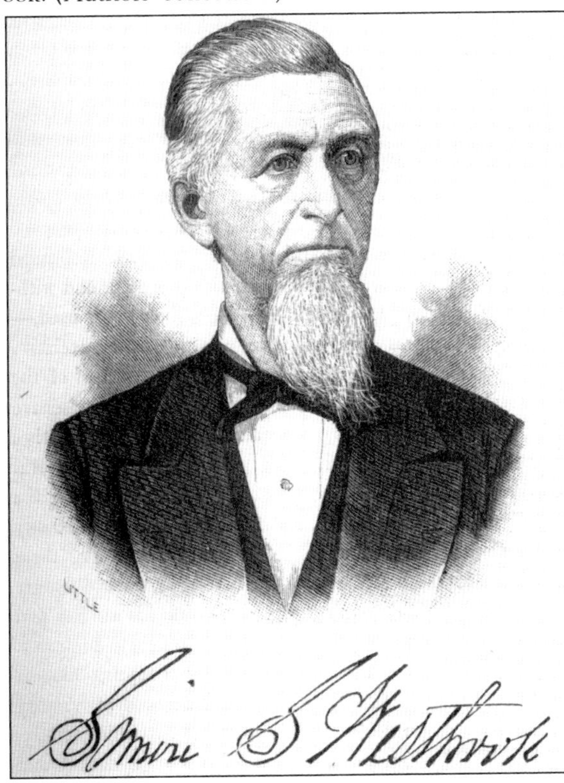

In July 1879, former Ulster County sheriff Simon S. Westbrook was signing certificates issued by the Home Gold and Silver Mining Company with offices at Esopus and the city of New York.[76] According to corporation papers, the company's capital investment was $2 million. This was raised in part by a sales agent who worked the weekend crowds gathered to watch the "diggings." There is gold on Hussey's Hill, that is true. How it came to be there is the question.

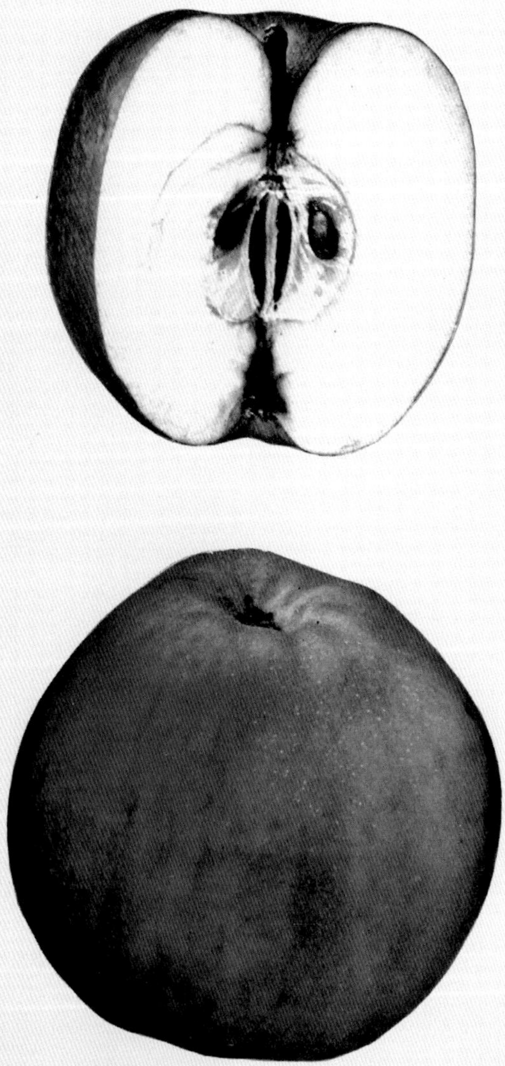

ESOPUS SPITZENBURG

Esopus Spitzenburg, a royal dessert, frequently appeared on the table of our third president, Thomas Jefferson. At its best for Christmas, this medium-sized red apple tinged with orange has a crisp juicy flesh that spritzes the taste buds with its rich, spicy flavor. The Spitzenburg, discovered in Esopus sometime between 1780 and 1790, is apparently of pre-colonial origin. It was found in a native orchard formerly cultivated by Amerindians. Apples were a favored crop on local farms such as Pelham, the 600-acre countryseat of Robert Livingston Pell. This 1840s state-of-the-art agricultural venture included an immense wharf with a warehouse where apples were sweated in preparation for market. Only the best were packed and shipped in locally produced wooden barrels and boxes, and they garnered a neat profit. According to an 1850 pomology report, the cost of production was 2½¢ per barrel, with apples selling for $8 per box of 100 in Europe and $8 per barrel (approximately 400 apples) in New York City. With upward of 25,000 apple trees, there was also plenty of fodder for Pell's large cider mill and sufficient local clientele to consume the product.

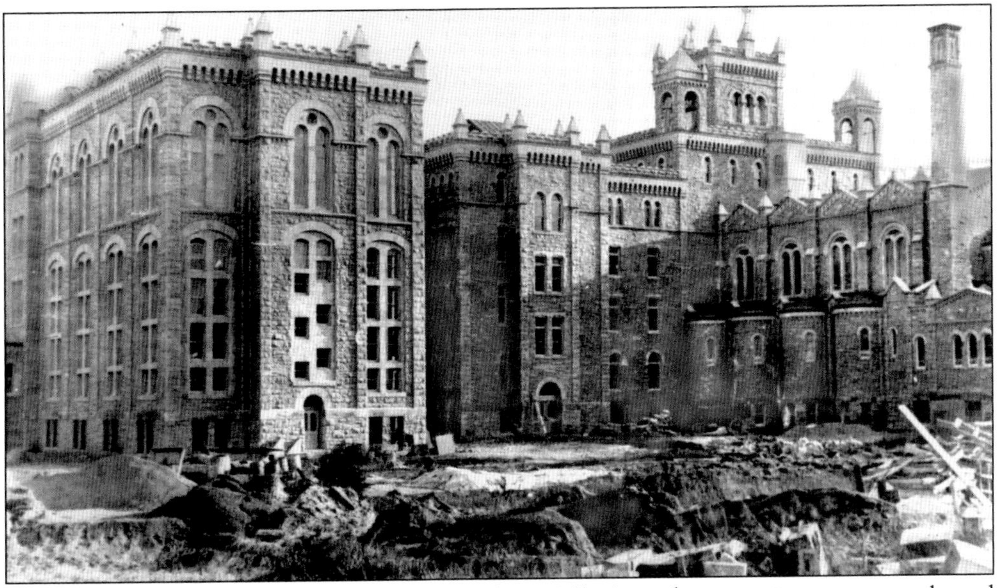

As the Victorian age faded, many of the Hudson Valley's mighty mansions were supplanted by edifices of divine majesty. In 1904–1907, the Mount (pictured above) helped to herald the advent of a new era. As assorted sectarian communities settled into an area long noted for its religious tolerance, the Redemptorist Brothers constructed a seminary on the site of Pell's mansion. In addition to their studies, these men continued to farm the land with a spirit of self-sufficiency and good stewardship. (Courtesy of the Mount.)

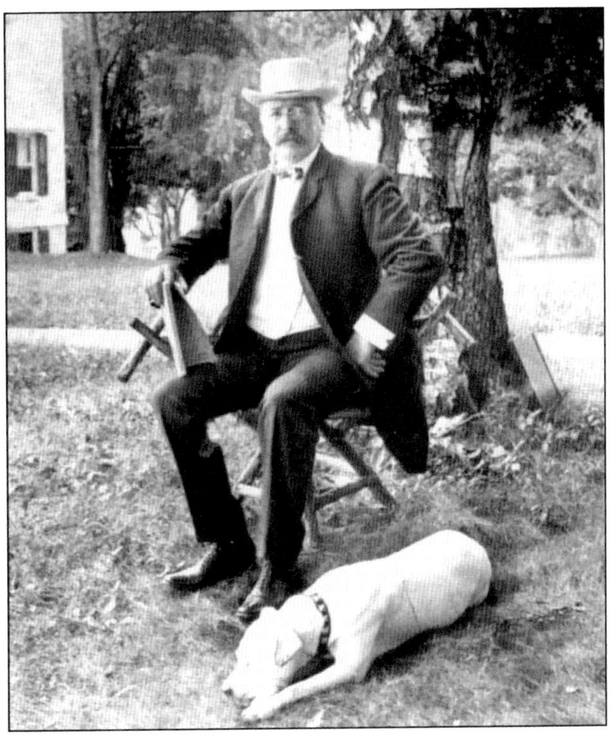

A big red-headed farm boy from Cortland, New York, Alton B. Parker came to Ulster County in 1871 to teach school. Here he met and married Mary Schoonmaker, daughter of a local judge. Parker returned to school to fulfill his boyhood dream of being a lawyer. He rose through the ranks to become Chief Justice of the New York Court of Appeals. This photograph of Parker and Senator was taken for his presidential run against Teddy Roosevelt in 1904.[77]

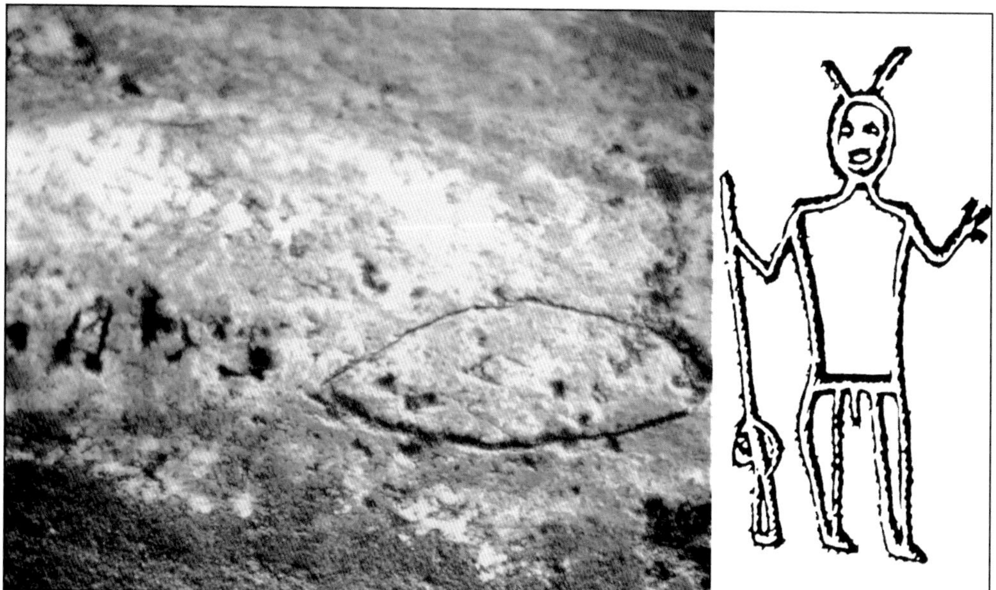

Indian Rock sits on the western bank of the Hudson River. This geodetic benchmark's legend concerning the Indian etched figure (seen to the right in a drawing done by E.M. Ruttenberg) has many variations. The figure is described as being "28 inches high, the legs 7½ inches, as is the diameter of the head." The author has visited Indian Rock since childhood and never found distinct evidence of that carving. Perhaps it has totally worn away. There are, however, fish, numbers, dates, and arrows carved upon the rock. (Authors' collection.)

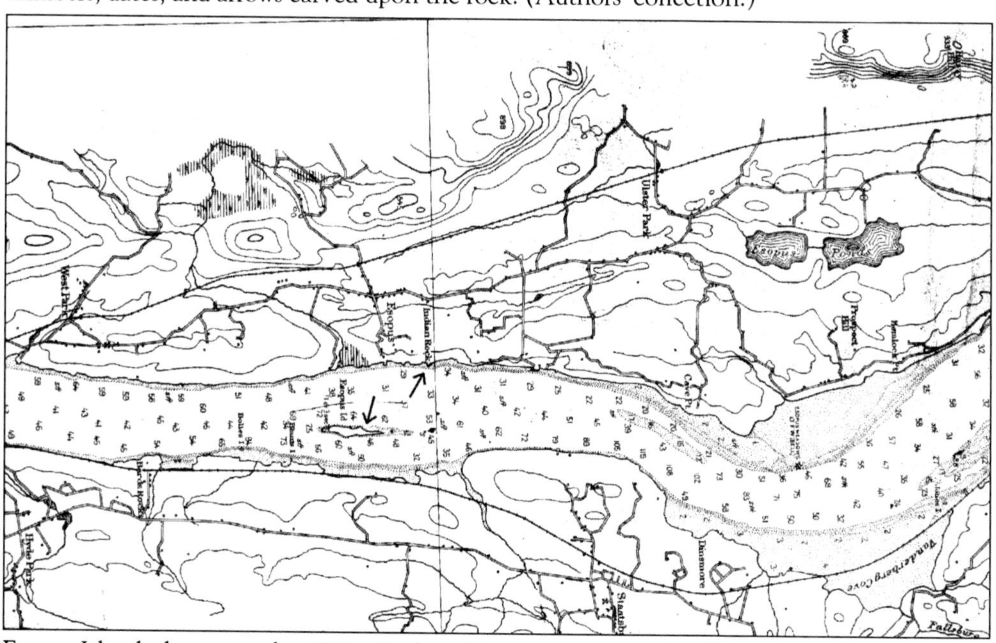

Esopus Island, shown on the 1920s Hudson River chart above, has been a temporary home to many. The Amerindians knew it as Raphoes, a springtime gathering spot for shad fishing. To Captain Kidd, it was a river outpost as he recruited privateers from the whaling ports of the Hudson River. Called Pell's Island in the 1800s, "Oesopus" was a summer camp to Aleister Crowley's pagan Magick in 1918. Today, it is a reservation owned by New York State.[78]

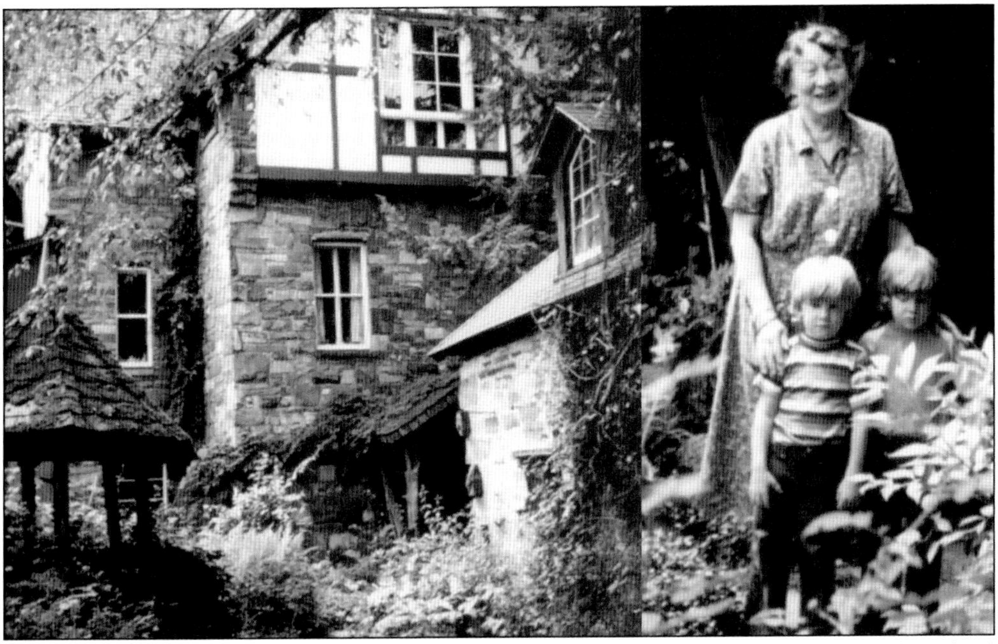

Elizabeth Burroughs Kelly, the granddaughter of John Burroughs, poses with David and Michael Ford on the grounds of Riverby, the West Park estate of John Burroughs, in September 1974. The buildings built by John are just beginning to deteriorate, and the grounds are overgrown. Elizabeth recalled fondly the estate as it was in her grandfather's time. Burroughs resided here from 1873 until his death in 1921. He taught in the local schools and was West Park's first postmaster, beginning in 1891.

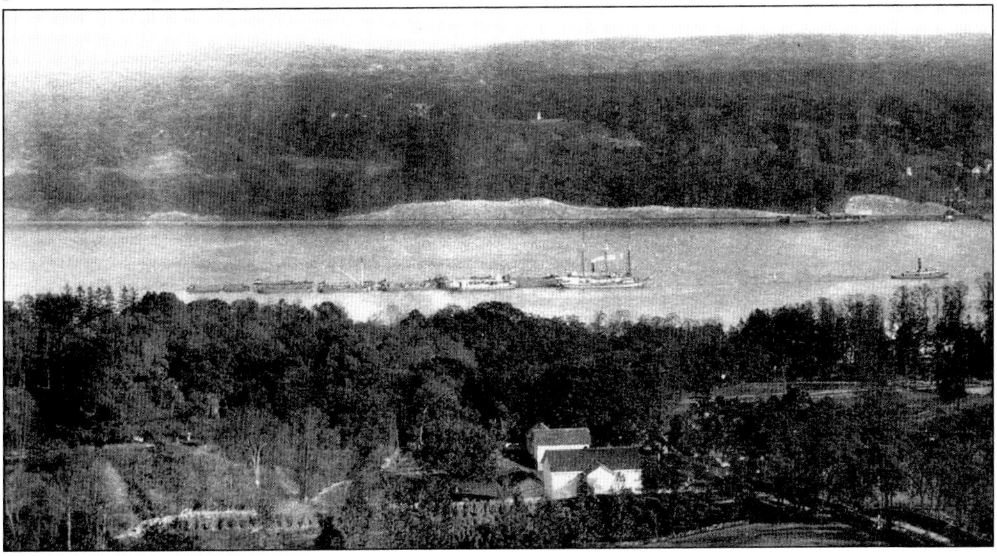

This is a 1905 Hudson River view from West Park and a familiar sight to naturalist John Burroughs, who preferred to pen his essays at Slabsides, his rustic retreat. The Burroughs family shared Riverby's scenic vantage with many guests. Presidents and farmers were entertained with equally gracious hospitality. Walt Whitman indulged himself with "Mrs. B's delicious coffee, with the cream and fresh picked fruit for breakfast." America's first saint, Mother Cabrini, was also a contemporary of John Burroughs at West Park. (Authors' collection.)

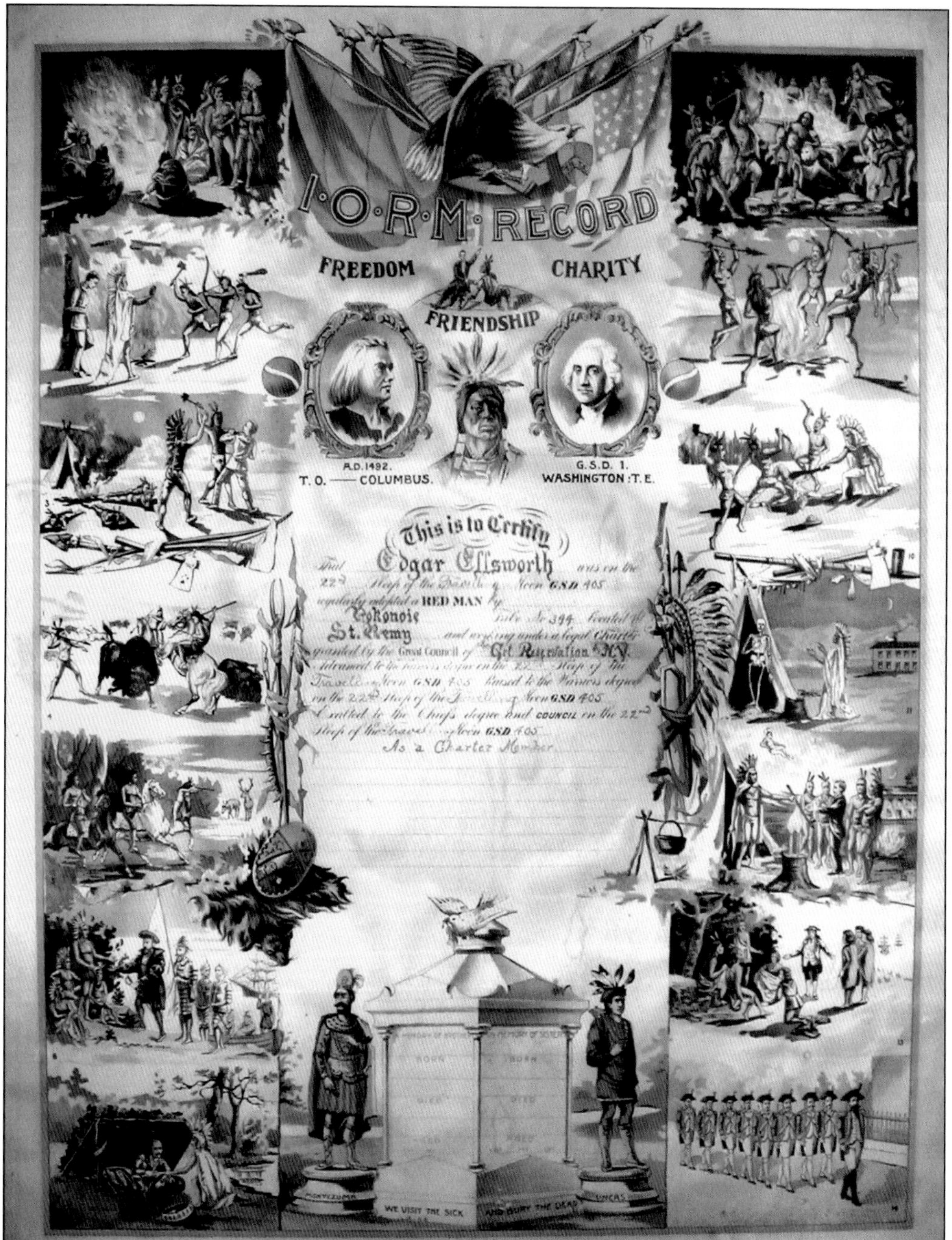

Pictured is an original membership certificate of the Improved Order of Redmen, Tribe No. 344. It was issued to Edgar Ellsworth as a charter member on October 22, 1896. The date is written in a secret code. The certificate measures about two by three feet in size and is printed in full color.

Six

Community Pride

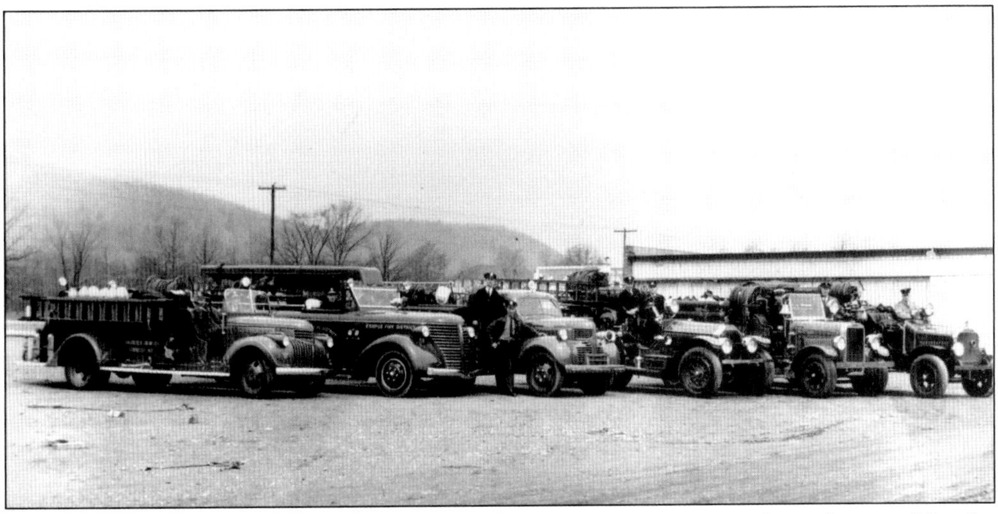

The strong commitment to community service and pride in Esopus is best illustrated by the members of the five fire districts in the town. Above we see representative trucks from each of the five districts massed for a group photograph at Aero Lake. The year is 1947. These represented about half of the combined firefighting machinery in the town. The Connelly firemen with the Sanford pumper are Ed McKinley (left) and Jim Carlson (right); with Esopus's 1940 American Lafrance are Frank Dumser and Ralph Coutant; with Rifton's 1944 Dodge are an unidentified person and Emil Wagner; with St. Remy's 1924 American Lafrance pumper are George King and Wally Wood; with Port Ewen's 1928 Sanford are Bud Dubois and Ed Mains; with Port Ewen's 1929 Mack ladder is Harry VanOrmer. Espopus's dedicated firefighters were joined in 1983 by the Town of Esopus Volunteer Ambulance Squad (TEVAS). (Clark Mains collection.)

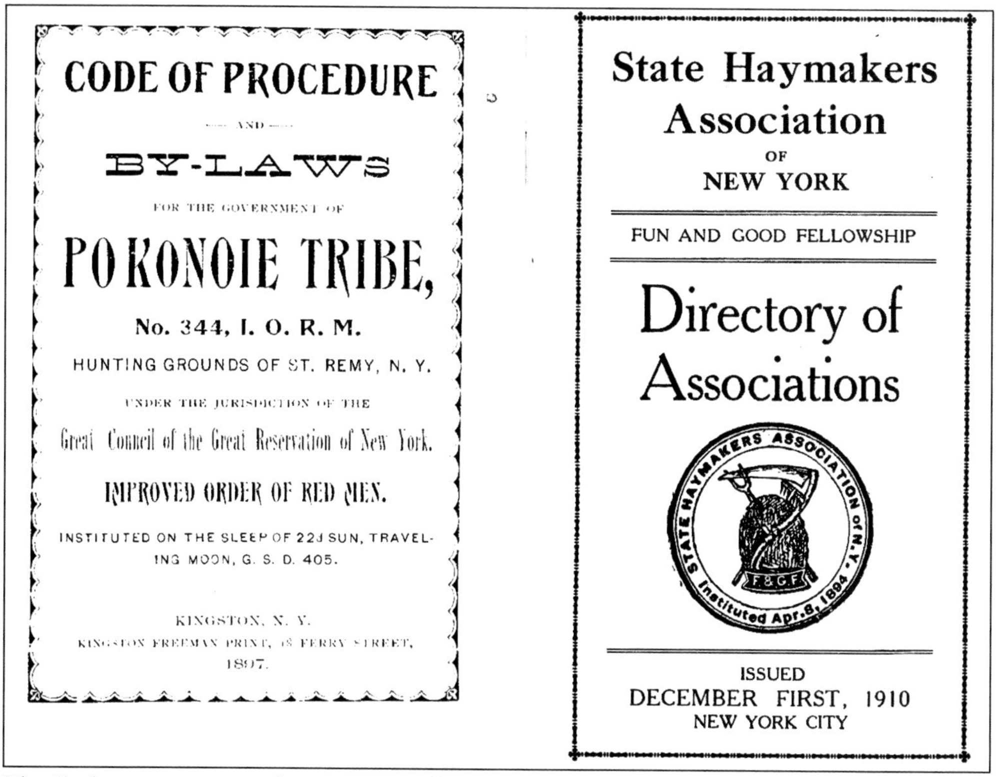

CODE OF PROCEDURE

AND

BY-LAWS

FOR THE GOVERNMENT OF

POKONOIE TRIBE,

No. 344, I. O. R. M.

HUNTING GROUNDS OF ST. REMY, N. Y.

UNDER THE JURISDICTION OF THE

Great Council of the Great Reservation of New York.

IMPROVED ORDER OF RED MEN.

INSTITUTED ON THE SLEEP OF 22d SUN, TRAVELING MOON, G. S. D. 405.

KINGSTON, N. Y.

KINGSTON FREEMAN PRINT, 18 FERRY STREET,

1897.

State Haymakers Association

OF

NEW YORK

FUN AND GOOD FELLOWSHIP

Directory of Associations

ISSUED

DECEMBER FIRST, 1910

NEW YORK CITY

The Redmen were one of many secret fraternal organizations in Esopus. Esopus boasts two Redmen's halls, an order of Haymakers, Knights of Pythias and Pythian Sisters, Mechanics, Odd Fellows, Rebecca Lodge, Sons and Daughters of Liberty, and the Independent Order of Good Templars. We also had more open organizations such as the Grange, organized in March 1908, and numerous church organizations. (Authors' collection.)

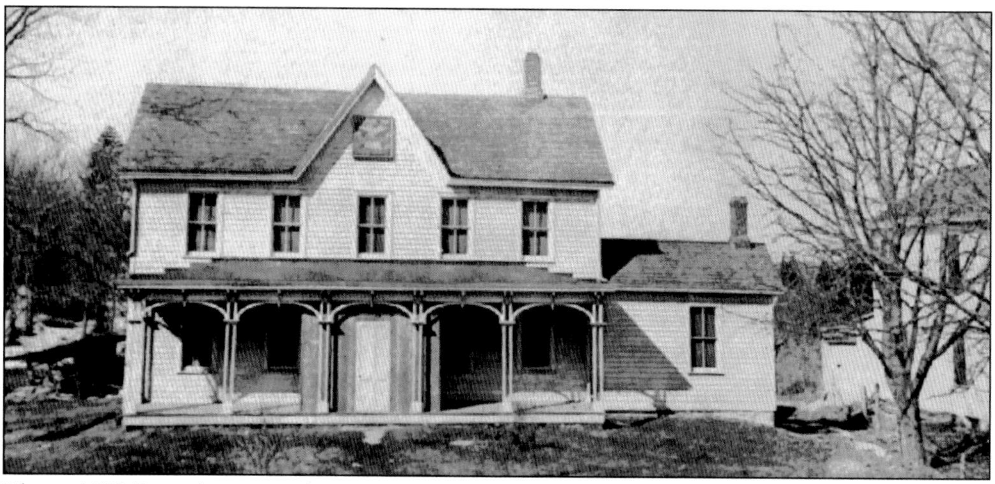

This *c.* 1870 Roosa homestead is now a part of the St. Remy Fire Station No. 1. In 1944, the town organized the five fire companies into tax-supported districts. In July 1945,[79] the commissioners of St. Remy purchased the Redmen's hall for use as their new fire station. The Redmen moved to other quarters until the dissolution of the local chapter in April 1957. Notice the lodge emblem on the front gable in this *c.* 1905 photograph. (Authors' collection.)

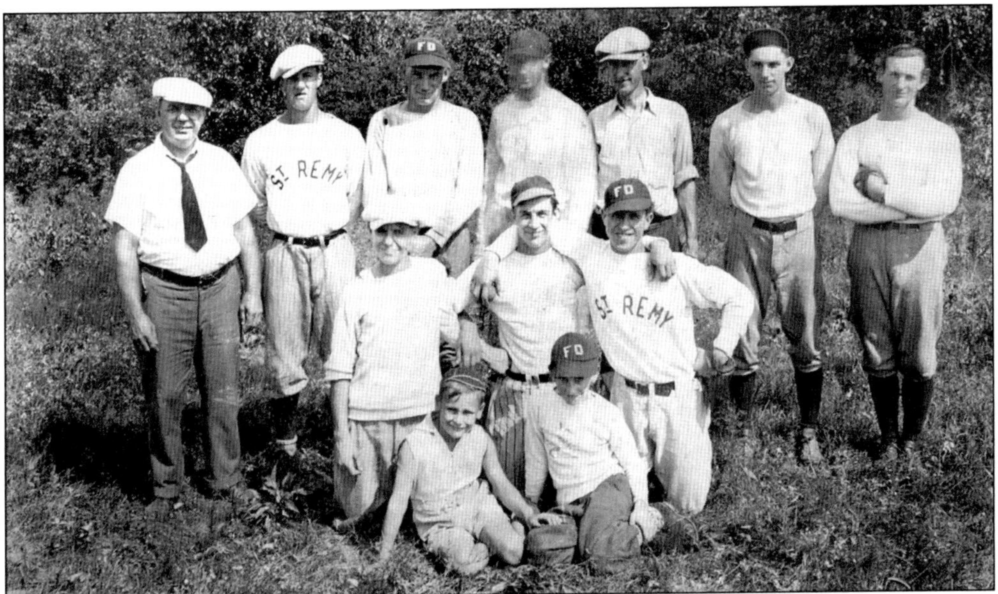

Many residents are familiar with the softball teams fielded by our town fire departments in the 1980s and 1990s. These are members of the St. Remy ball team from the late 1940s. From left to right are the following: (front row) two unidentified people; (middle row) an unidentified person (possibly Phil Fischer Jr. or George White), Myron York, and an unidentified person; (back row) Phil Fischer Sr., ? Ennist, Walter Helmich, John Helmich, Ernest Frost, Pete Helmich, and Jim Helmich. George White still has an original uniform. (Authors' collection.)

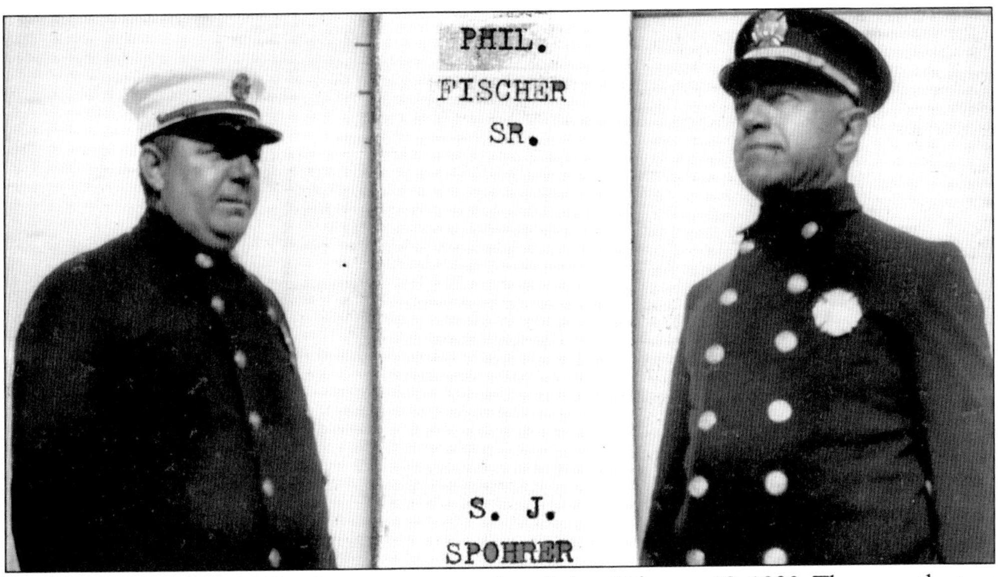

The St. Remy Volunteer Fire Department was founded on February 18, 1930. These are the two organizers: Phil Fischer Sr. (left) and Sebastian J. Spohrer. The Von Beck Engine Company (in Connelly) was the first fire department in the town. It was founded by George Von Beck and Jacob Fox in 1856. Von Beck supplied funding and a building, while Fox provided expertise and recruitment. The Port Ewen Fire Department was organized in 1896; Esopus, in 1939; Rifton, in 1943.

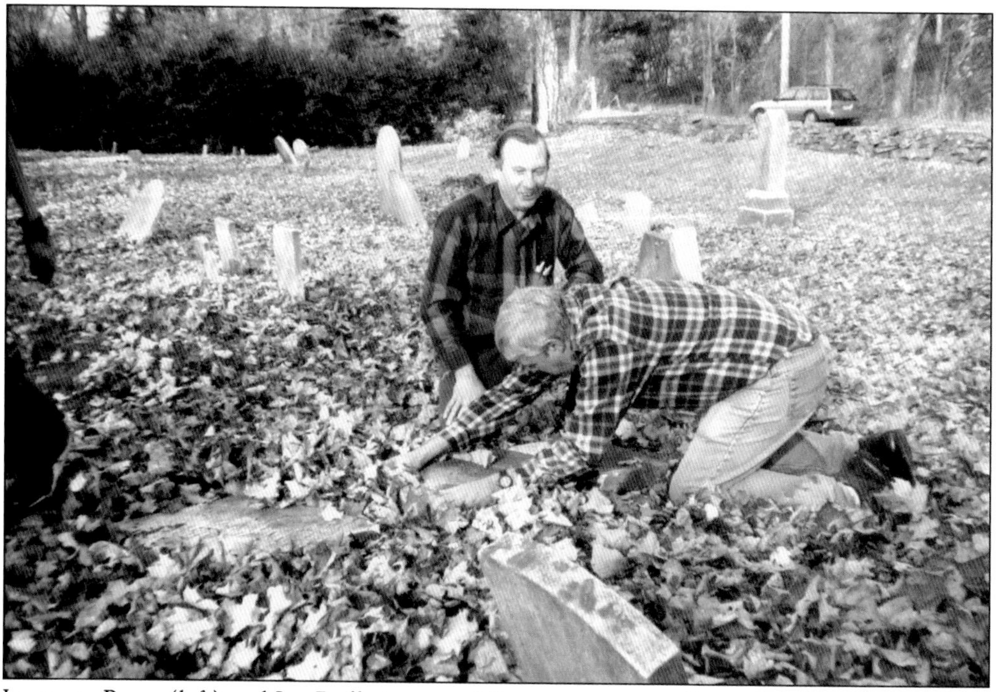

Laurence Rowe (left) and Joe Ruffini reset a fallen gravestone at Perrine's Cemetery in Rifton. Both men are the fathers of Eagle Scouts. Rowe helped Ruffini's son Frank restore the old Rock School as his Eagle project. Now Frank is returning the favor as expert help for Kenneth Rowe's project of restoring the cemetery. The Scouts and dads also cut brush, removed debris, and moved an entire stone wall four feet farther from the highway. (Photograph by Susan B. Wick.)

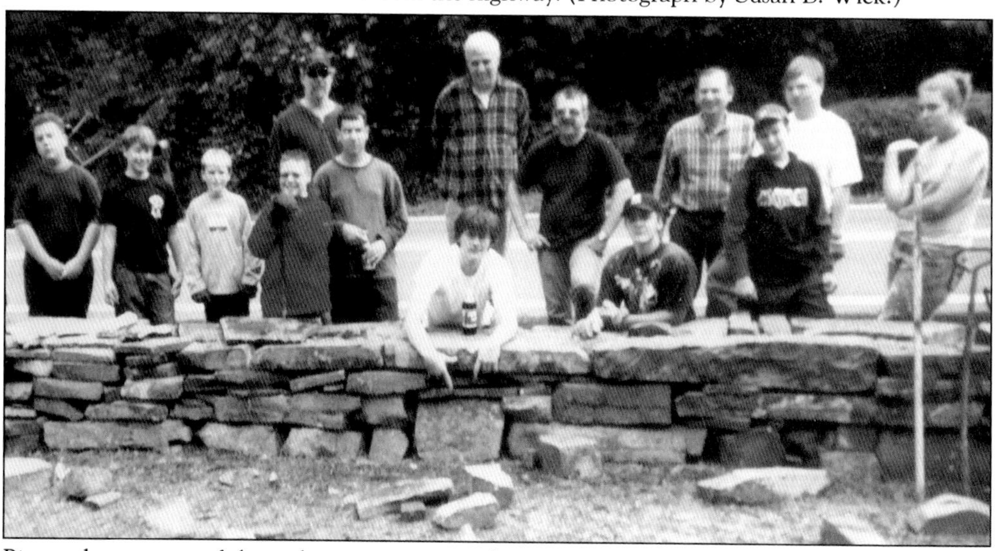

Pictured are many of the volunteer crew members. From left to right are Josh Harrison, Tim Metty, James Newman, Brian Conner, Mike Gerhart, Joe Harrison, Kenneth Rowe, Joe Ruffini, Mike Harrison, Frank Ruffini, Larry Rowe, Scott Gerhart, T.J. Wasik, and Amy Ruffini. In addition to relocating and rebuilding the stone wall, Kenneth also designed a new iron entryway. The Scouts, with expert assistance from local craftsmen, then helped to fabricate it and to secure it in place. (Kenneth Rowe collection.)

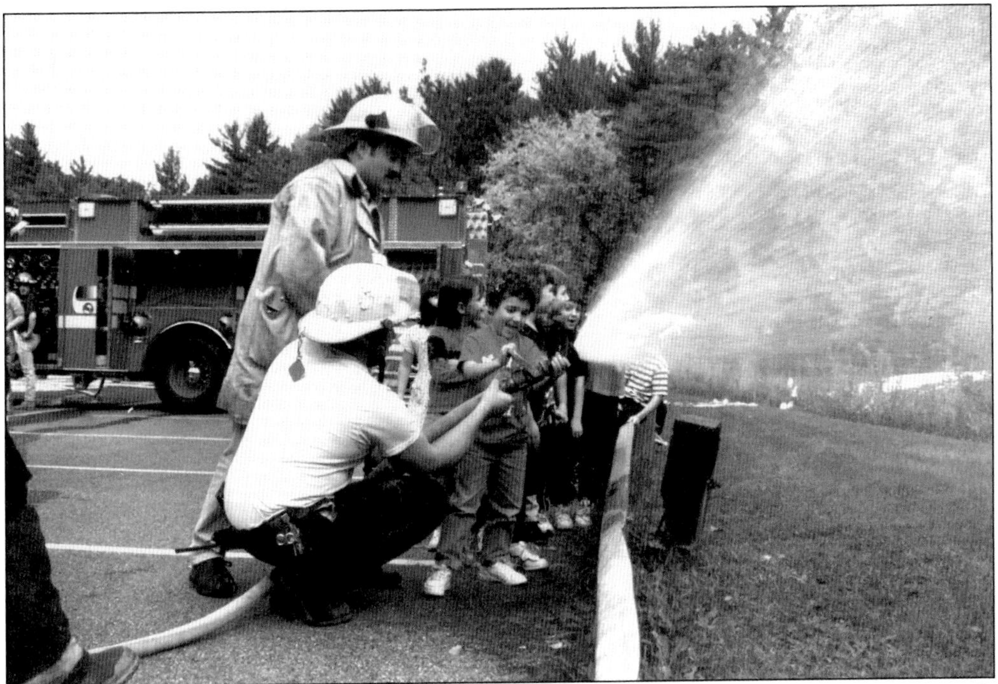

Karl R. Wick, St. Remy fire chief, and Michael Litts, assistant chief, show the second-grade class at Anna Devine School how to adjust the pattern of a fire nozzle. Each fall, the Rifton, Tillson, and St. Remy Fire Departments and the Esopus ambulance service conduct a fire-safety session and equipment demonstrations for the students and staff. The Port Ewen Fire Department conducts similar sessions at the Robert Graves School. (Photograph by Susan B. Wick.)

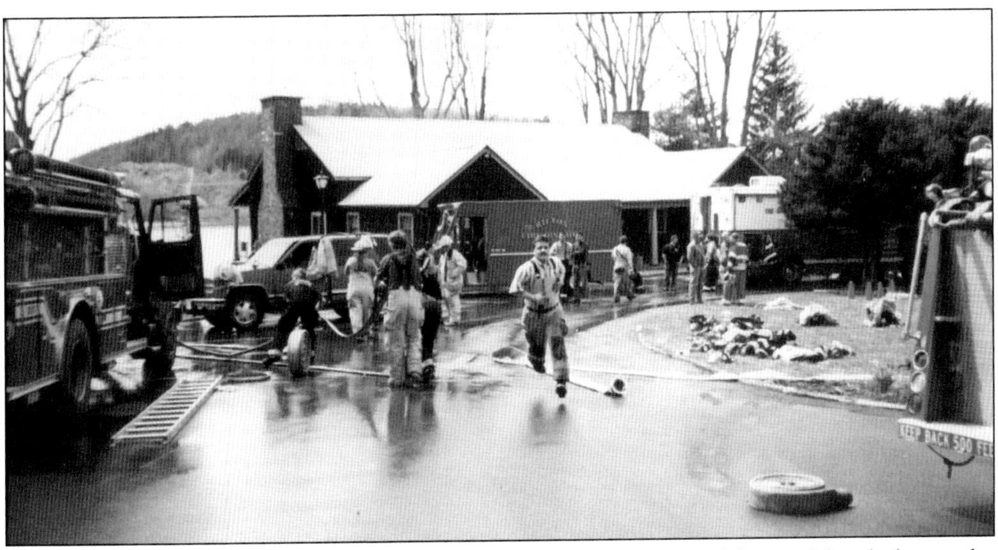

This award-winning photograph was taken during a large structural fire and brush fire at the Central Hudson Recreation Center in Rifton. The firefighter floating in midair is Ernie Navarra of the Bloomington Fire Department. In all, 15 area fire companies fought this fire, coming from as far away as Clintondale to lend a hand. Firefighters know what community spirit is all about. Please thank your volunteers the next time you see them. (Photograph by Susan B. Wick.)

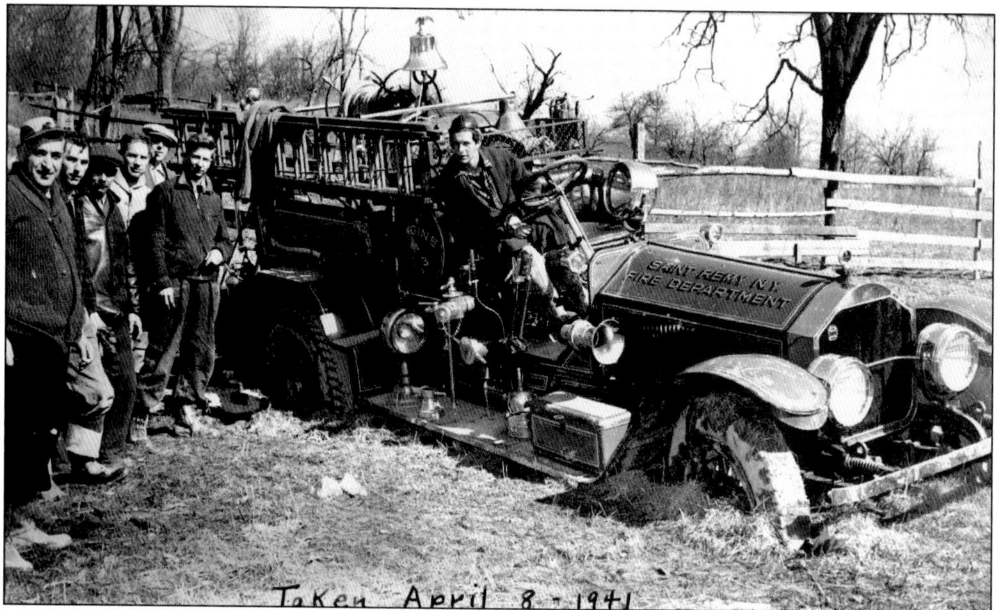

Mud can stop even our bravest. This is the St. Remy American Lafrance engine the day after the fire shown below. The engine was headed for a pond to pump water to the fire when the soft spring ground swallowed it up to the axles. The crew managed to pull it out in a few hours. From left to right are an unidentified man (possibly Sam Barnett), Phil Fischer Jr., Cornelius Helmich, an unidentified man (possibly Walter Helmich or Doc Bovie), Harry Havlin (with cigar), Jimmy Helmich, and an unidentified driver.

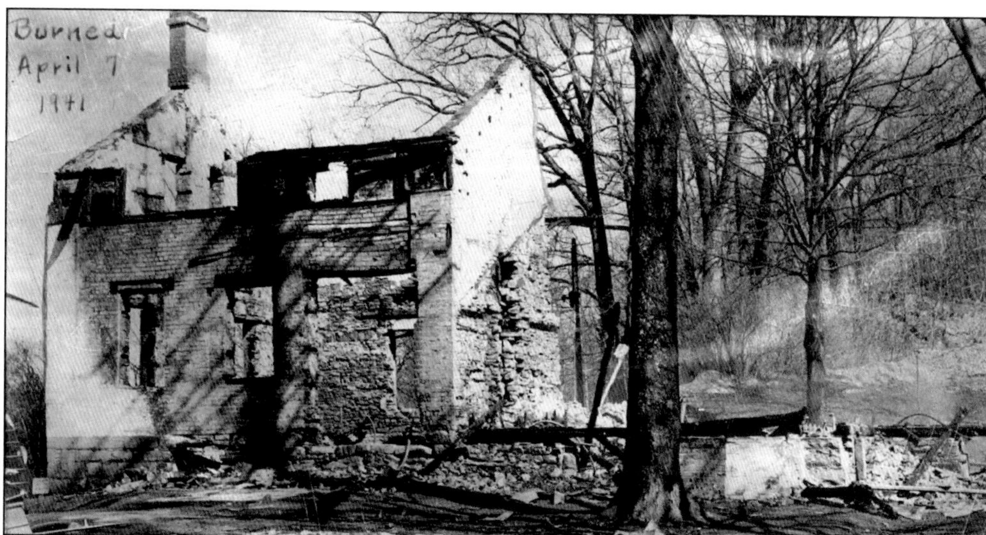

Here is what can happen when an arsonist's match meets an old house. The Bomer house was located on the Oak Grove Farm (now the Oak Tree Farm) between St. Remy and Rifton. Mr. Bomer had just finished renovating the house, and someone who did not like him was overheard making the comment, "No siree, you'll never live in this place." Two days later, it burned to the ground. The arsonist was never brought to justice.[80] (Authors' collection.)

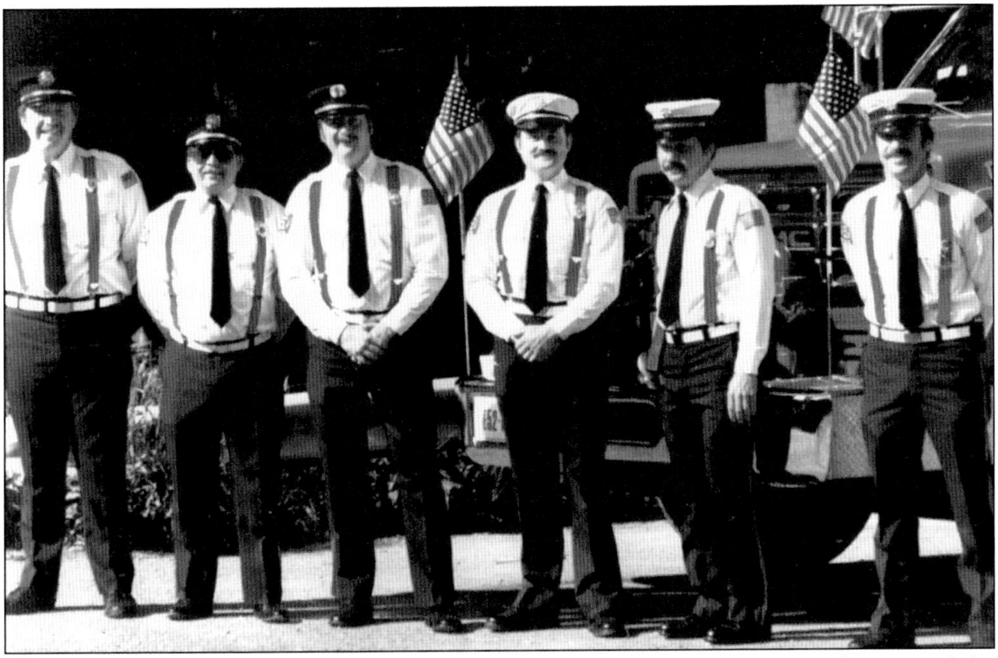

The line officers of the St. Remy Fire Department are pictured here prior to the start of the town's 1979 Memorial Day parade in Port Ewen. From left to right are Lt. Michael Gage, Lt. James Cosgrove, Capt. Frank Bunten, First Assistant Chief Karl R. Wick, Second Assistant Chief Vincent T. Dabrowski, and Chief John York. Missing is Capt. Gerard Richter. The truck is a 1981 GMC pumper-tanker, and this was its first parade. (Authors' collection.)

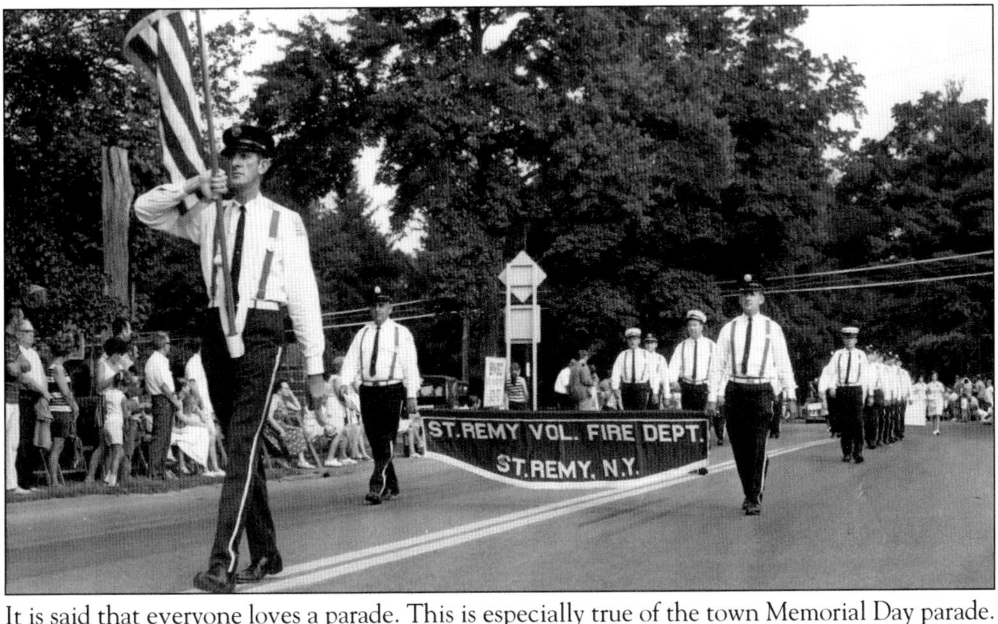

It is said that everyone loves a parade. This is especially true of the town Memorial Day parade. Leading the way in 1969 is Joe Sills. Carrying the banner are Gabe Guido and Bob Ennist. Next is Chief Walter Kaufmann, followed by Assistant Chief Cas Landi and Assistant Chief John York. Other officers that year were Capt. Fred Kirk, Capt. George Moxham, Lt. William York, Lt. Charles Henniger, and Captain of Fire Police Karl Koemm. (Authors' collection.)

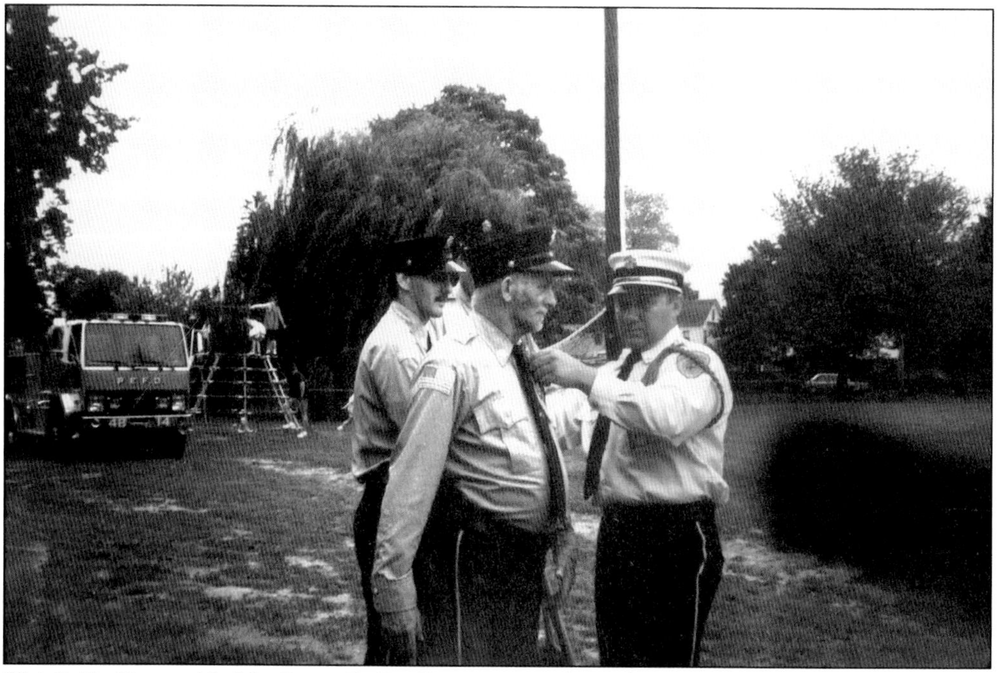

Chief Mike Fitzgerald of the Connelly Fire Department adjusts the insignia of firefighter Chuck Riley at the 1999 Flag Day celebration at Ross Park. In the rear is firefighter Fred Coddington. The town fire departments provide expertise, braving the heat and smoke of fire, and protection against wayward sparks at the flag retirement ceremonies. (Photograph by Susan B. Wick.)

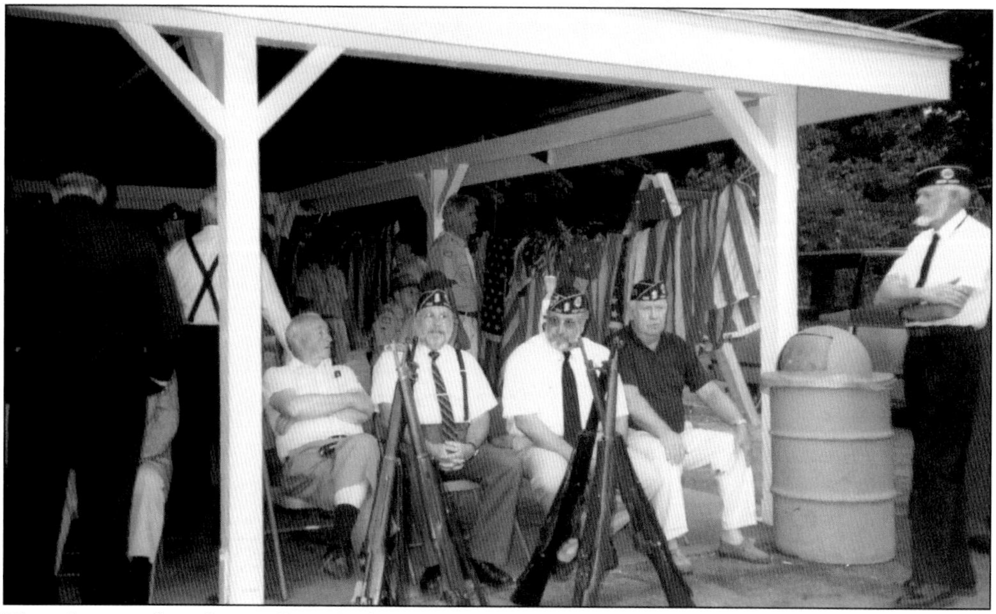

This photograph, taken at Ross Park in 1999, is dedicated to Councilman John Loughlin, who passed away in the fall of 2002. From left to right are Bob Richter, Dennis Helm, Ira Weiner, Bernie Cockley, and John Loughlin (standing). The Legionnaires are taking part in a flag exchange program masterminded by Dick Williams (also known as "Mr. Flag"). Residents could bring an old flag for proper disposal and receive a new one in return. (Photograph by Susan B. Wick.)

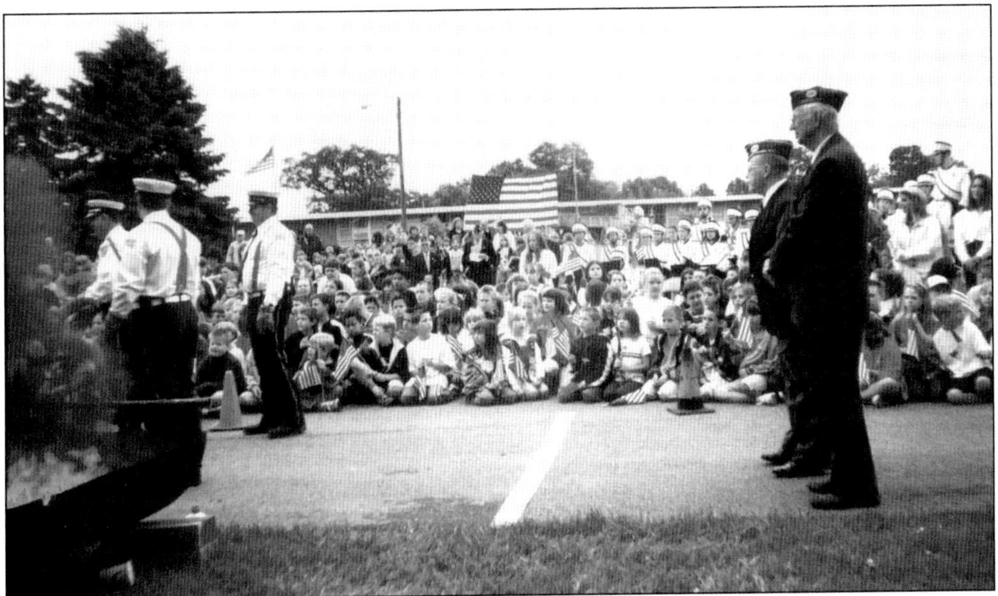

Flag Day honors the adoption of the first American flag in 1777 by the Continental Congress. It means much more than this, however. It is an enthusiastic celebration of freedom and democracy. Opening with the school band playing "Castle Hill Overture," about 500 students at the Port Ewen Elementary School participated in the year 2000 Flag Day festivities. Seen to the left are the fire chiefs of the town, and at the right stand Gil Krom and Jack Spinnenweber Sr. (Authors' collection.)

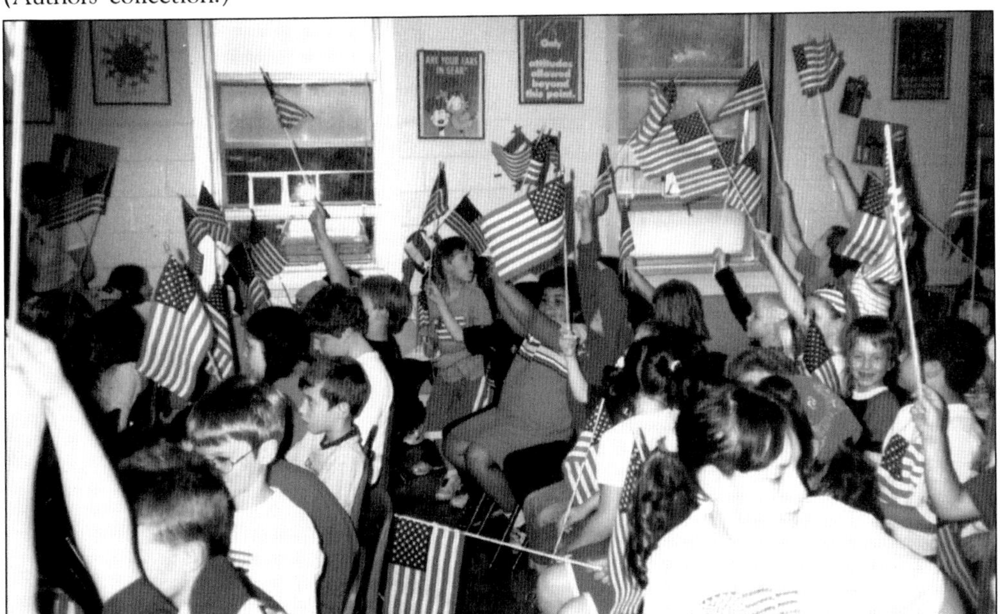

A rainy day did not dampen the spirits of these young patriots gathered in the Anna Devine School cafeteria for Flag Day 2002. The large room was filled with hundreds of waving flags and jubilant faces. After the speeches from the stage, students and adults alike watched through windows as the Rifton and St. Remy Fire Departments assisted Legionnaires and Scouts in giving 600 old and tattered flags a proper end. (Authors' collection.)

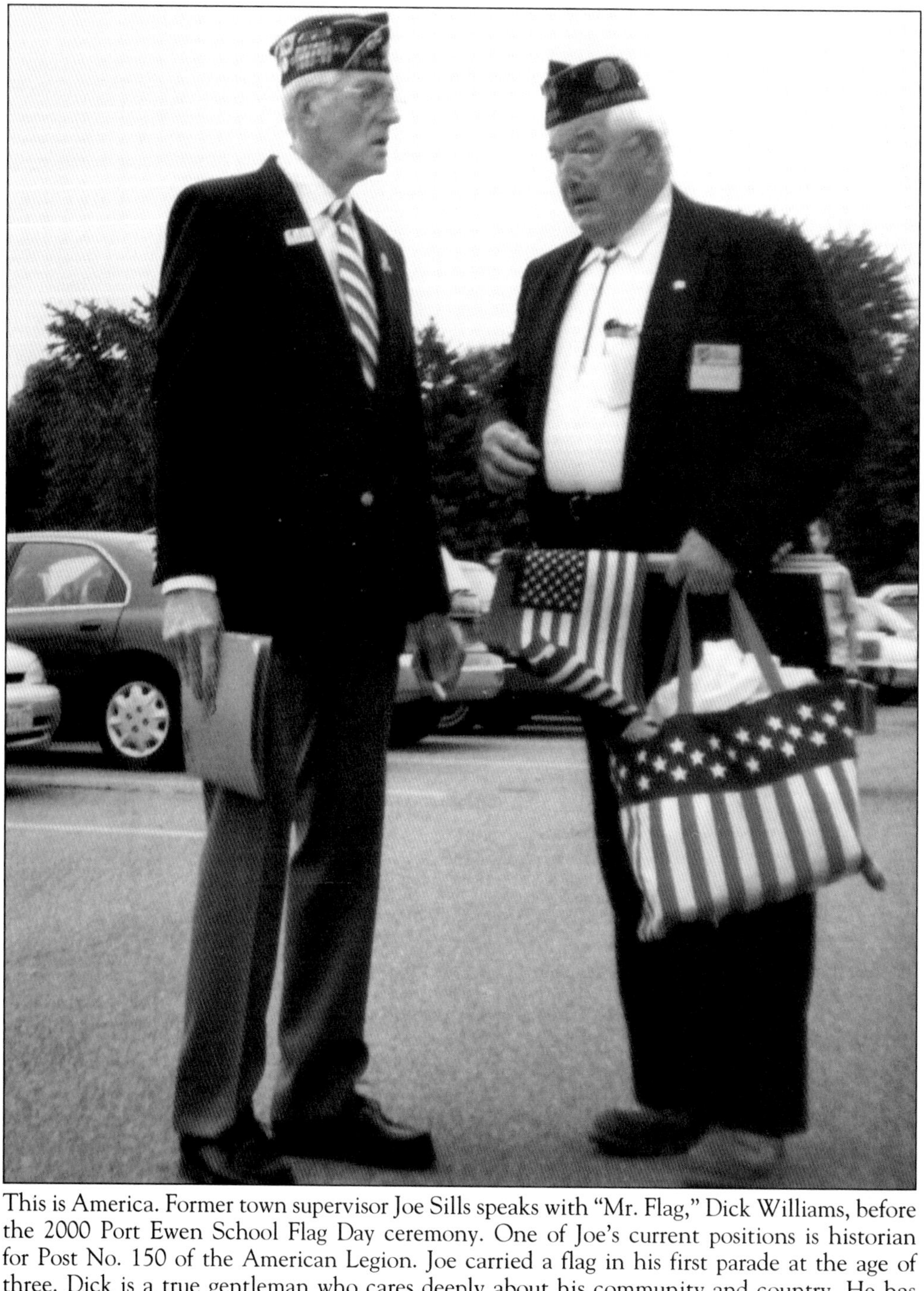

This is America. Former town supervisor Joe Sills speaks with "Mr. Flag," Dick Williams, before the 2000 Port Ewen School Flag Day ceremony. One of Joe's current positions is historian for Post No. 150 of the American Legion. Joe carried a flag in his first parade at the age of three. Dick is a true gentleman who cares deeply about his community and country. He has been coordinating flag retirement ceremonies since 1950. During that time, he has properly disposed of well over 12,500 flags and given out about 10,000 replacements. As part of his fencing business, he also sold flagpoles and flags. Mr. Flag believes that everyone should be able to fly a flag. He personally installed the pole at Cas Landi Park in St. Remy, and he makes sure that old glory flies proudly in every park in the town of Esopus. (Photograph by the author.)

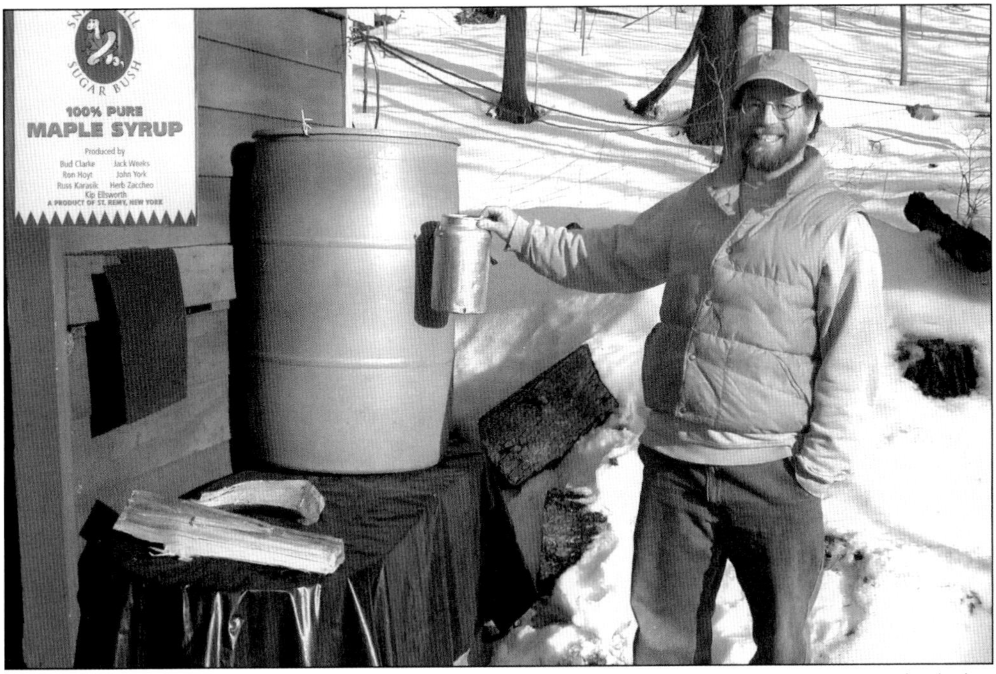

Hidden away on Snake Hill is the Pokonoie Sugar Shack, established in 1996 by Bud Clarke, Russ Karasik, Ron Hoyt, Jack Weeks, John York, and Herb Zaccheo. The friends make maple syrup for fun and personal use. Russ Karasik is showing us how much sap is required to make a single quart of syrup. Most of the sap is carried to the boiler by special plastic tubing, although they still use a few buckets and spiles (small wooden or metal spouts for drawing off sap from a sugar maple). (Photograph by the author.)

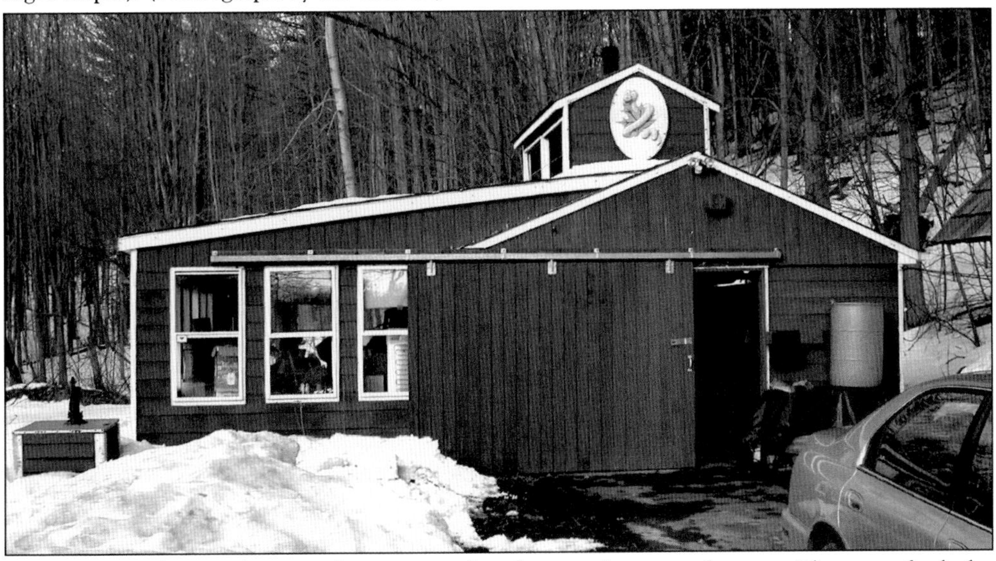

Here is the sap house where maple sap is wondrously turned into maple syrup. The group feeds the evaporator with 14 cords of pine each season. The snake carving on the gable is the creation of founding member Bud Clarke. The group has also successfully petitioned the federal government to rename the old Dwarfskill running under Pokonoie Road to Sugarbush Creek, a fitting name indeed. In 2003, the group produced 123 gallons of syrup. (Photograph by the author.)

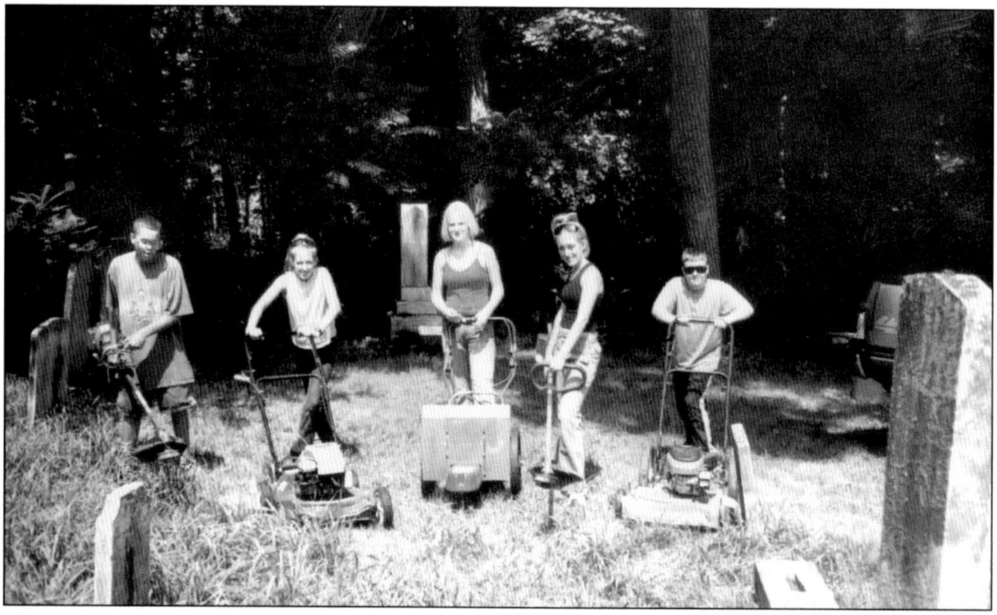

The St. Remy Reformed Church (seventh grade through high school) Sunday school class is cleaning up the old Greenkill Burying Ground during the summer of 2001. Mowing, weeding and resetting fallen stones have become an annual project for these fine young people and their teachers. Reading the ancient stones is an added treat. From left to right are Aaron Knox, Dorian Dodd, Amy Brechter, Deanndra Dodd, and Michael Brechter. The teachers involved in the project were Marty Jordan and Gary VanAken. (Gary VanAken collection.)

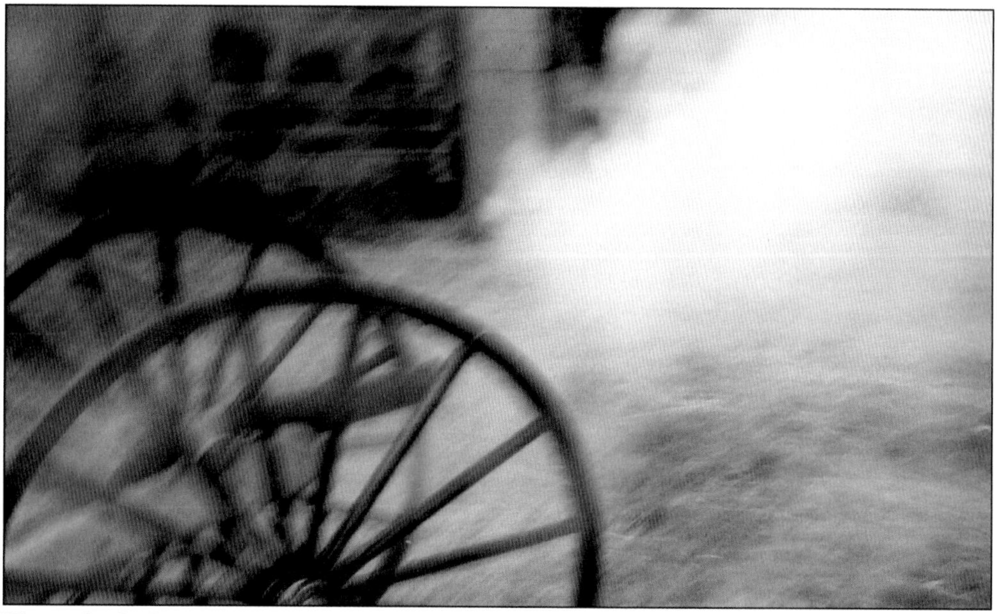

This is the St. Remy cannon moments after firing. The wheels are blurry because they are turning from the recoil. The carriage is certainly antique but probably not original to the cannon, which sports a bore of "only" one inch. This was a ceremonial cannon used by the Redmen and other local civic groups. Its small size is deceptive. The report, flash, and smoke from a cannon of this size are very impressive. (Authors' collection.)

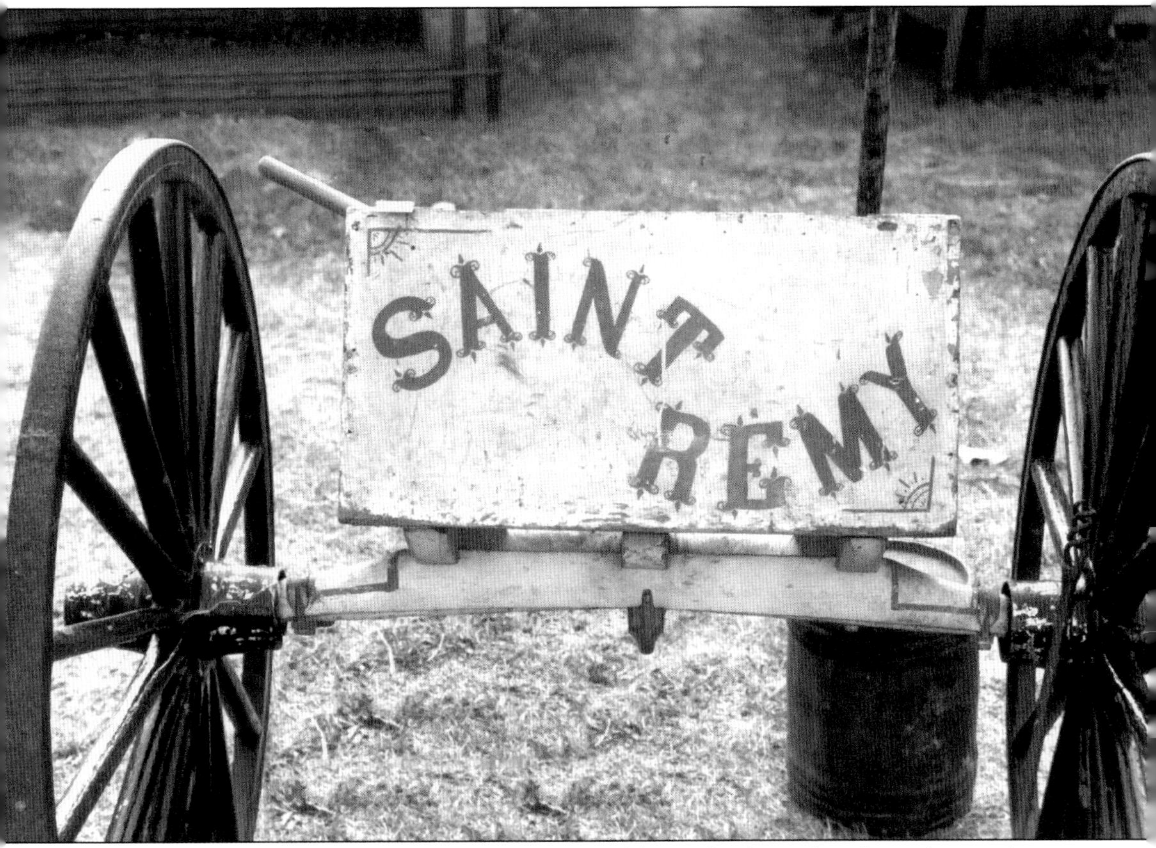

Now it is time for the St. Remy historians to bid a fond farewell. The authors hope that you have enjoyed this photo album. They have many more pictures to share and invite the reader to visit the Web site at www.stremy.net, where further information about the town of Esopus and the photographs is offered.

ACKNOWLEDGMENTS

The authors would like to extend a special thanks to their friends and colleagues who assisted them with photographs, information, specialty documents, and artifacts: Samuel Haines Carman and Alberta Mercer Carman; Dorothy Dumond; Monika Kaufmann; Don and Shirley Briggs; Beatrice and Martin Jordan; Raymond Krom; "Hype" Terpening; Roesner Wheeler; Wilson Tinney; Florence Prehn; Florence Dixon; Isabel Krom; Myron York; John and Bill York; David Cummins; Mr. and Mrs. Willis DeHart; Catherine Haber; Geoffrey Megargee; Bob Scherer; and the Local History Section librarians at Ulster County Community College, Kingston Area Library, Ulster County Genealogical Society, and Port Ewen Library.

After an interview in 1995, Margaret Ryan presented the author with her collection of Esopus photographs.

Thank you all those listed, and thank you to everyone else for your encouragement and support.

SUGGESTED READINGS

Town of Esopus Story, 1979. Town of Esopus Bicentennial Committee.
Maple Lanes, 1989. Woodcrest School Press.
Timbers of Time, 1977. Patricia Bartles Miller. The ERPF Catskill Cultural Center Inc.
History of Ulster County New York, 1880. Nathaniel Bartlett Sylvester. Everts and Peck.
Atlas of Ulster County, 1875. J.H. Beers and Company.
Commemorative Biographical Record of Ulster County NY, 1896. J.H. Beers and Company.
Coalboats to Tidewater: The Story of the Delaware & Hudson Canal, 1981. Manville B. Wakefield.
Footsteps across Cement, 1976. Ann Gilchrist.
Sojourner Truth: Slave, Prophet, Legend, 1993. Carlton Mabee and Susan Mabee Newhouse. New York University Press.
Growing Up in Tillson, 1992. Huguenot Historical Society.
The Dutch and Quaker Colonies in America, 1903. John Fiske. Houghton, Mifflin and Company.
American Pioneers and Patriots Peter Stuyvesant, 1873. John S.C. Abbott. Dodd and Mead.
A History of Ulster County under the Dominion of the Dutch, 1923. Augustus Van Buren.
Southeastern New York, 1946. Lewis Historical Publishing Company.

Other valuable sources of information include the Web site www.stremy.net and the Ulster County Archives.

ENDNOTES

1. A loose extrapolation from Jones Patent division. Twenty houses and one school in the southeast one-fifth of town in 1784. Average household at 7.4 yields: 20 x 5 x 7.4 = 740 inhabitants.
2. Ulster County Legislative Manuals, 1898, 1934, and 1967.
3. Fiske, p. 60.
4. June 24, 1682. See Fried's *The Early History of Kingston*, p. 81.
5. Permission to purchase from the Indians was granted on January 12, 1681. The deed was completed in 1682 from the "Osoopus Savages." Liber 2, p. 629.
6. Liber C, p. 440.
7. Washington marched his troops northward along what is now Route 32 in Rosendale not Route 9W in Esopus. They were half a day too late.
8. The reaffirmation agreement is in the Ulster County Archives.
9. *History of Ulster County New York*, p. 110 et al.
10. *Sojourner Truth: Slave, Prophet, Legend.*
11. U.S. Postal Service Ledger, pp. 371, 537.
12. Certificate of Incorporation, Ulster County Clerk Box 3-77 et. al. The corporation owned three steamboats in 1888: the *Ettie Wright*, the *Charles A. Shultz*, and the *Eltinge Anderson*.
13. Each person could sign only one petition per district each year. A brief study of these petitions shows some of the same names appearing on petitions in several jurisdictions.
14. Liber 3, p. 413.
15. Liber 4, p. 110.
16. *Maine Antique Digest*, July 1996.
17. Minutes of the board of supervisors, petition for payment for lands taken from Freer farm for a new road, Ulster County Archives.
18. See Wakefield's *Coalboats to Tidewater: The Story of the Delaware & Hudson Canal.*
19. His actual signature was Dimond not Diamond, as it is commonly misspelled.
20. Several bridges of the Town lattice style can be seen spanning the creeks west of Concord, New Hampshire. Most are open to foot traffic.
21. Ulster County Archives, road petitions 12 folder box. Petition and notice from Freer to VanAken for damages in building road to the bridge.
22. Ulster County Hall of Records.
23. *Commemorative Biographical Record.*
24. Topographical map, "Kingston West," 1980.
25. See Sylvester's *History of Ulster County New York.*
26. See *Hudson River Atlas*, 1891.
27. Ferrymen licenses, Ulster County Archives.
28. These same rates would have been posted on a large two- by three-foot sign at the landings. Similar signs can be seen in the Museum of New Hampshire History in Concord, New Hampshire.
29. James Perrine constructed the hotel and tavern in the 1820s.
30. The B & J Arnold cotton mill was in operation from 1827 to 1828. The Dashville Custom and Flouring Mill was in operation from 1830 to 1835.
31. Melody Savage, U.S. Postal Service research associate, September 7, 1999.
32. *Ulster County Directory*, 1978.
33. From an 1853 map of Ulster County.
34. The 1915 census et al. for the town of Esopus.

35. See Sylvester's *History of Ulster County New York*.
36. From an 1811 highway list for the town of Esopus.
37. Plate 21, *Hudson River Atlas*, 1891; *Commemorative Biographical Record*.
38. Brochure in author's collection.
39. Proceedings of the Ulster County Historical Society, 1945–1946.
40. Liber 69, p. 472 et al.
41. Ulster County Clerk Box 2-54.
42. Exception to lot 47N George Eddy Deed. Also confirmation deed to trustees 1816.
43. Tax records for that year.
44. The original was located across from the Haines Blacksmith Shop, one-quarter mile south.
45. Liber 4, p. 235, November 6, 1804, $1.
46. From census records and an interview with Beatrice Jordan, whose grandmother was five years old when she came to St. Remy.
47. From an interview with Beatrice Jordan in February 1993.
48. Liber 57, p. 182.
49. From an interview with Lydia Zerbst, a former owner.
50. Census records from 1875, town of Esopus.
51. The 1910 tax list from the town of Esopus.
52. From an interview with Katie Brandt.
53. Liber 248, p. 547; Liber 302, p. 496.
54. From an interview with Isabell Krom in March 2003.
55. Ulster County census records.
56. February 25, 1860; Liber 110, p. 650 et al. $250.
57. From an interview with Martin Jordan in March 2003.
58. Spelling from Surrogate's Court of Ulster County.
59. "Scorch," an informal term meaning to drive or ride very fast (in this case, more than six miles per hour).
60. *Maple Lanes* and *The Town of Esopus Story*.
61. The 1790 census.
62. From an interview with Martin Jordan in March 2003.
63. In-house document dated May 15, 1924.
64. Dimick estate papers from a private collection.
65. From an interview with Roesner Wheeler in February 2003.
66. Growing up in Tillson.
67. Ibid, estate papers.
68. A 1924 U.S. Geographical Survey topographical map.
69. From interviews with several old-timers. In 1979, one of the authors shared half a bottle of carefully preserved Rifton Applejack with Samuel Carman. It was simply the best whiskey ever made—smooth as silk, tasty, and quite a kick.
70. Court documents filed with Ulster County clerk.
71. From an interview with Martin Jordan (Duke's son) in February 2003.
72. From an interview with Roesner Wheeler in February 2003.
73. Honorary life member of Hasbrouck Engine Company No. 1 of Connelly; *Boyhood Memories of South Rondout*.
74. Assorted papers, Ulster County Archives.
75. Rear of postcard says, "fourth anniversary" and is postmarked 1937.
76. Ulster County Corporation and land records; *Treasure Tales of the Shawangunks and Catskills*, by Harold Harris, 1998.
77. *They Also Ran*, by Irving Stone, Doubleday, 1943.
78. New York State Consolidated Laws. Article 2, Section 2, "Public Lands."
79. Deed from J. Clyne Frost, Hawley Krom, et al., trustees of the Redmen; Liber 653, p. 114.
80. See our Web site for further details. Space does not permit us to provide them here.